JUSTICE SOCIETY of AMERICA

THE BAD SEED

BILL WILLINGHAM & MATTHEW STURGES
WRITERS

JESUS MERINO
ARTIST & COVERS

ALLEN PASSALAQUA
COLORIST

ROB LEIGH
LETTERER

MIKE CARLIN Editor-original series
RACHEL GLUCKSTERN Associate Editor-original series
BOB HARRAS Group Editor-Collected Editions
BOB JOY Editor
ROBBIN BROSTERMAN Design Director-Books

DC COMICS

DIANE NELSON President
DAN DIDIO and JIM LEE Co-Publishers
GEOFF JOHNS Chief Creative Officer
PATRICK CALDON EVP-Finance and Administration
JOHN ROOD EVP-Sales, Marketing and Business Development
AMY GENKINS SVP-Business and Legal Affairs
STEVE ROTTERDAM SVP-Sales and Marketing
JOHN CUNNINGHAM VP-Marketing
TERRI CUNNINGHAM VP-Managing Editor
ALISON GILL VP-Manufacturing
DAVID HYDE VP-Publicity
SUE POHJA VP-Book Trade Sales
ALYSSE SOLL VP-Advertising and Custom Publishing
BOB WAYNE VP-Sales
MARK CHIARELLO Art Director

Cover by Jesus Merino

JUSTICE SOCIETY OF AMERICA: THE BAD SEED
Published by DC Comics.

DC Comics, 1700 Broadway, New York, NY 10019
A Warner Bros. Entertainment Company
Printed by World Color Press, Inc., Dubuque, IA, USA 4/21/10.
First printing.
ISBN: 978-1-4012-2714-2

SUSTAINABLE FORESTRY INITIATIVE
Certified Chain of Custody
Promoting Sustainable Forest Management

Fiber used in this product line meets the sourcing requirements of the SFI program.
www.sfiprogram.org NFS-SPICOC-C0001801

THE BAD SEED Part One

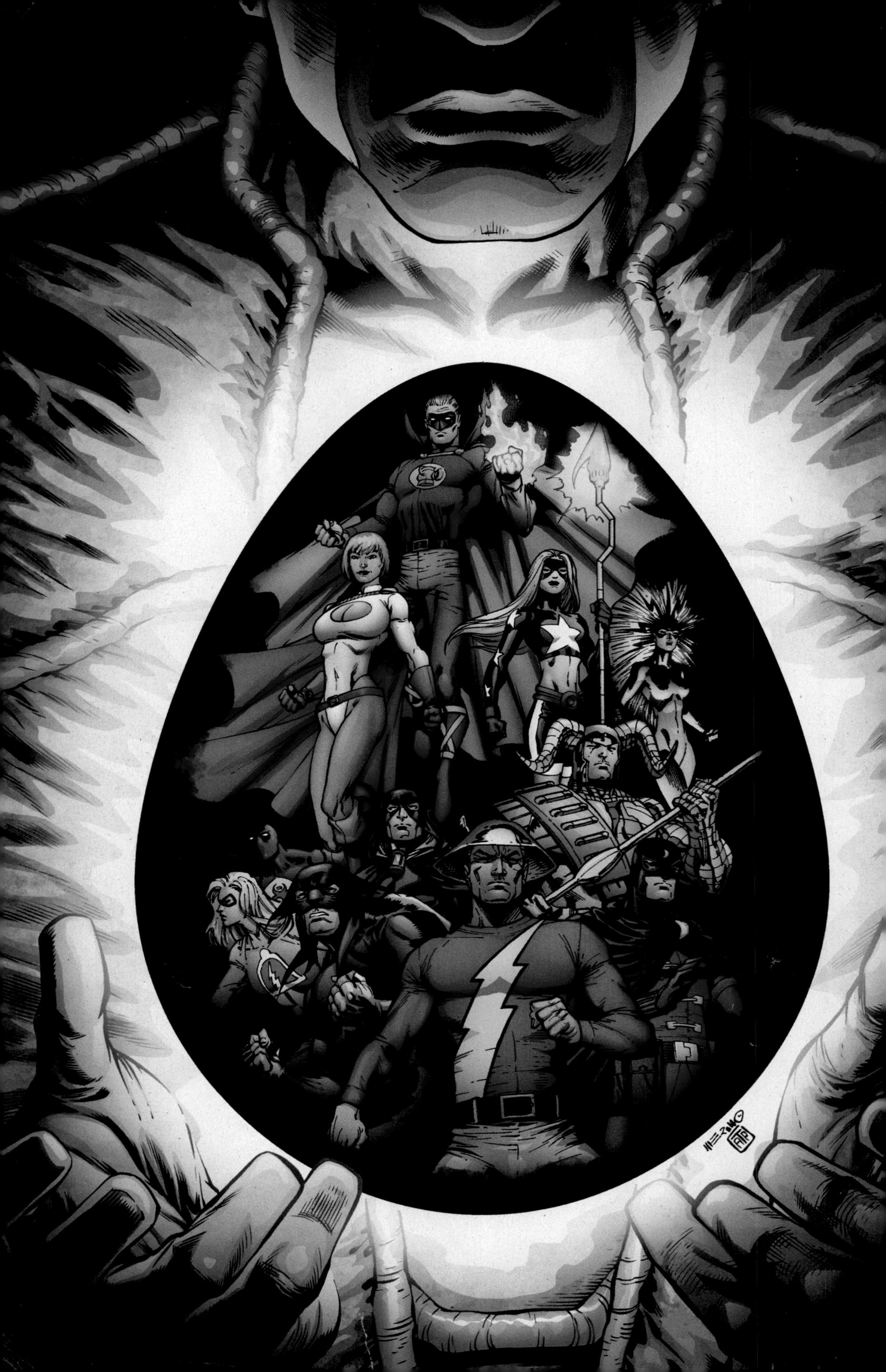

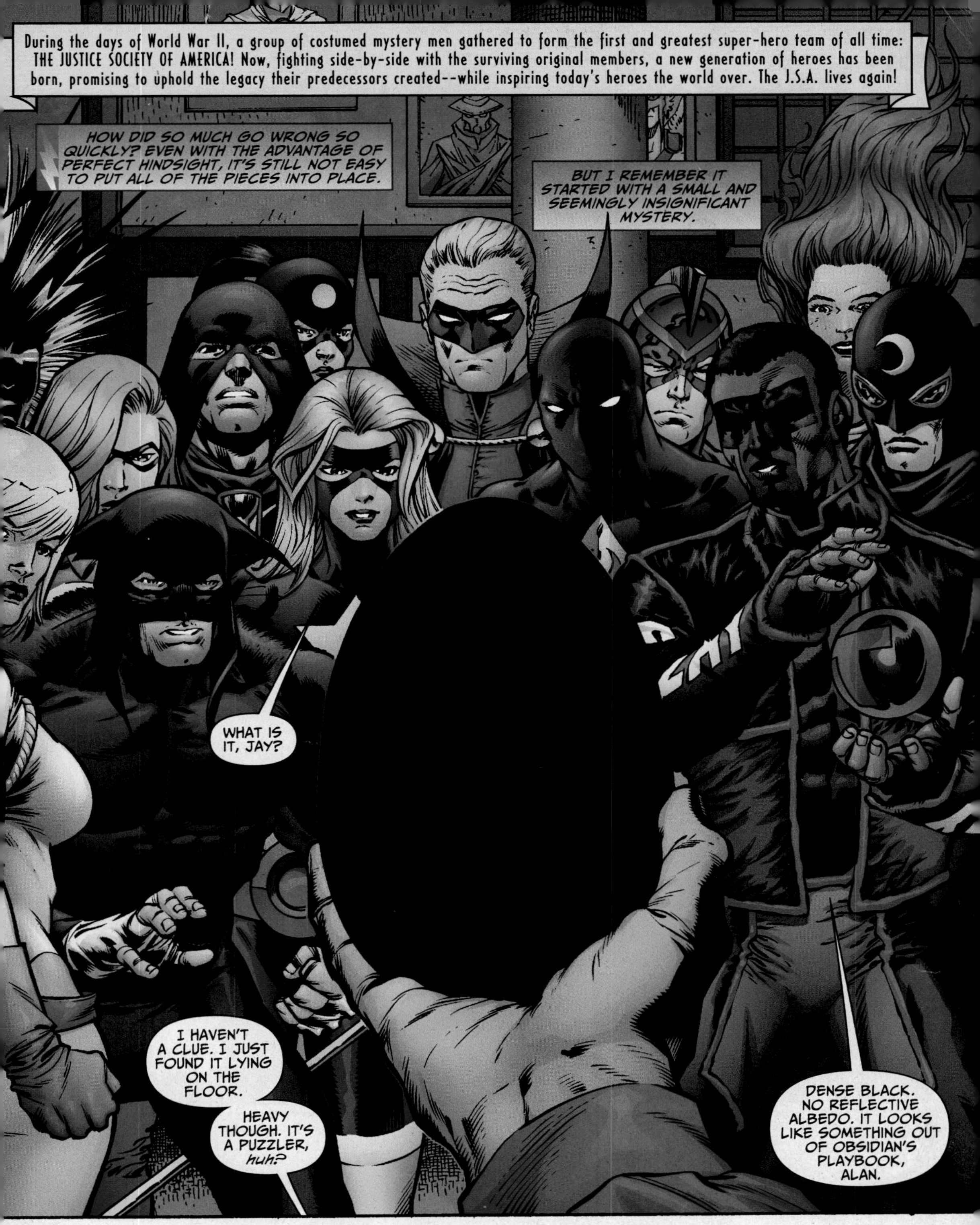
During the days of World War II, a group of costumed mystery men gathered to form the first and greatest super-hero team of all time: THE JUSTICE SOCIETY OF AMERICA! Now, fighting side-by-side with the surviving original members, a new generation of heroes has been born, promising to uphold the legacy their predecessors created--while inspiring today's heroes the world over. The J.S.A. lives again!
HOW DID SO MUCH GO WRONG SO QUICKLY? EVEN WITH THE ADVANTAGE OF PERFECT HINDSIGHT, IT'S STILL NOT EASY TO PUT ALL OF THE PIECES INTO PLACE.
BUT I REMEMBER IT STARTED WITH A SMALL AND SEEMINGLY INSIGNIFICANT MYSTERY.
WHAT IS IT, JAY?
I HAVEN'T A CLUE. I JUST FOUND IT LYING ON THE FLOOR.
HEAVY THOUGH. IT'S A PUZZLER, *huh?*
DENSE BLACK. NO REFLECTIVE ALBEDO. IT LOOKS LIKE SOMETHING OUT OF OBSIDIAN'S PLAYBOOK, ALAN.

FRESH MEAT

PART 1 OF THE BAD SEED

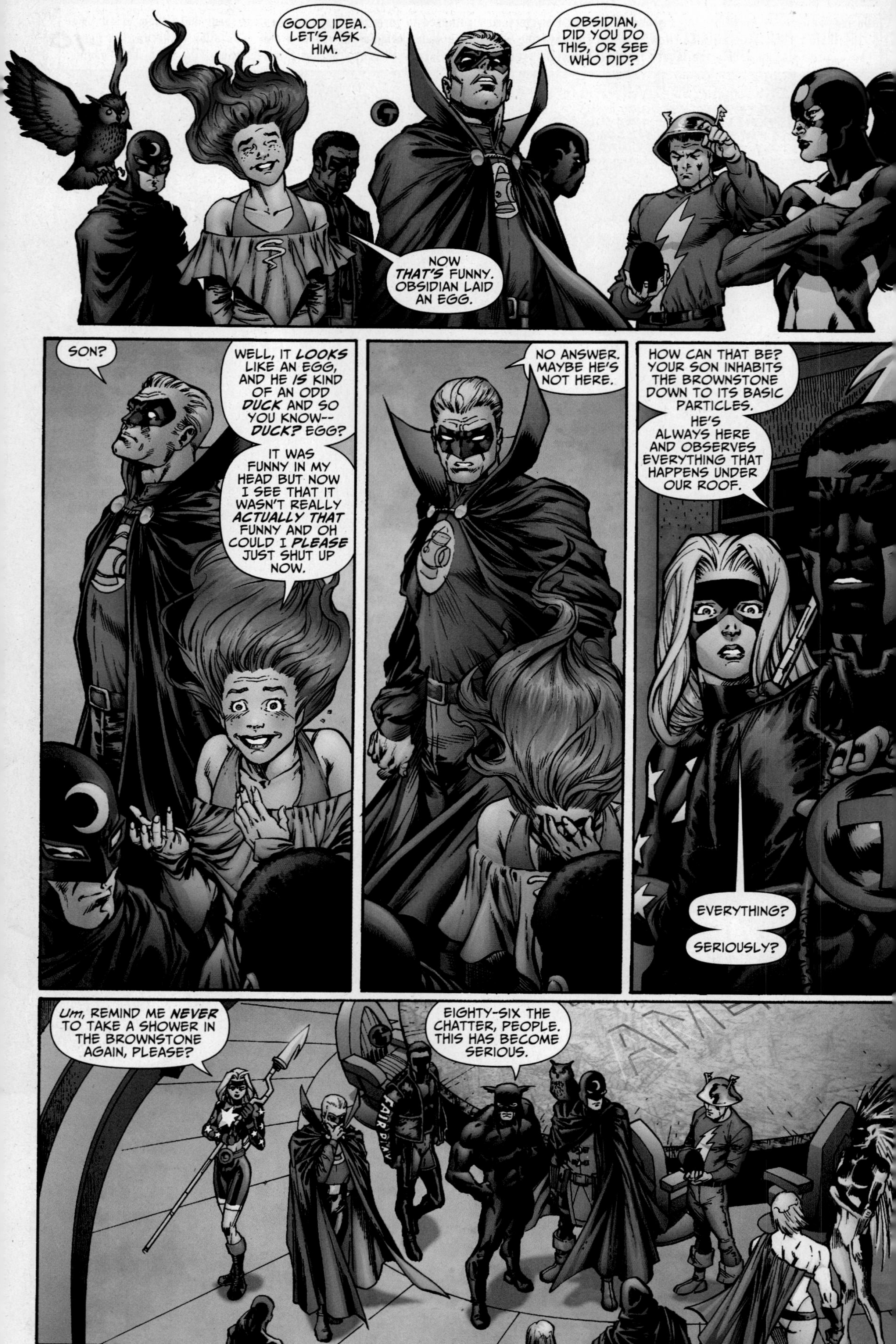
GOOD IDEA. LET'S ASK HIM.
OBSIDIAN, DID YOU DO THIS, OR SEE WHO DID?
NOW THAT'S FUNNY. OBSIDIAN LAID AN EGG.
SON?
WELL, IT LOOKS LIKE AN EGG, AND HE IS KIND OF AN ODD DUCK AND SO YOU KNOW-- DUCK? EGG?
IT WAS FUNNY IN MY HEAD BUT NOW I SEE THAT IT WASN'T REALLY ACTUALLY THAT FUNNY AND OH COULD I PLEASE JUST SHUT UP NOW.
NO ANSWER. MAYBE HE'S NOT HERE.
HOW CAN THAT BE? YOUR SON INHABITS THE BROWNSTONE DOWN TO ITS BASIC PARTICLES.
HE'S ALWAYS HERE AND OBSERVES EVERYTHING THAT HAPPENS UNDER OUR ROOF.
EVERYTHING?
SERIOUSLY?
Um, REMIND ME NEVER TO TAKE A SHOWER IN THE BROWNSTONE AGAIN, PLEASE?
EIGHTY-SIX THE CHATTER, PEOPLE. THIS HAS BECOME SERIOUS.
FAIR PLAY

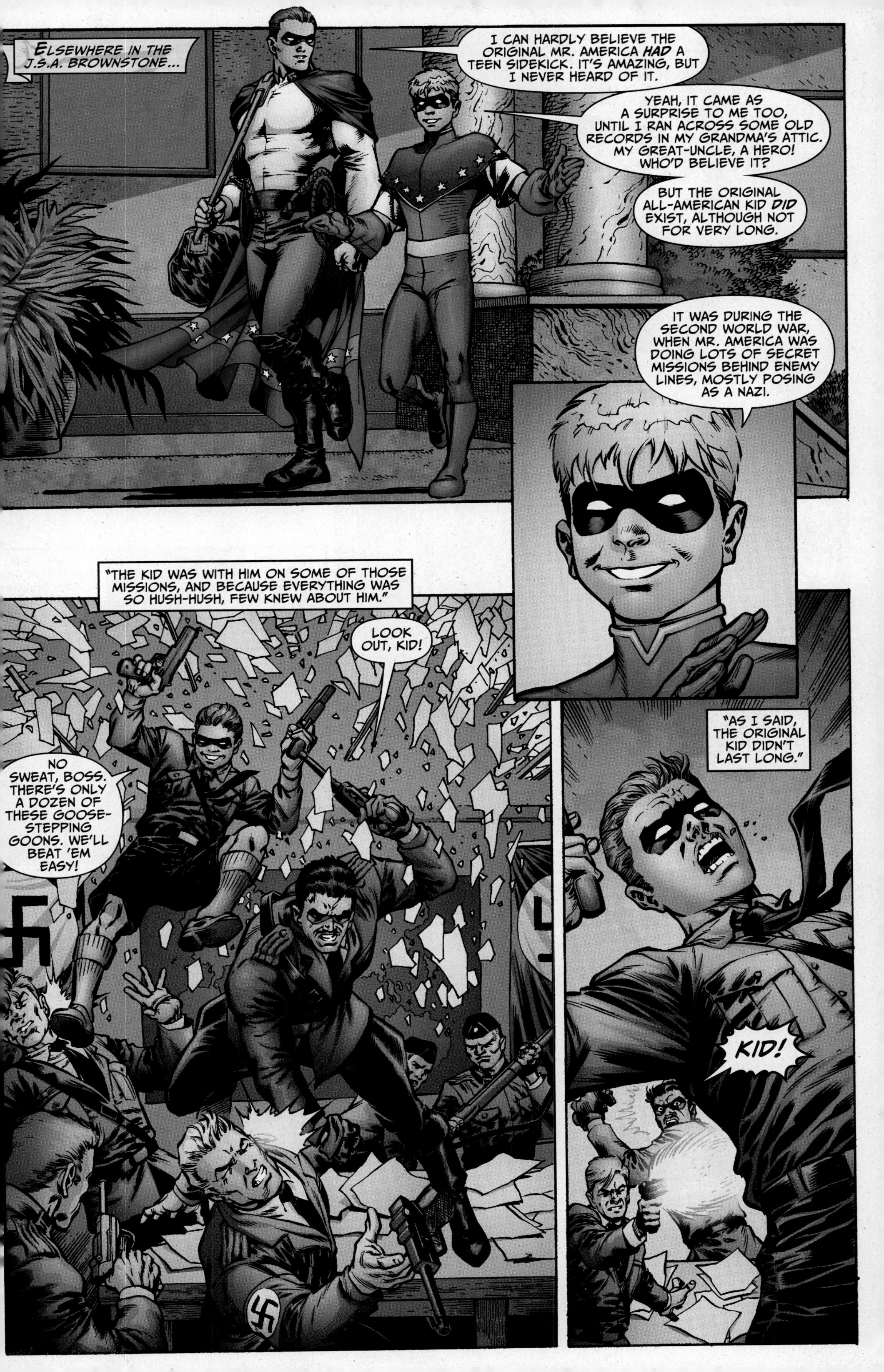
ELSEWHERE IN THE J.S.A. BROWNSTONE...
I CAN HARDLY BELIEVE THE ORIGINAL MR. AMERICA HAD A TEEN SIDEKICK. IT'S AMAZING, BUT I NEVER HEARD OF IT.
YEAH, IT CAME AS A SURPRISE TO ME TOO, UNTIL I RAN ACROSS SOME OLD RECORDS IN MY GRANDMA'S ATTIC. MY GREAT-UNCLE, A HERO! WHO'D BELIEVE IT?
BUT THE ORIGINAL ALL-AMERICAN KID DID EXIST, ALTHOUGH NOT FOR VERY LONG.
IT WAS DURING THE SECOND WORLD WAR, WHEN MR. AMERICA WAS DOING LOTS OF SECRET MISSIONS BEHIND ENEMY LINES, MOSTLY POSING AS A NAZI.
"THE KID WAS WITH HIM ON SOME OF THOSE MISSIONS, AND BECAUSE EVERYTHING WAS SO HUSH-HUSH, FEW KNEW ABOUT HIM."
LOOK OUT, KID!
NO SWEAT, BOSS. THERE'S ONLY A DOZEN OF THESE GOOSE-STEPPING GOONS. WE'LL BEAT 'EM EASY!
"AS I SAID, THE ORIGINAL KID DIDN'T LAST LONG."
KID!

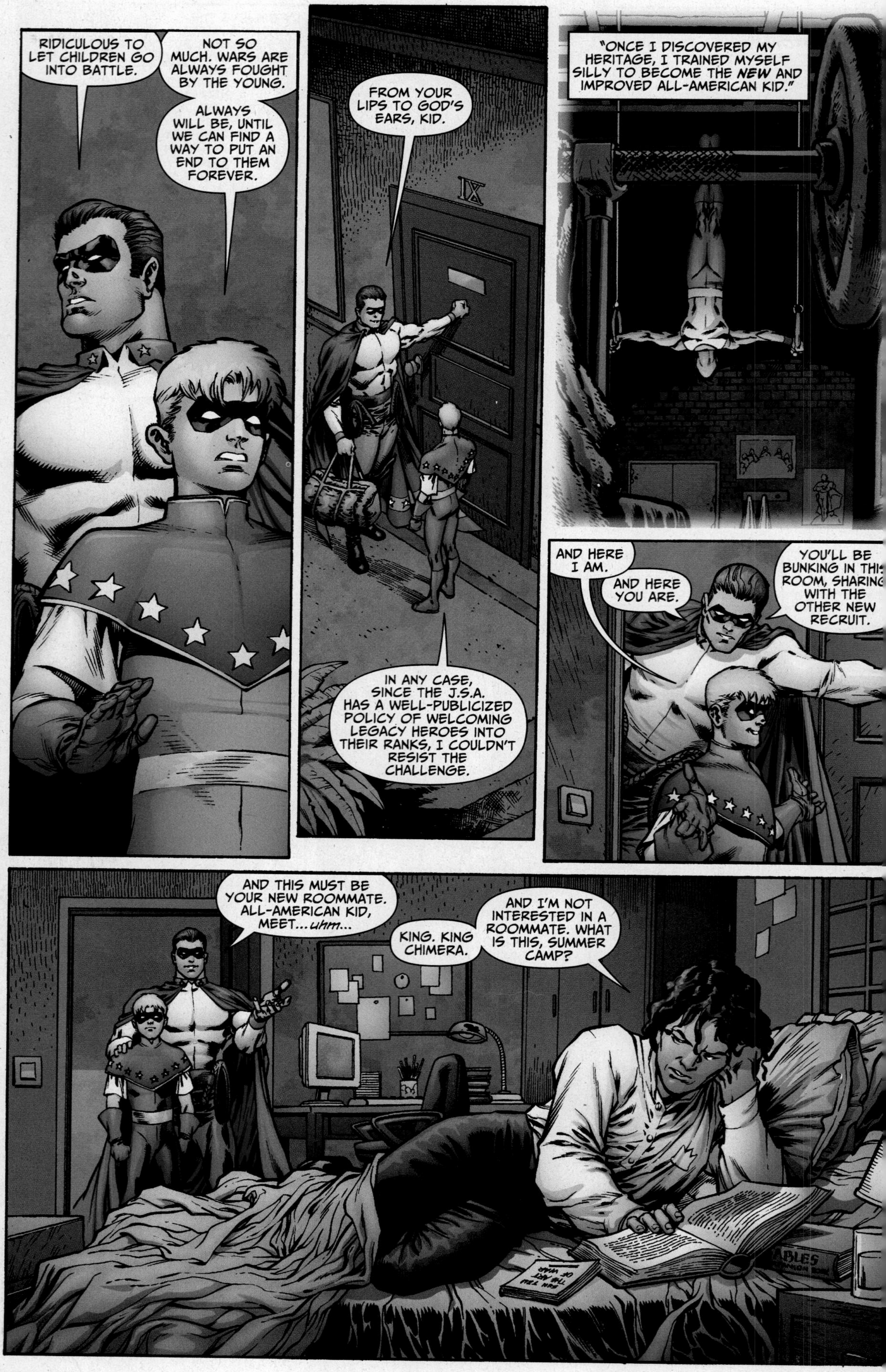
RIDICULOUS TO LET CHILDREN GO INTO BATTLE.
NOT SO MUCH. WARS ARE ALWAYS FOUGHT BY THE YOUNG.
ALWAYS WILL BE, UNTIL WE CAN FIND A WAY TO PUT AN END TO THEM FOREVER.
FROM YOUR LIPS TO GOD'S EARS, KID.
IX
IN ANY CASE, SINCE THE J.S.A. HAS A WELL-PUBLICIZED POLICY OF WELCOMING LEGACY HEROES INTO THEIR RANKS, I COULDN'T RESIST THE CHALLENGE.
"ONCE I DISCOVERED MY HERITAGE, I TRAINED MYSELF SILLY TO BECOME THE *NEW* AND IMPROVED ALL-AMERICAN KID."
AND HERE I AM.
AND HERE YOU ARE.
YOU'LL BE BUNKING IN THIS ROOM, SHARING WITH THE OTHER NEW RECRUIT.
AND THIS MUST BE YOUR NEW ROOMMATE. ALL-AMERICAN KID, MEET... *uhm...*
KING. KING CHIMERA.
AND I'M NOT INTERESTED IN A ROOMMATE. WHAT IS THIS, SUMMER CAMP?

AT MISTER TERRIFIC'S PROMPTING, GREEN LANTERN DID A DEEP SCAN OF THE MYSTERY ARTIFACT.

OH NO.

WHAT'S WRONG, ALAN?

THIS ISN'T SOMETHING OBSIDIAN MADE, IT *IS* HIM.

THIS IS TODD, ALTHOUGH IN AN EXTREMELY DEGRADED STATE.

WHAT CAUSED IT?

I DON'T KNOW. I HAD TO BREAK OFF MY EXAMINATION PREMATURELY, BECAUSE IT WAS CAUSING HIM INTENSE PAIN, DEGRADING HIM EVEN FURTHER.

THE EQUIPMENT CONJURED BY MY RING IS MADE OF PURE LIGHT, WHILE HE'S MADE OF RAW DARKNESS AND--WELL-- THE TWO DON'T EXACTLY MIX.

SINCE ALL I CAN DO IS HURT MY SON BY TRYING TO FIND OUT WHAT HAPPENED TO HIM, I THINK YOU AND DOCTOR MID-NITE SHOULD TAKE OVER THE INVESTIGATION.

WE'LL GET TO THE BOTTOM OF THIS, ALAN.

YAAHRROOOOGAYAAHRROOOGA

EMERGENCY ALARM!

WHAT NOW?

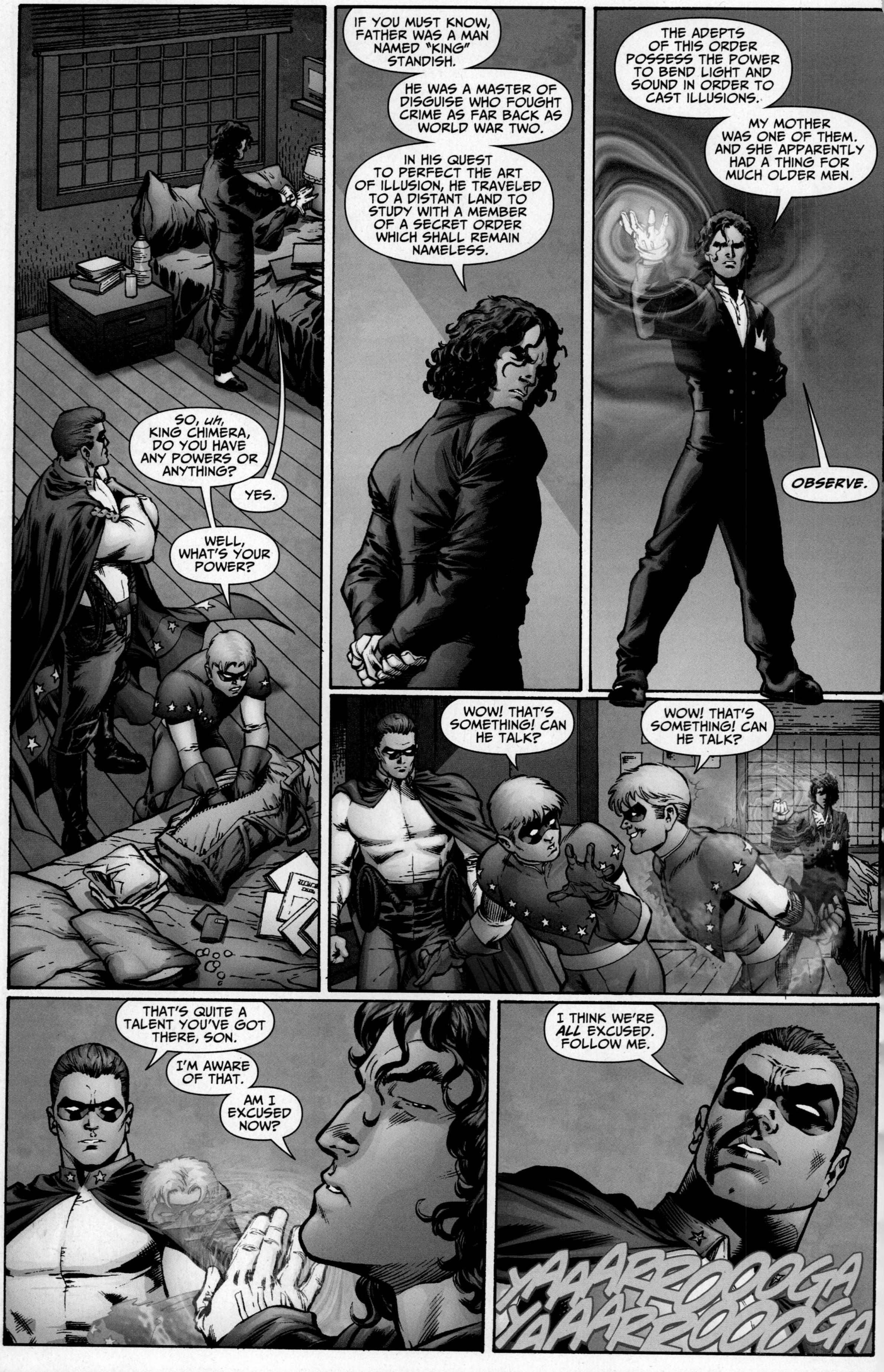
SO, uh, KING CHIMERA, DO YOU HAVE ANY POWERS OR ANYTHING?
YES.
WELL, WHAT'S YOUR POWER?
IF YOU MUST KNOW, FATHER WAS A MAN NAMED "KING" STANDISH.
HE WAS A MASTER OF DISGUISE WHO FOUGHT CRIME AS FAR BACK AS WORLD WAR TWO.
IN HIS QUEST TO PERFECT THE ART OF ILLUSION, HE TRAVELED TO A DISTANT LAND TO STUDY WITH A MEMBER OF A SECRET ORDER WHICH SHALL REMAIN NAMELESS.
THE ADEPTS OF THIS ORDER POSSESS THE POWER TO BEND LIGHT AND SOUND IN ORDER TO CAST ILLUSIONS.
MY MOTHER WAS ONE OF THEM. AND SHE APPARENTLY HAD A THING FOR MUCH OLDER MEN.
OBSERVE.
WOW! THAT'S SOMETHING! CAN HE TALK?
WOW! THAT'S SOMETHING! CAN HE TALK?
THAT'S QUITE A TALENT YOU'VE GOT THERE, SON.
I'M AWARE OF THAT.
AM I EXCUSED NOW?
I THINK WE'RE ALL EXCUSED. FOLLOW ME.
YAAARROOOGA
YAAARROOOGA

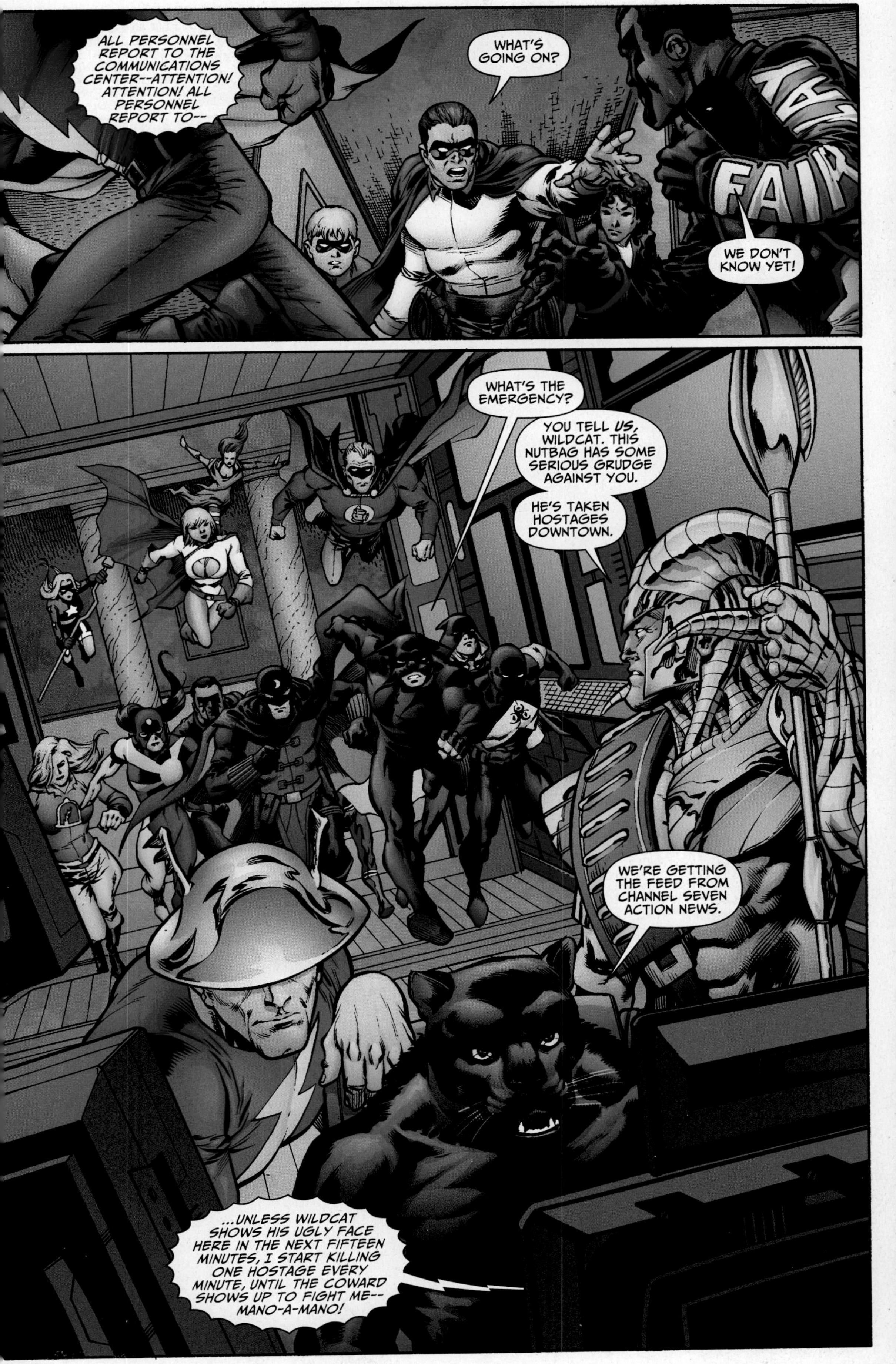
ALL PERSONNEL REPORT TO THE COMMUNICATIONS CENTER--ATTENTION! ATTENTION! ALL PERSONNEL REPORT TO--
WHAT'S GOING ON?
WE DON'T KNOW YET!
WHAT'S THE EMERGENCY?
YOU TELL US, WILDCAT. THIS NUTBAG HAS SOME SERIOUS GRUDGE AGAINST YOU.
HE'S TAKEN HOSTAGES DOWNTOWN.
WE'RE GETTING THE FEED FROM CHANNEL SEVEN ACTION NEWS.
...UNLESS WILDCAT SHOWS HIS UGLY FACE HERE IN THE NEXT FIFTEEN MINUTES, I START KILLING ONE HOSTAGE EVERY MINUTE, UNTIL THE COWARD SHOWS UP TO FIGHT ME--MANO-A-MANO!

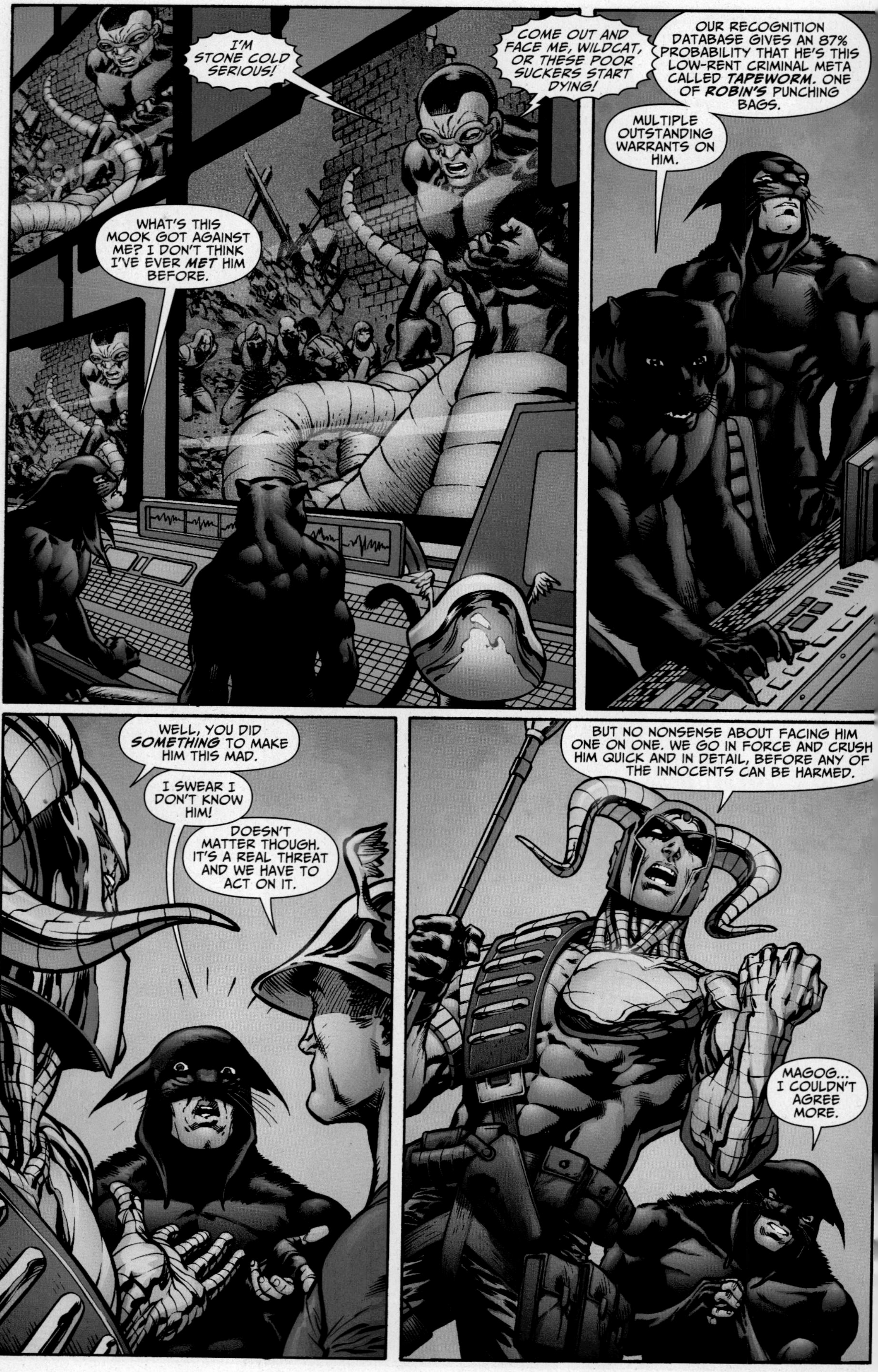
I'M STONE COLD SERIOUS!
COME OUT AND FACE ME, WILDCAT, OR THESE POOR SUCKERS START DYING!
WHAT'S THIS MOOK GOT AGAINST ME? I DON'T THINK I'VE EVER MET HIM BEFORE.
OUR RECOGNITION DATABASE GIVES AN 87% PROBABILITY THAT HE'S THIS LOW-RENT CRIMINAL META CALLED TAPEWORM. ONE OF ROBIN'S PUNCHING BAGS.
MULTIPLE OUTSTANDING WARRANTS ON HIM.
WELL, YOU DID SOMETHING TO MAKE HIM THIS MAD.
I SWEAR I DON'T KNOW HIM!
DOESN'T MATTER THOUGH. IT'S A REAL THREAT AND WE HAVE TO ACT ON IT.
BUT NO NONSENSE ABOUT FACING HIM ONE ON ONE. WE GO IN FORCE AND CRUSH HIM QUICK AND IN DETAIL, BEFORE ANY OF THE INNOCENTS CAN BE HARMED.
MAGOG... I COULDN'T AGREE MORE.

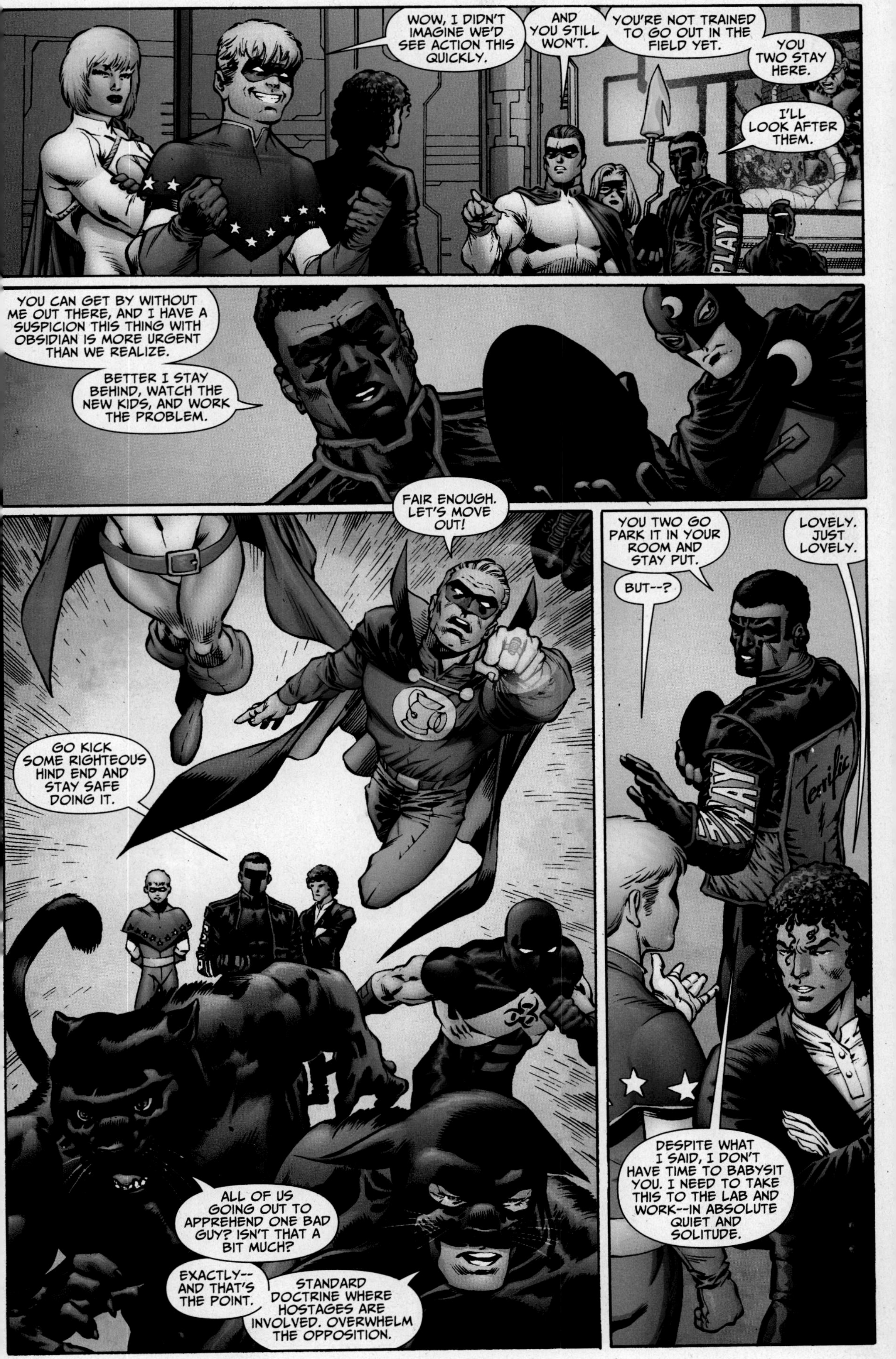
WOW, I DIDN'T IMAGINE WE'D SEE ACTION THIS QUICKLY.
AND YOU STILL WON'T.
YOU'RE NOT TRAINED TO GO OUT IN THE FIELD YET.
YOU TWO STAY HERE.
I'LL LOOK AFTER THEM.
PLAY
YOU CAN GET BY WITHOUT ME OUT THERE, AND I HAVE A SUSPICION THIS THING WITH OBSIDIAN IS MORE URGENT THAN WE REALIZE.
BETTER I STAY BEHIND, WATCH THE NEW KIDS, AND WORK THE PROBLEM.
FAIR ENOUGH. LET'S MOVE OUT!
GO KICK SOME RIGHTEOUS HIND END AND STAY SAFE DOING IT.
ALL OF US GOING OUT TO APPREHEND ONE BAD GUY? ISN'T THAT A BIT MUCH?
EXACTLY-- AND THAT'S THE POINT.
STANDARD DOCTRINE WHERE HOSTAGES ARE INVOLVED. OVERWHELM THE OPPOSITION.
YOU TWO GO PARK IT IN YOUR ROOM AND STAY PUT.
BUT--?
LOVELY. JUST LOVELY.
PLAY
Terrific
DESPITE WHAT I SAID, I DON'T HAVE TIME TO BABYSIT YOU. I NEED TO TAKE THIS TO THE LAB AND WORK--IN ABSOLUTE QUIET AND SOLITUDE.

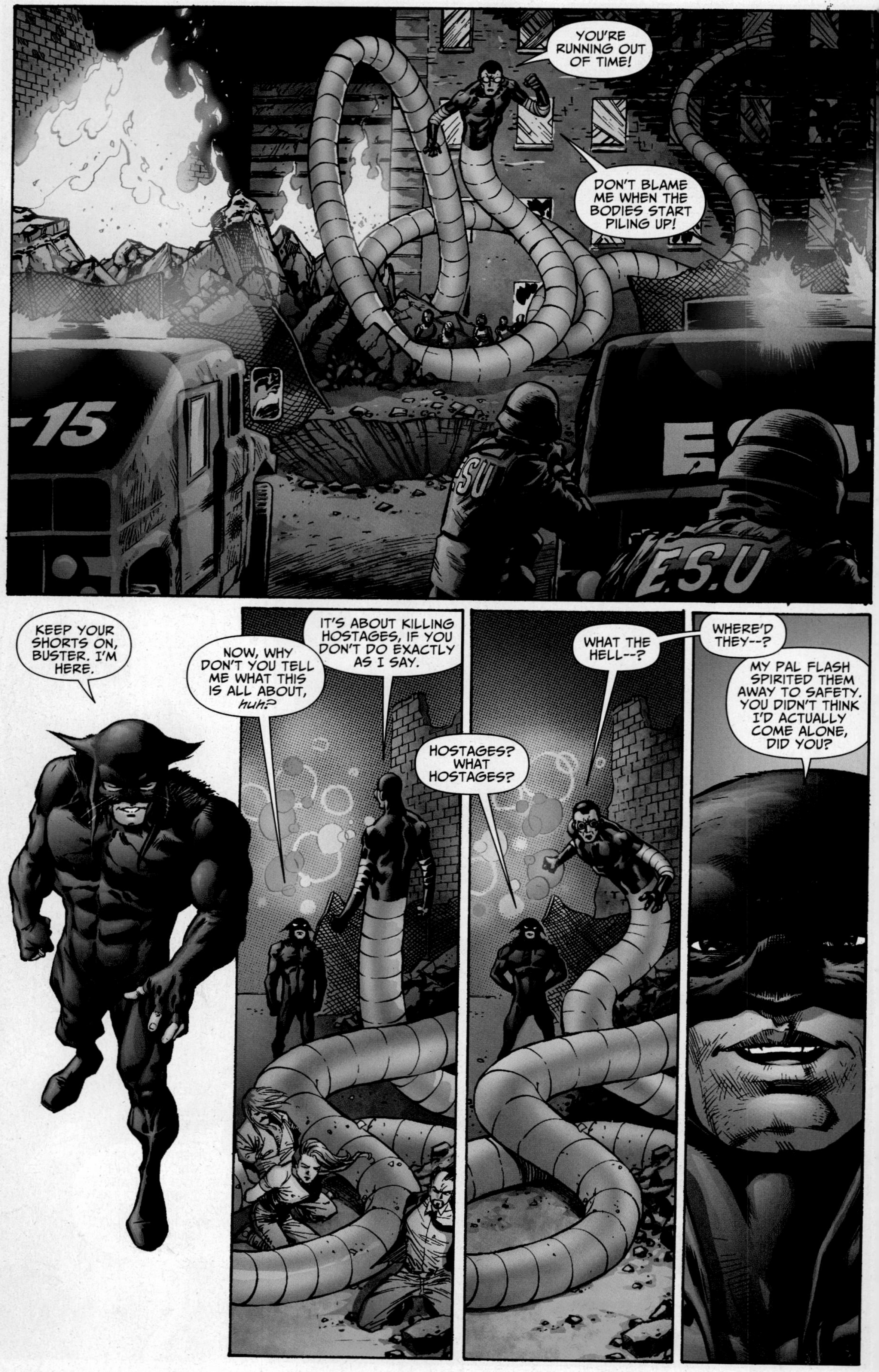
YOU'RE RUNNING OUT OF TIME!
DON'T BLAME ME WHEN THE BODIES START PILING UP!
-15
ESU
E.S.U
KEEP YOUR SHORTS ON, BUSTER. I'M HERE.
NOW, WHY DON'T YOU TELL ME WHAT THIS IS ALL ABOUT, *huh?*
IT'S ABOUT KILLING HOSTAGES, IF YOU DON'T DO EXACTLY AS I SAY.
HOSTAGES? WHAT HOSTAGES?
WHAT THE HELL--?
WHERE'D THEY--?
MY PAL FLASH SPIRITED THEM AWAY TO SAFETY. YOU DIDN'T THINK I'D ACTUALLY COME ALONE, DID YOU?

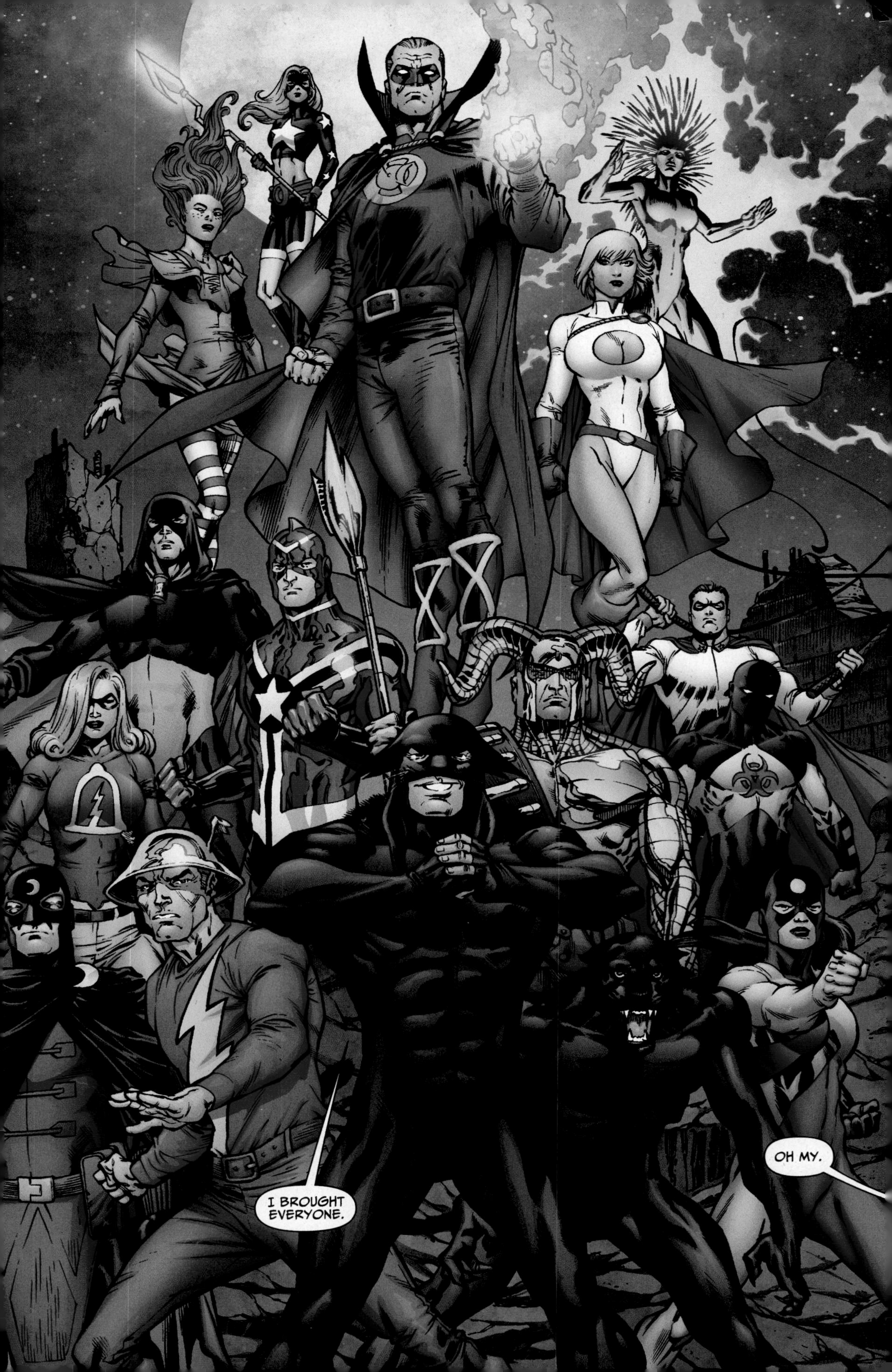
I BROUGHT EVERYONE.
OH MY.

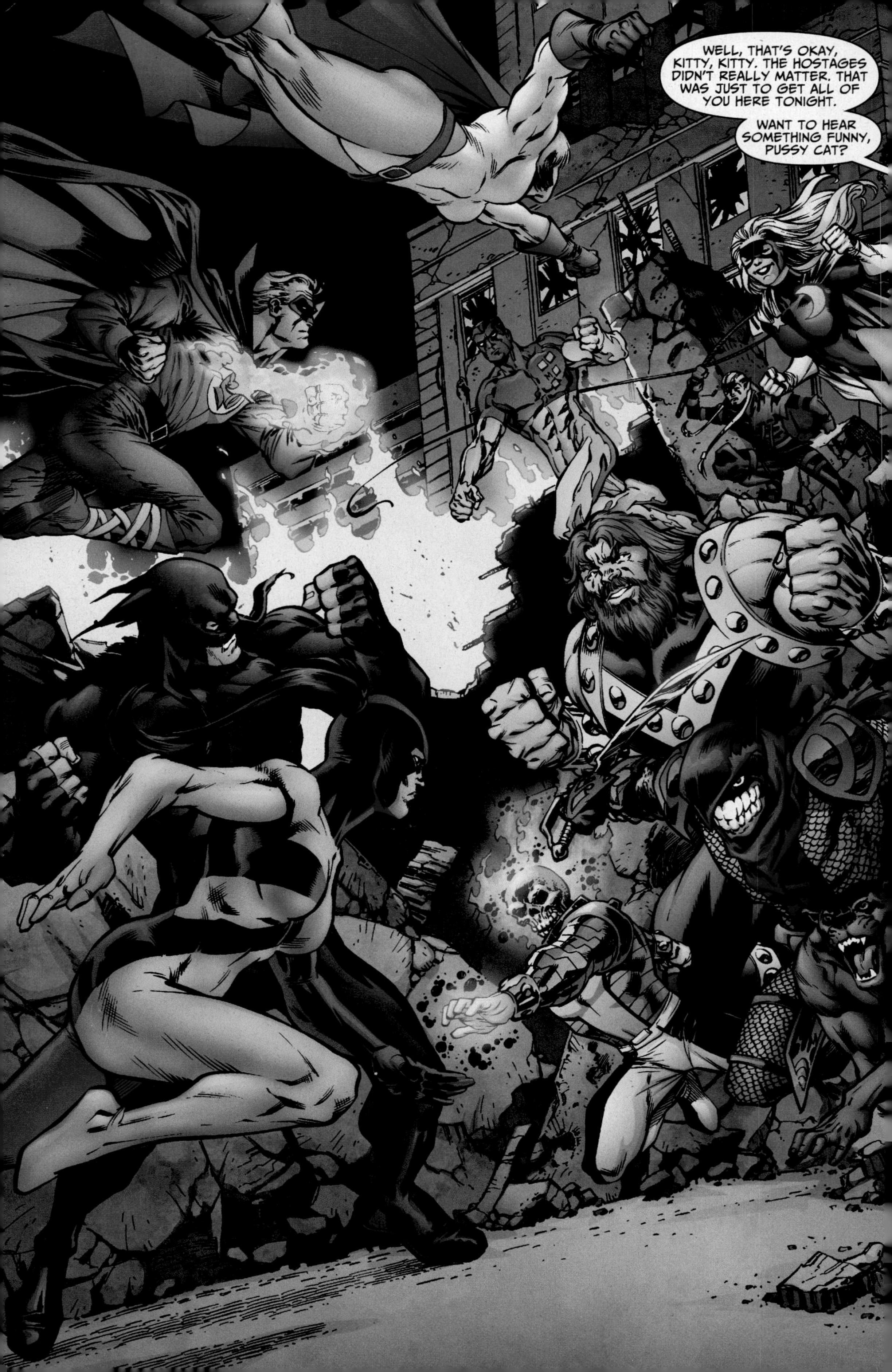
WELL, THAT'S OKAY, KITTY, KITTY. THE HOSTAGES DIDN'T REALLY MATTER. THAT WAS JUST TO GET ALL OF YOU HERE TONIGHT.
WANT TO HEAR SOMETHING FUNNY, PUSSY CAT?

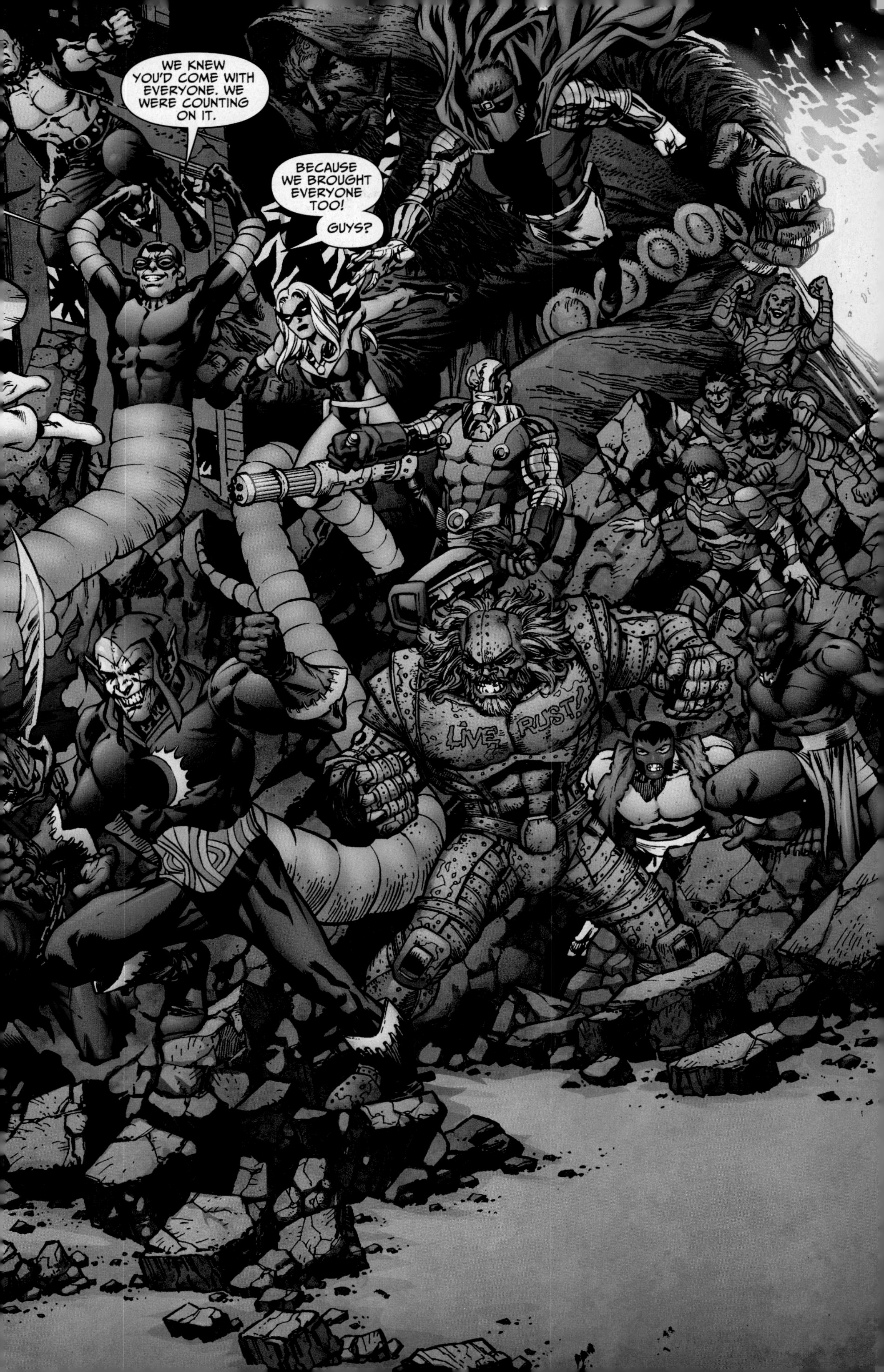
WE KNEW YOU'D COME WITH EVERYONE. WE WERE COUNTING ON IT.
BECAUSE WE BROUGHT EVERYONE TOO!
GUYS?
LIVE RUST!

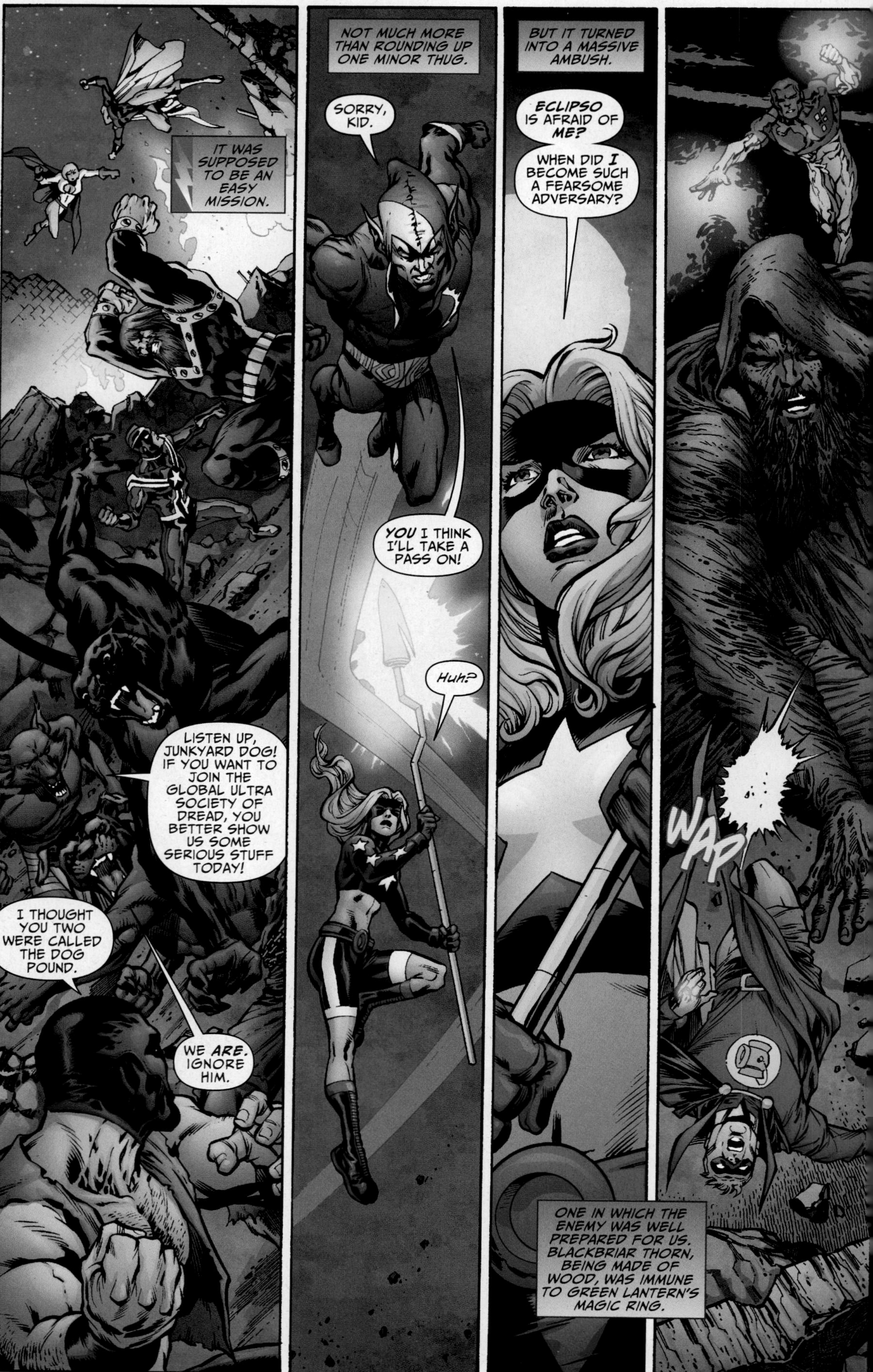
IT WAS SUPPOSED TO BE AN EASY MISSION.
LISTEN UP, JUNKYARD DOG! IF YOU WANT TO JOIN THE GLOBAL ULTRA SOCIETY OF DREAD, YOU BETTER SHOW US SOME SERIOUS STUFF TODAY!
I THOUGHT YOU TWO WERE CALLED THE DOG POUND.
WE ARE. IGNORE HIM.
NOT MUCH MORE THAN ROUNDING UP ONE MINOR THUG.
SORRY, KID.
YOU I THINK I'LL TAKE A PASS ON!
Huh?
BUT IT TURNED INTO A MASSIVE AMBUSH.
ECLIPSO IS AFRAID OF ME?
WHEN DID I BECOME SUCH A FEARSOME ADVERSARY?
WAP
ONE IN WHICH THE ENEMY WAS WELL PREPARED FOR US. BLACKBRIAR THORN, BEING MADE OF WOOD, WAS IMMUNE TO GREEN LANTERN'S MAGIC RING.

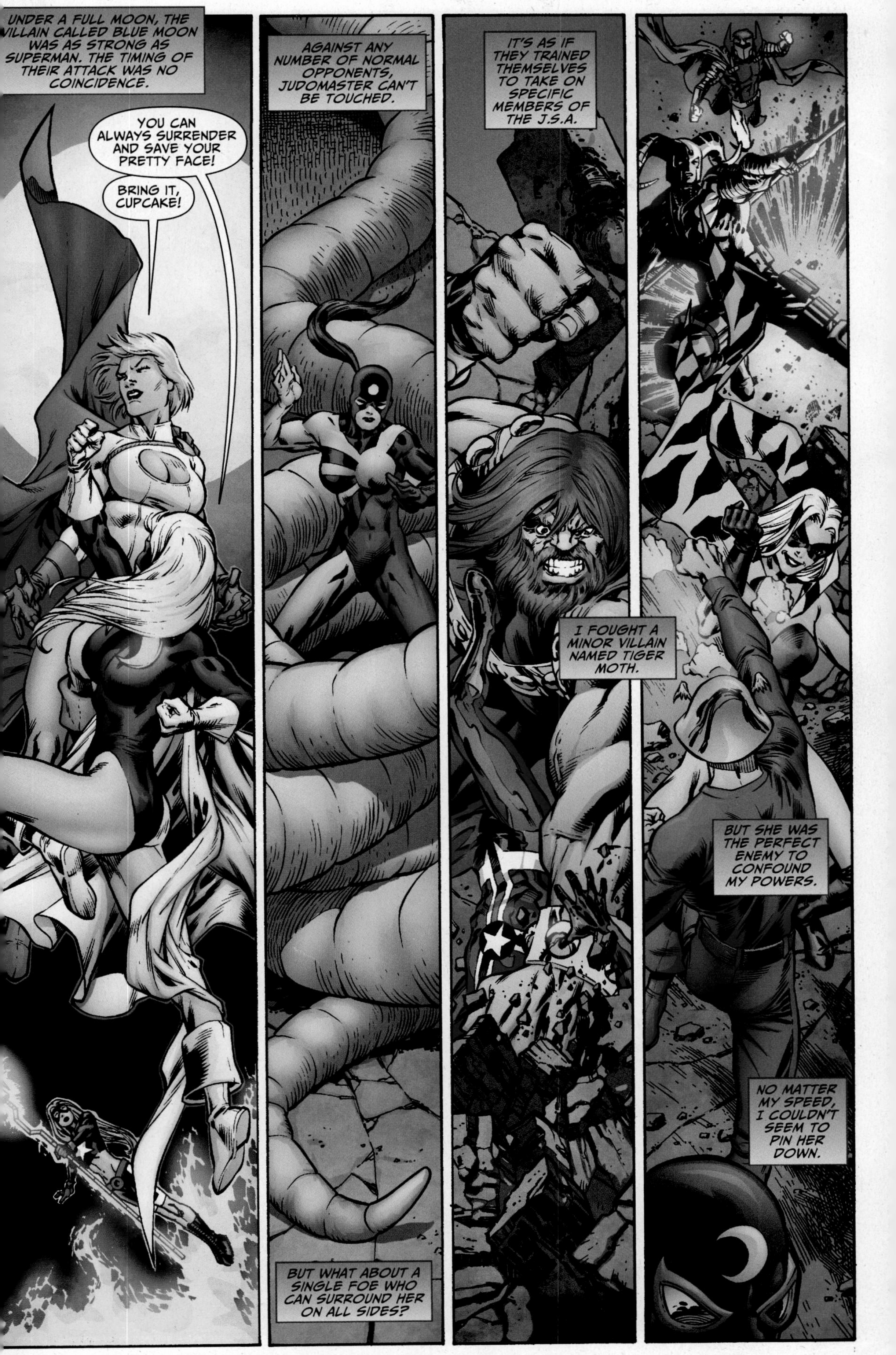
UNDER A FULL MOON, THE VILLAIN CALLED BLUE MOON WAS AS STRONG AS SUPERMAN. THE TIMING OF THEIR ATTACK WAS NO COINCIDENCE.
YOU CAN ALWAYS SURRENDER AND SAVE YOUR PRETTY FACE!
BRING IT, CUPCAKE!
AGAINST ANY NUMBER OF NORMAL OPPONENTS, JUDOMASTER CAN'T BE TOUCHED.
BUT WHAT ABOUT A SINGLE FOE WHO CAN SURROUND HER ON ALL SIDES?
IT'S AS IF THEY TRAINED THEMSELVES TO TAKE ON SPECIFIC MEMBERS OF THE J.S.A.
I FOUGHT A MINOR VILLAIN NAMED TIGER MOTH.
BUT SHE WAS THE PERFECT ENEMY TO CONFOUND MY POWERS.
NO MATTER MY SPEED, I COULDN'T SEEM TO PIN HER DOWN.

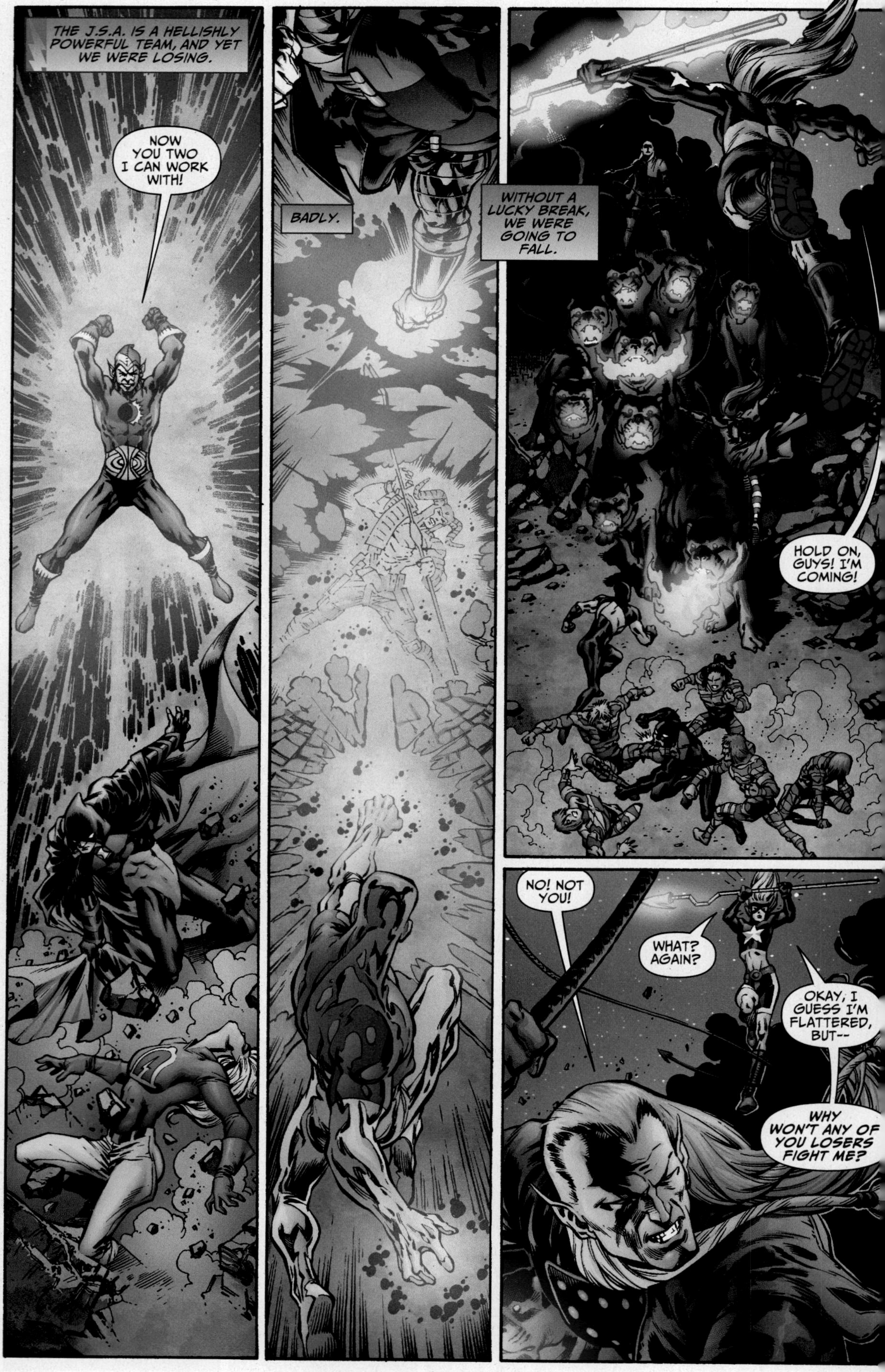
THE J.S.A. IS A HELLISHLY POWERFUL TEAM, AND YET WE WERE LOSING.
NOW YOU TWO I CAN WORK WITH!
BADLY.
WITHOUT A LUCKY BREAK, WE WERE GOING TO FALL.
HOLD ON, GUYS! I'M COMING!
NO! NOT YOU!
WHAT? AGAIN?
OKAY, I GUESS I'M FLATTERED, BUT--
WHY WON'T ANY OF YOU LOSERS FIGHT ME?

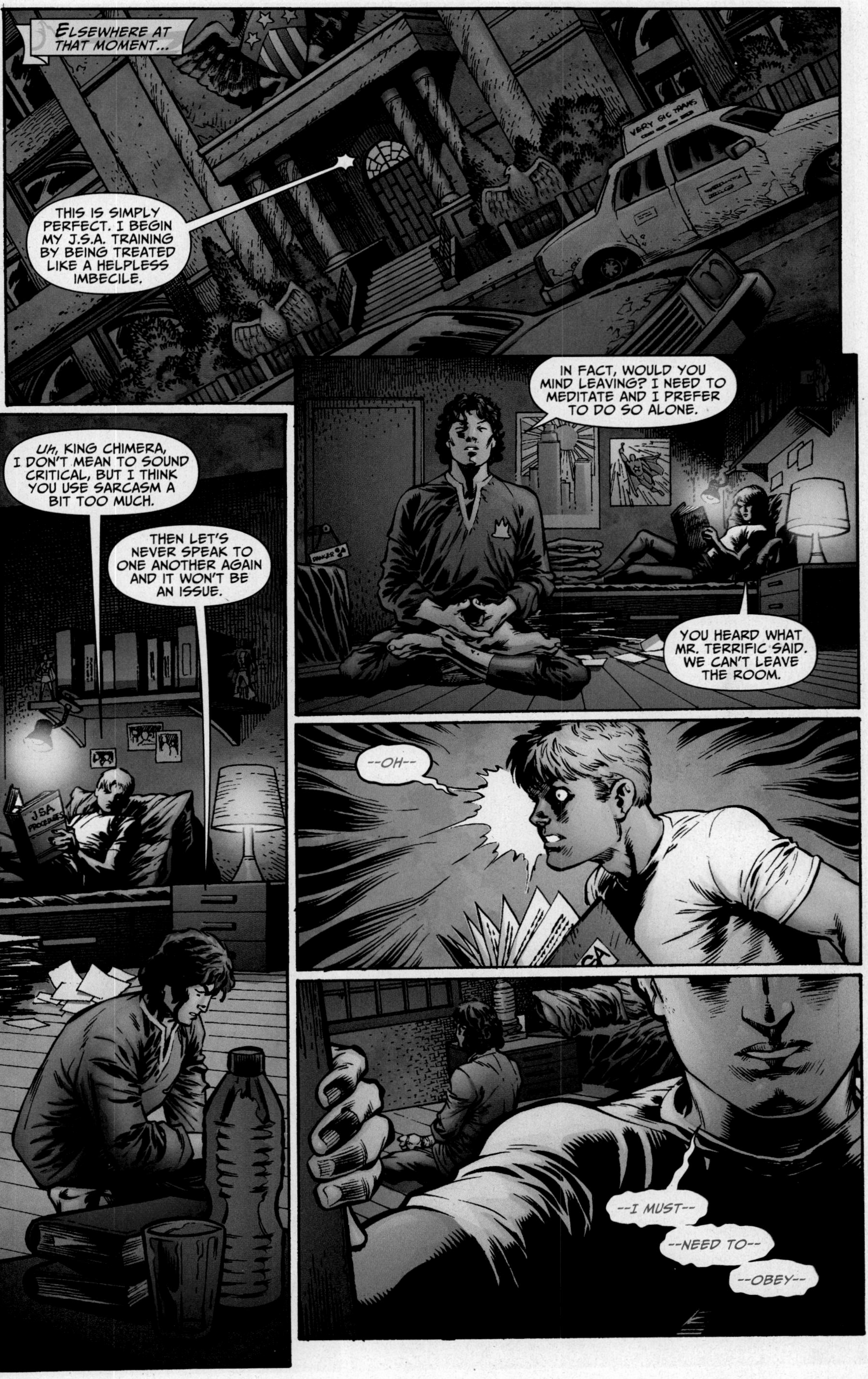
ELSEWHERE AT THAT MOMENT...
VERY SIG TAXIS
THIS IS SIMPLY PERFECT. I BEGIN MY J.S.A. TRAINING BY BEING TREATED LIKE A HELPLESS IMBECILE.
IN FACT, WOULD YOU MIND LEAVING? I NEED TO MEDITATE AND I PREFER TO DO SO ALONE.
YOU HEARD WHAT MR. TERRIFIC SAID. WE CAN'T LEAVE THE ROOM.
Uh, KING CHIMERA, I DON'T MEAN TO SOUND CRITICAL, BUT I THINK YOU USE SARCASM A BIT TOO MUCH.
THEN LET'S NEVER SPEAK TO ONE ANOTHER AGAIN AND IT WON'T BE AN ISSUE.
JSA PROCEDURES
--OH--
--I MUST--
--NEED TO--
--OBEY--

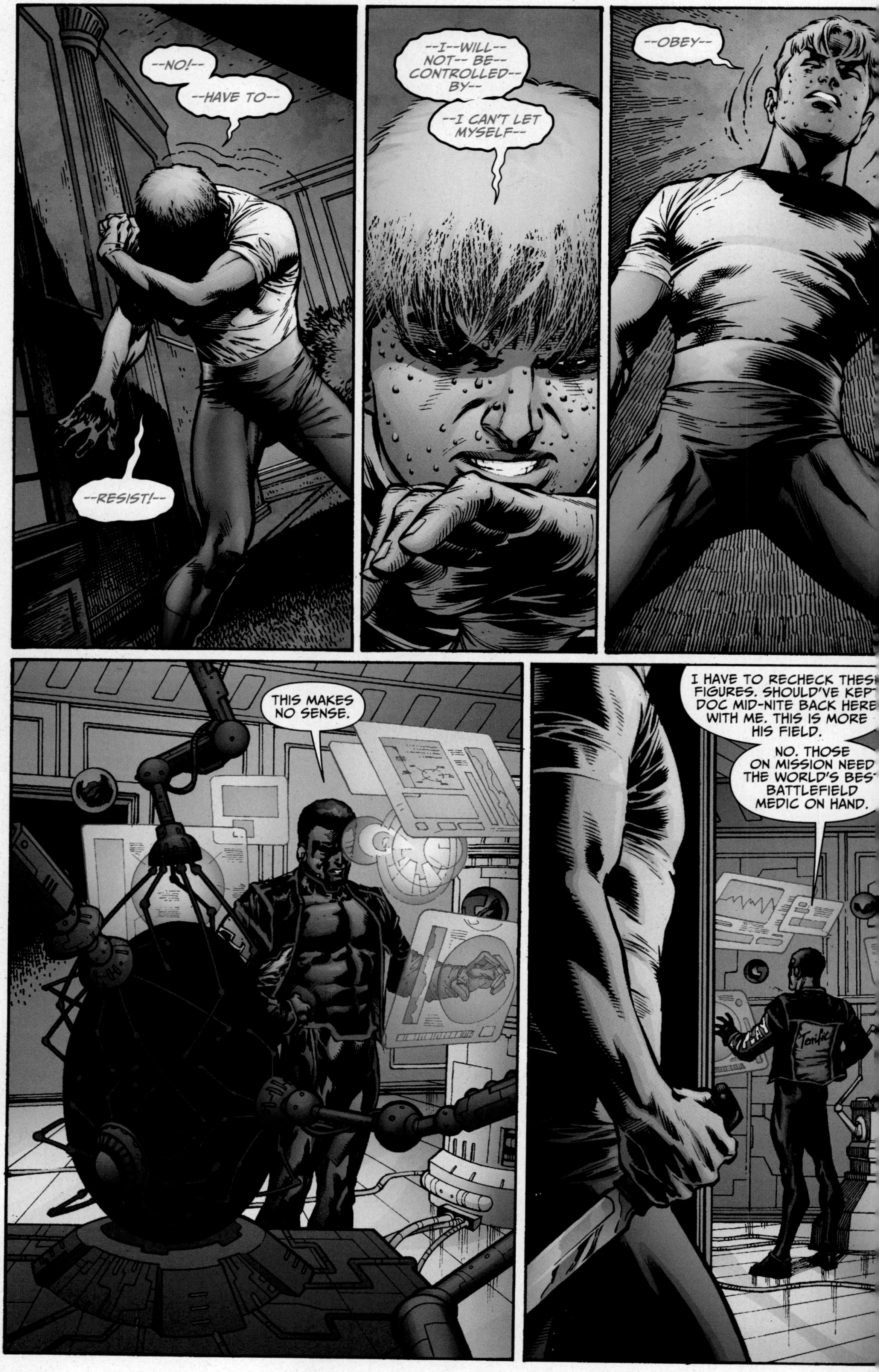
--NO!--
--HAVE TO--
--RESIST!--
--I--WILL-- NOT-- BE-- CONTROLLED-- BY--
--I CAN'T LET MYSELF--
--OBEY--
THIS MAKES NO SENSE.
I HAVE TO RECHECK THESE FIGURES. SHOULD'VE KEPT DOC MID-NITE BACK HERE WITH ME. THIS IS MORE HIS FIELD.
NO. THOSE ON MISSION NEED THE WORLD'S BEST BATTLEFIELD MEDIC ON HAND.

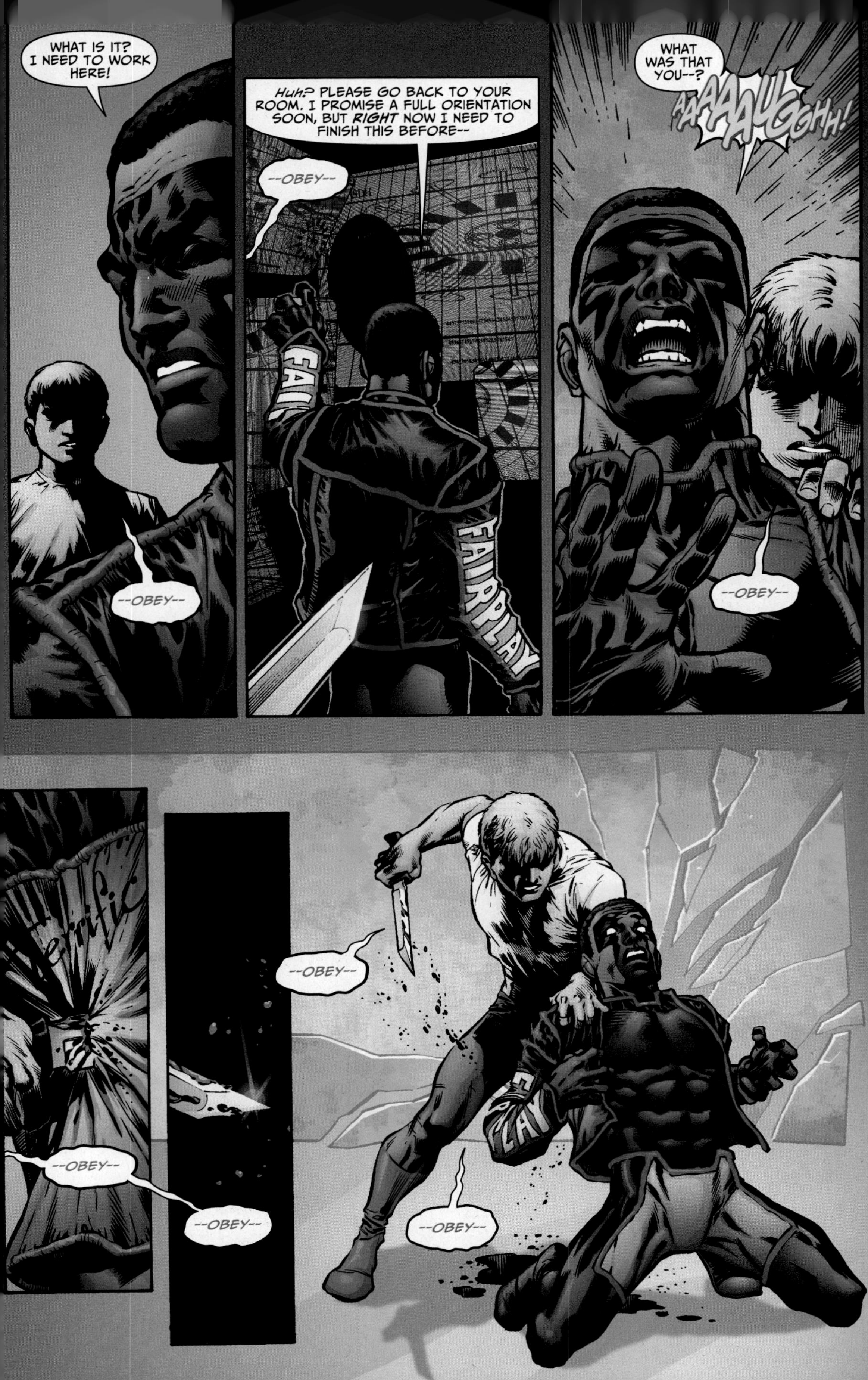
WHAT IS IT? I NEED TO WORK HERE!
--OBEY--
Huh? PLEASE GO BACK TO YOUR ROOM. I PROMISE A FULL ORIENTATION SOON, BUT RIGHT NOW I NEED TO FINISH THIS BEFORE--
--OBEY--
FAIRPLAY
WHAT WAS THAT YOU--?
AAAAAUUGGHH!
--OBEY--
--OBEY--
--OBEY--
--OBEY--
--OBEY--

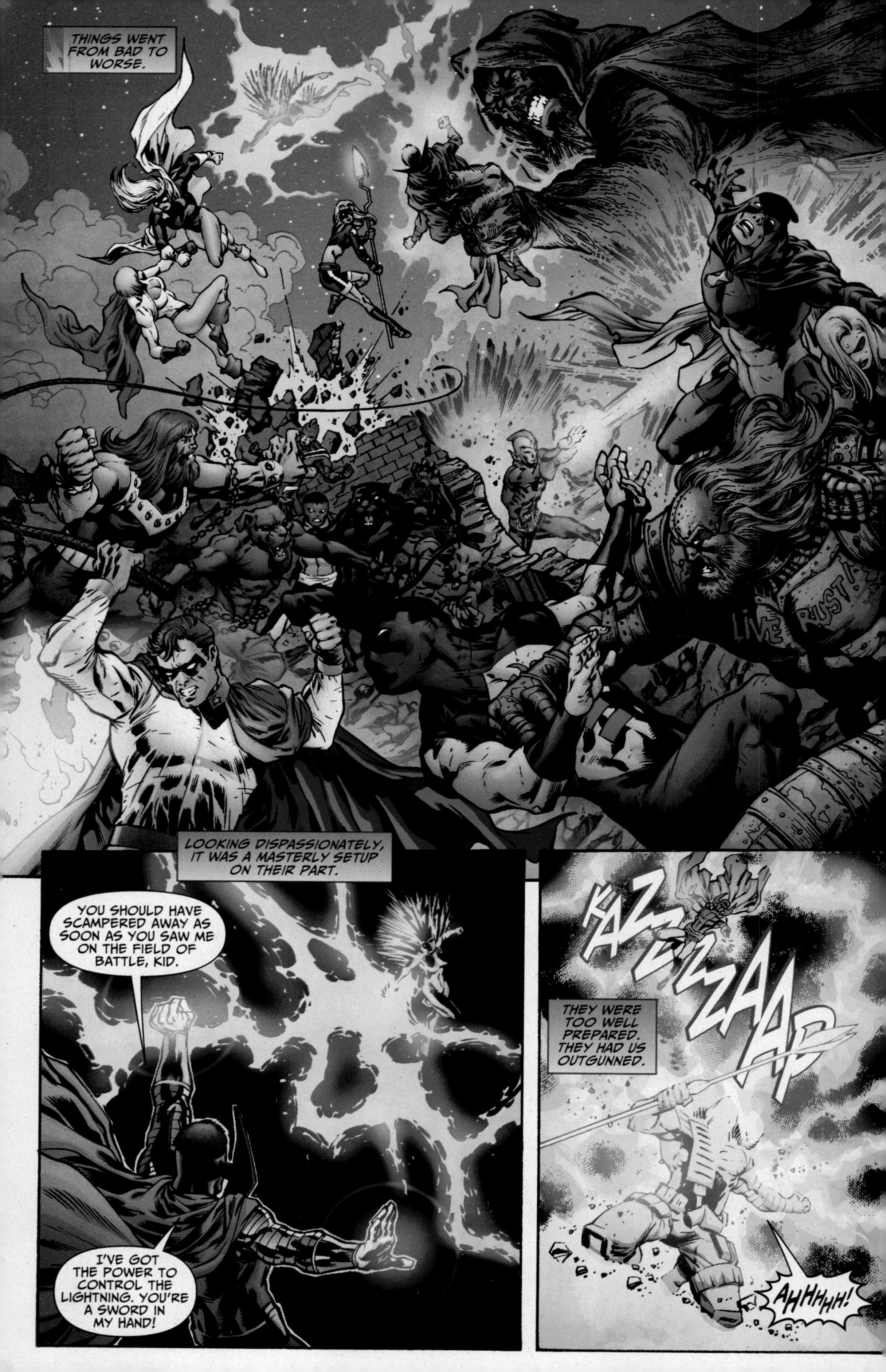
THINGS WENT FROM BAD TO WORSE.
LOOKING DISPASSIONATELY, IT WAS A MASTERLY SETUP ON THEIR PART.
YOU SHOULD HAVE SCAMPERED AWAY AS SOON AS YOU SAW ME ON THE FIELD OF BATTLE, KID.
I'VE GOT THE POWER TO CONTROL THE LIGHTNING. YOU'RE A SWORD IN MY HAND!
KAZZZZAAP
THEY WERE TOO WELL PREPARED. THEY HAD US OUTGUNNED.
AHHHHH!

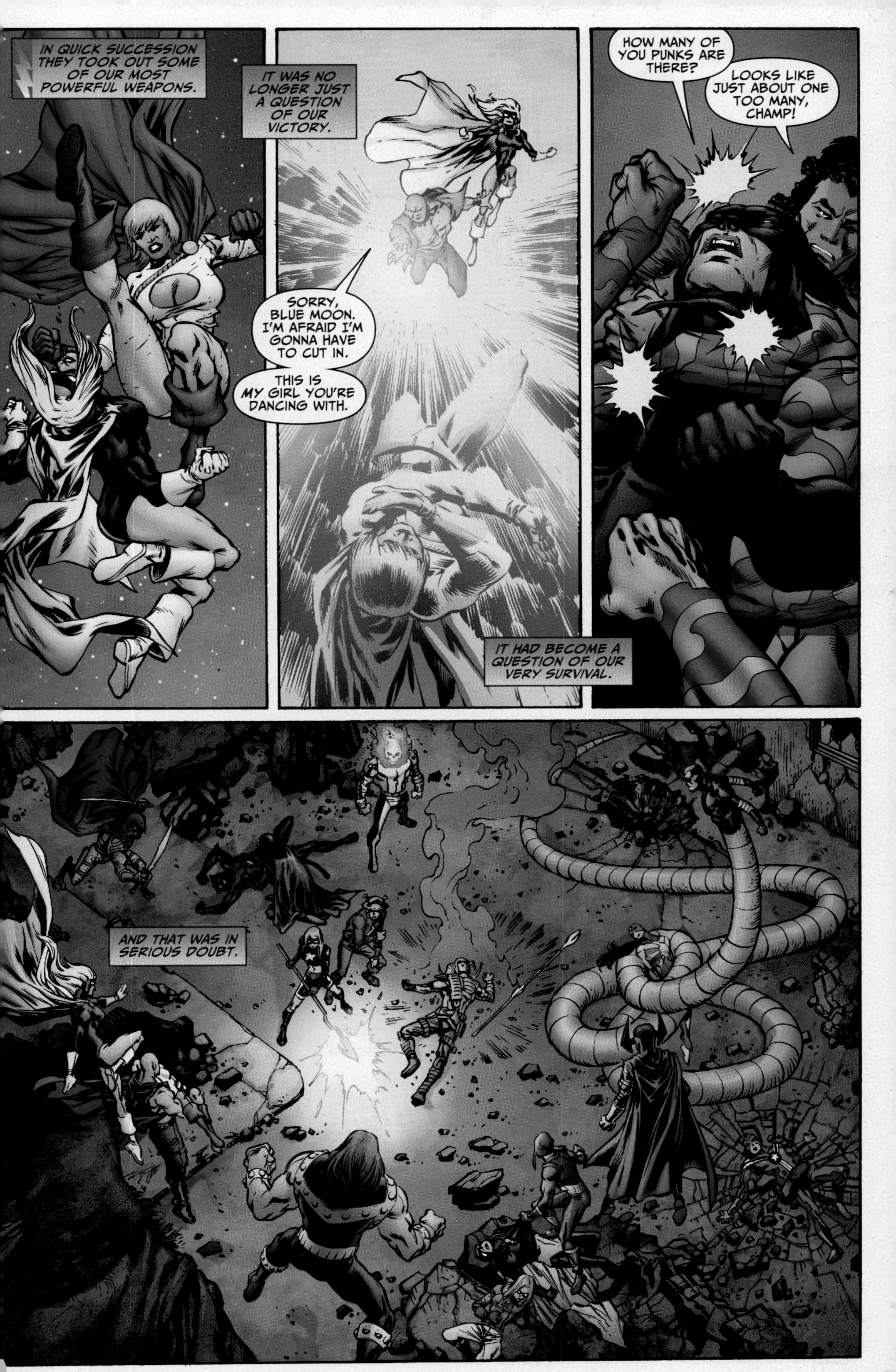
IN QUICK SUCCESSION THEY TOOK OUT SOME OF OUR MOST POWERFUL WEAPONS.
IT WAS NO LONGER JUST A QUESTION OF OUR VICTORY.
SORRY, BLUE MOON. I'M AFRAID I'M GONNA HAVE TO CUT IN.
THIS IS MY GIRL YOU'RE DANCING WITH.
IT HAD BECOME A QUESTION OF OUR VERY SURVIVAL.
HOW MANY OF YOU PUNKS ARE THERE?
LOOKS LIKE JUST ABOUT ONE TOO MANY, CHAMP!
AND THAT WAS IN SERIOUS DOUBT.

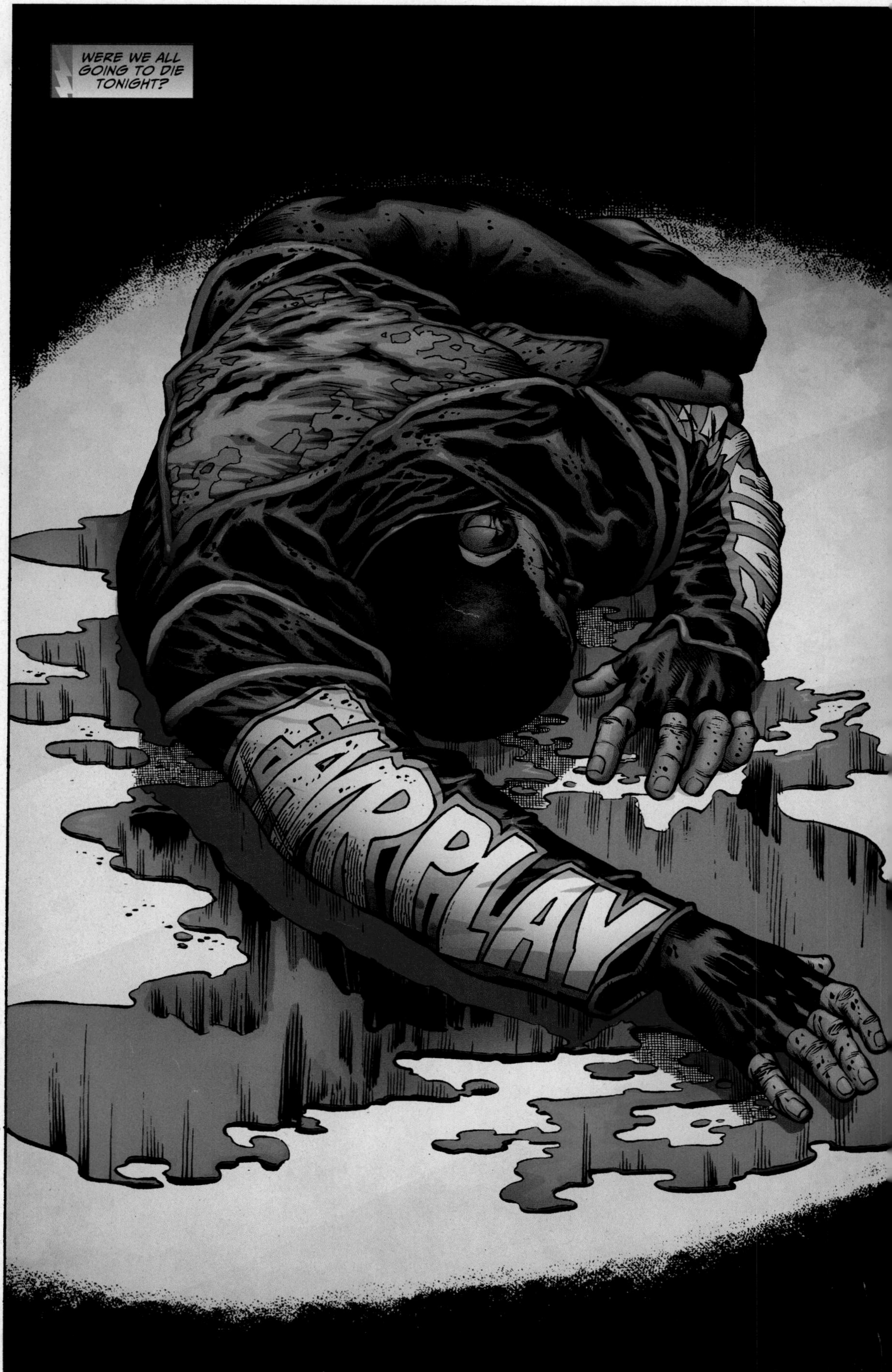
WERE WE ALL GOING TO DIE TONIGHT?
HARD PLAY

THE BAD SEED Part Two

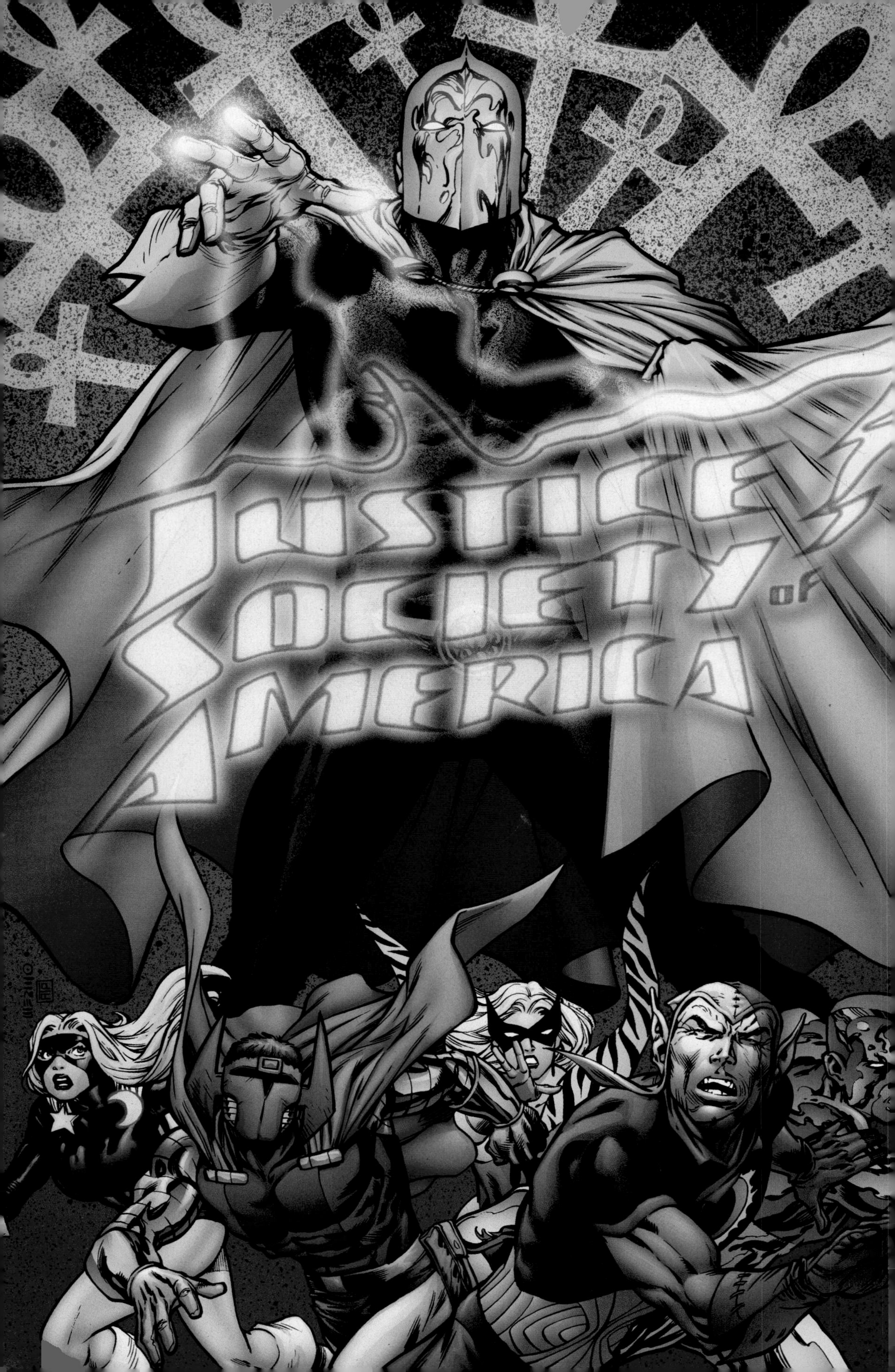
JUSTICE SOCIETY OF AMERICA

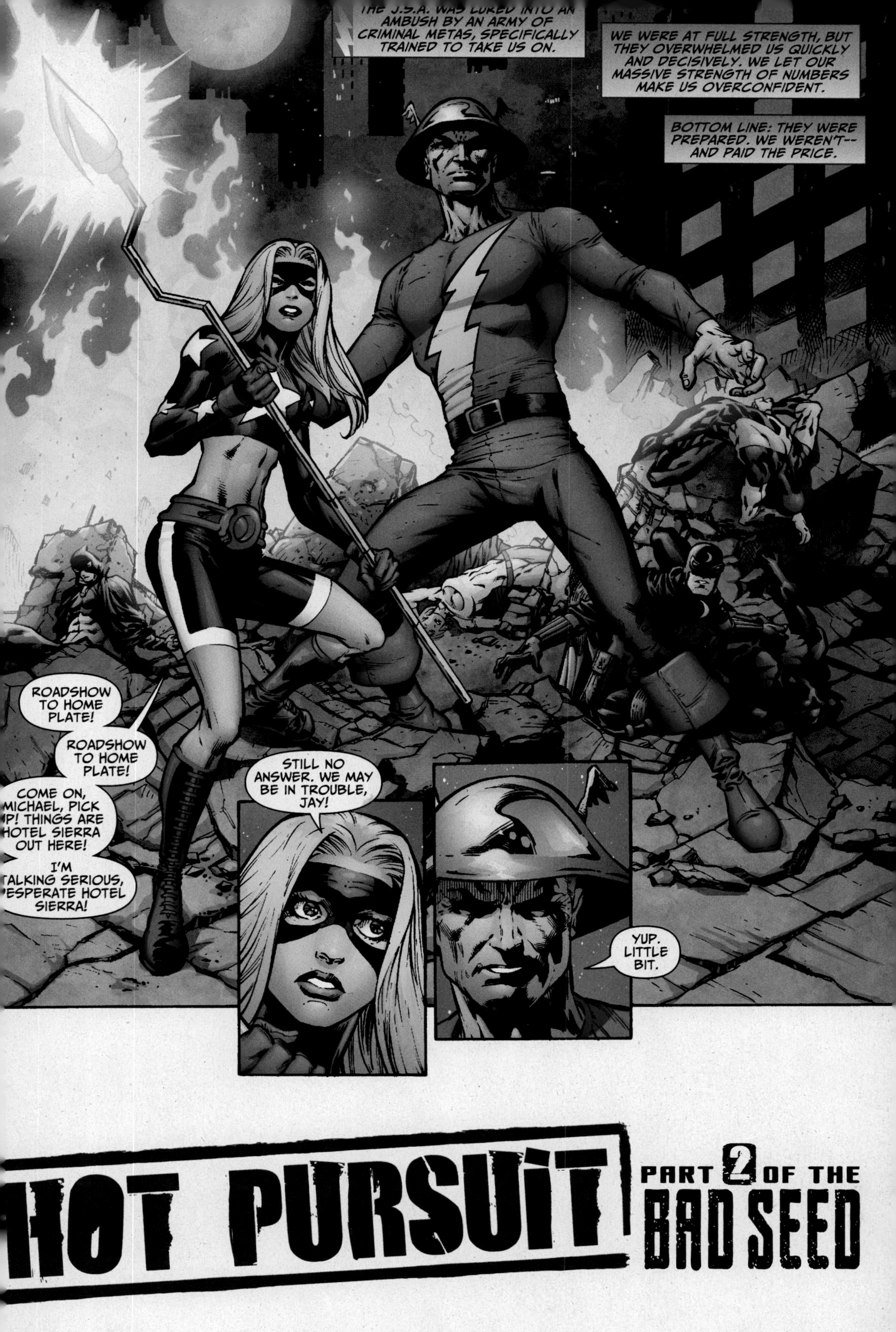
THE J.S.A. WAS LURED INTO AN AMBUSH BY AN ARMY OF CRIMINAL METAS, SPECIFICALLY TRAINED TO TAKE US ON.
WE WERE AT FULL STRENGTH, BUT THEY OVERWHELMED US QUICKLY AND DECISIVELY. WE LET OUR MASSIVE STRENGTH OF NUMBERS MAKE US OVERCONFIDENT.
BOTTOM LINE: THEY WERE PREPARED. WE WEREN'T-- AND PAID THE PRICE.
ROADSHOW TO HOME PLATE!
ROADSHOW TO HOME PLATE!
COME ON, MICHAEL, PICK P! THINGS ARE HOTEL SIERRA OUT HERE!
I'M TALKING SERIOUS, ESPERATE HOTEL SIERRA!
STILL NO ANSWER. WE MAY BE IN TROUBLE, JAY!
YUP. LITTLE BIT.
HOT PURSUIT
PART 2 OF THE BAD SEED

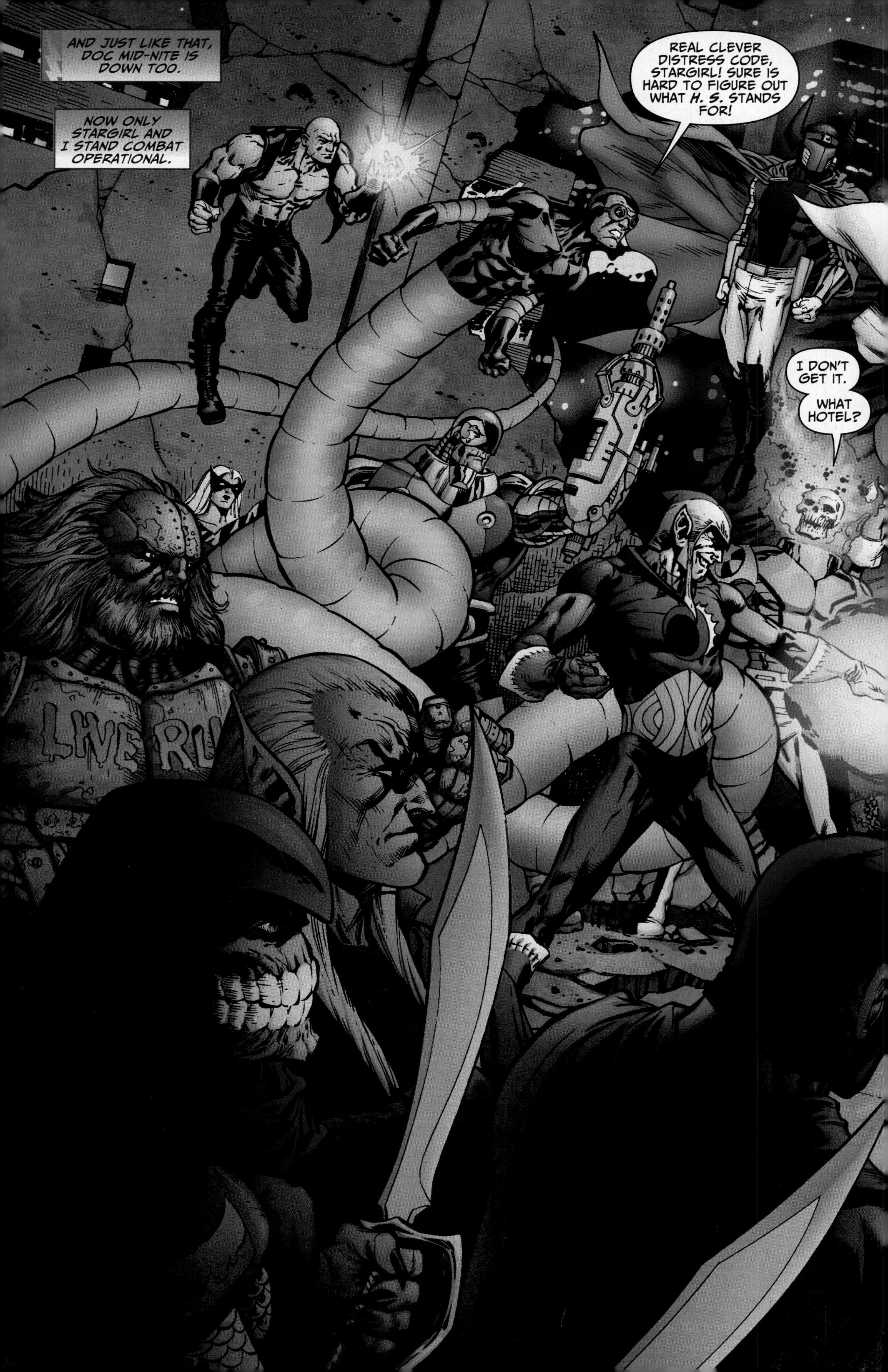
AND JUST LIKE THAT, DOC MID-NITE IS DOWN TOO.
NOW ONLY STARGIRL AND I STAND COMBAT OPERATIONAL.
REAL CLEVER DISTRESS CODE, STARGIRL! SURE IS HARD TO FIGURE OUT WHAT H. S. STANDS FOR!
I DON'T GET IT.
WHAT HOTEL?

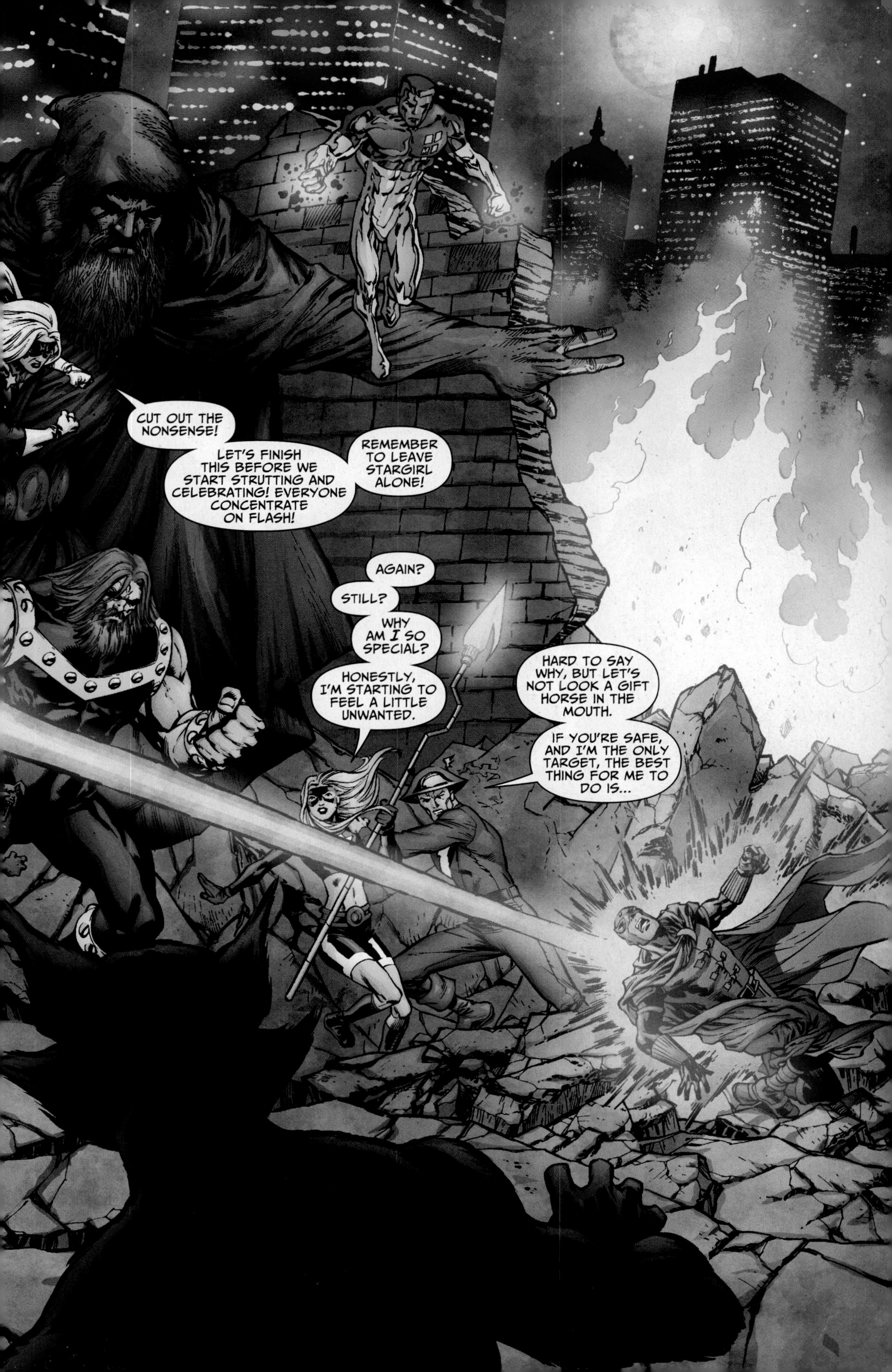

CUT OUT THE NONSENSE!
LET'S FINISH THIS BEFORE WE START STRUTTING AND CELEBRATING! EVERYONE CONCENTRATE ON FLASH!
REMEMBER TO LEAVE STARGIRL ALONE!
AGAIN?
STILL?
WHY AM I SO SPECIAL?
HONESTLY, I'M STARTING TO FEEL A LITTLE UNWANTED.
HARD TO SAY WHY, BUT LET'S NOT LOOK A GIFT HORSE IN THE MOUTH.
IF YOU'RE SAFE, AND I'M THE ONLY TARGET, THE BEST THING FOR ME TO DO IS...

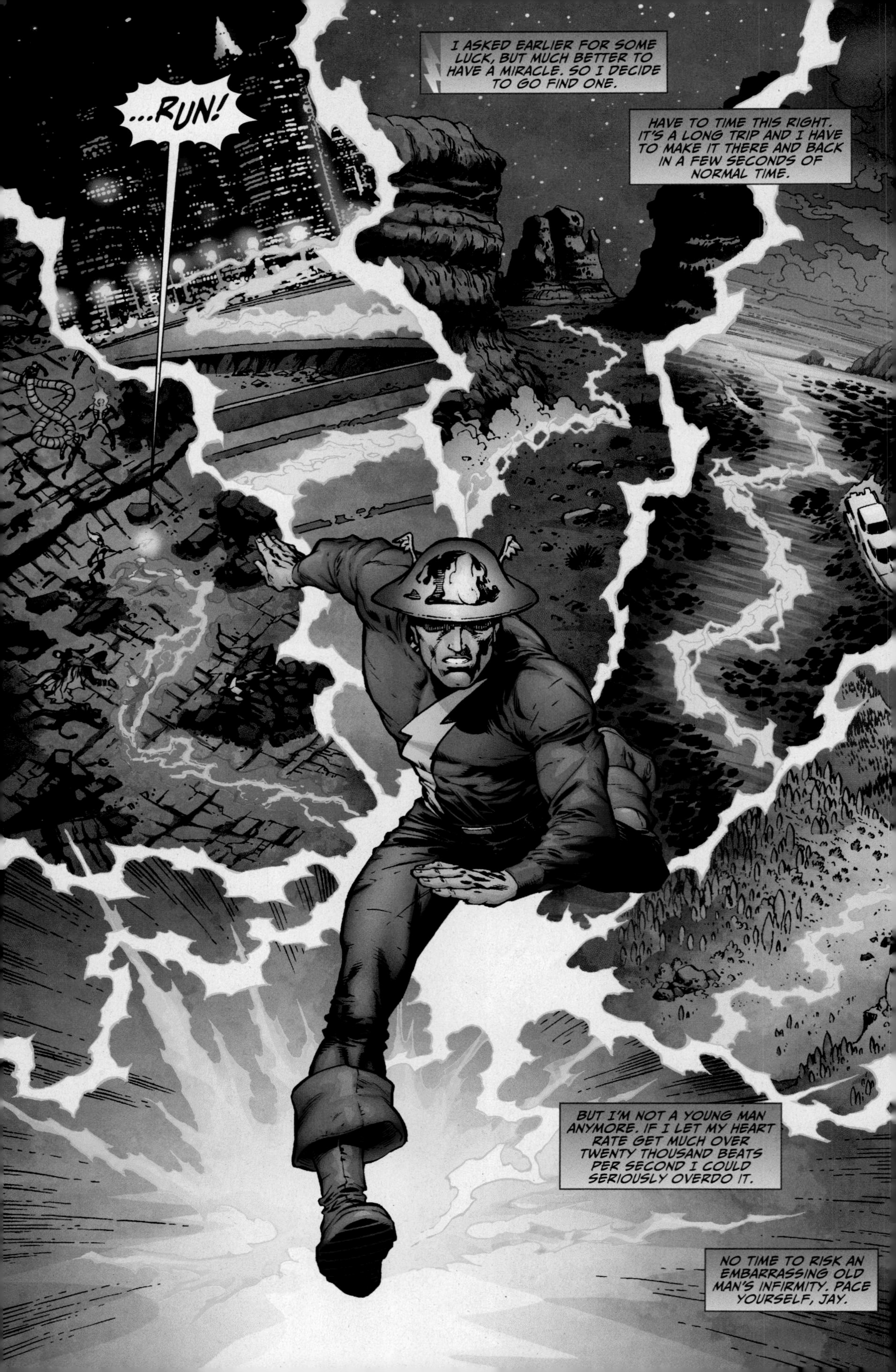
I ASKED EARLIER FOR SOME LUCK, BUT MUCH BETTER TO HAVE A MIRACLE. SO I DECIDE TO GO FIND ONE.
...RUN!
HAVE TO TIME THIS RIGHT. IT'S A LONG TRIP AND I HAVE TO MAKE IT THERE AND BACK IN A FEW SECONDS OF NORMAL TIME.
BUT I'M NOT A YOUNG MAN ANYMORE. IF I LET MY HEART RATE GET MUCH OVER TWENTY THOUSAND BEATS PER SECOND I COULD SERIOUSLY OVERDO IT.
NO TIME TO RISK AN EMBARRASSING OLD MAN'S INFIRMITY. PACE YOURSELF, JAY.

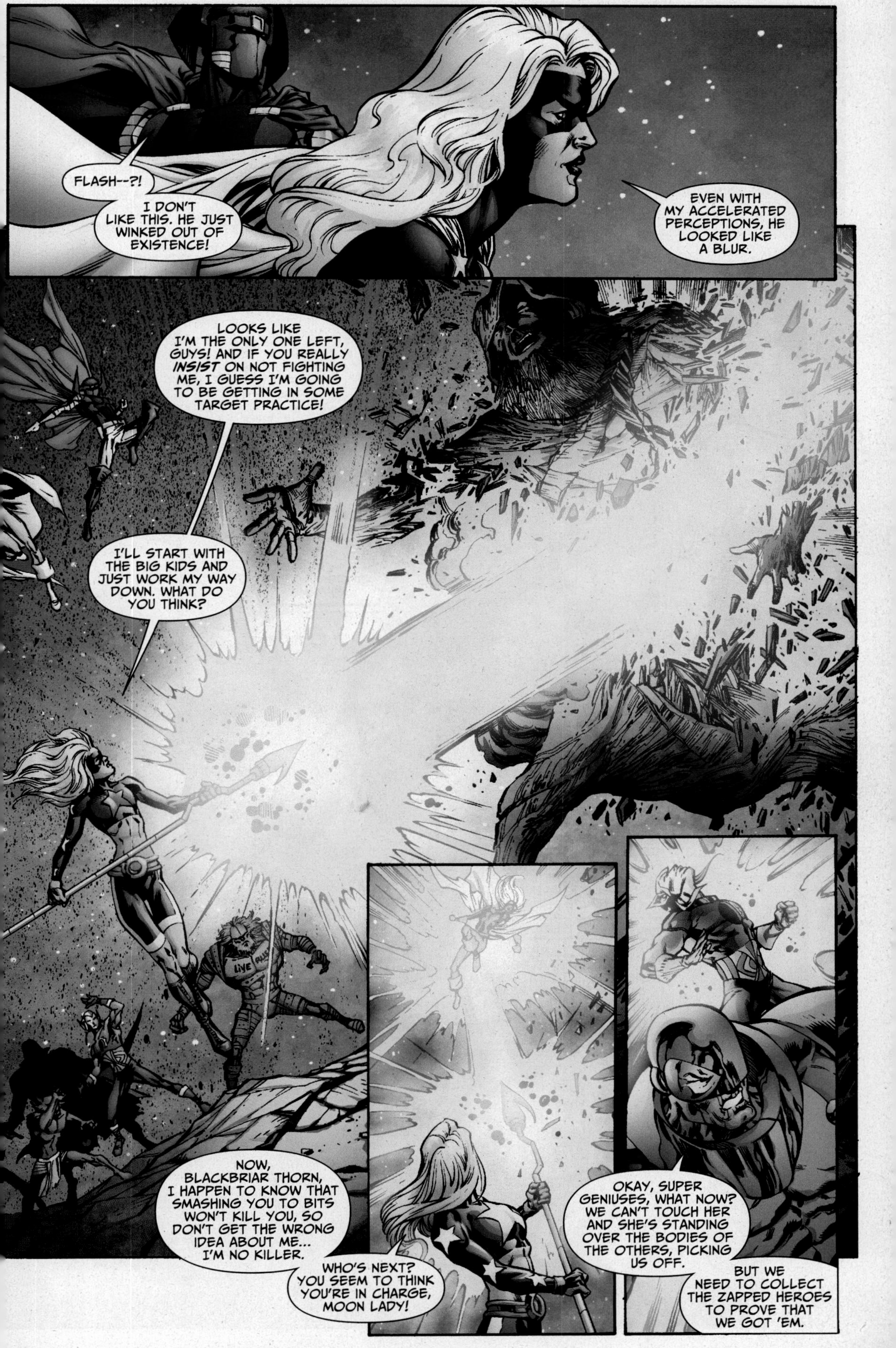
FLASH--?!
I DON'T LIKE THIS. HE JUST WINKED OUT OF EXISTENCE!
EVEN WITH MY ACCELERATED PERCEPTIONS, HE LOOKED LIKE A BLUR.
LOOKS LIKE I'M THE ONLY ONE LEFT, GUYS! AND IF YOU REALLY *INSIST* ON NOT FIGHTING ME, I GUESS I'M GOING TO BE GETTING IN SOME TARGET PRACTICE!
I'LL START WITH THE BIG KIDS AND JUST WORK MY WAY DOWN. WHAT DO YOU THINK?
NOW, BLACKBRIAR THORN, I HAPPEN TO KNOW THAT SMASHING YOU TO BITS WON'T KILL YOU, SO DON'T GET THE WRONG IDEA ABOUT ME... I'M NO KILLER.
WHO'S NEXT? YOU SEEM TO THINK YOU'RE IN CHARGE, MOON LADY!
OKAY, SUPER GENIUSES, WHAT NOW? WE CAN'T TOUCH HER AND SHE'S STANDING OVER THE BODIES OF THE OTHERS, PICKING US OFF.
BUT WE NEED TO COLLECT THE ZAPPED HEROES TO PROVE THAT WE GOT 'EM.

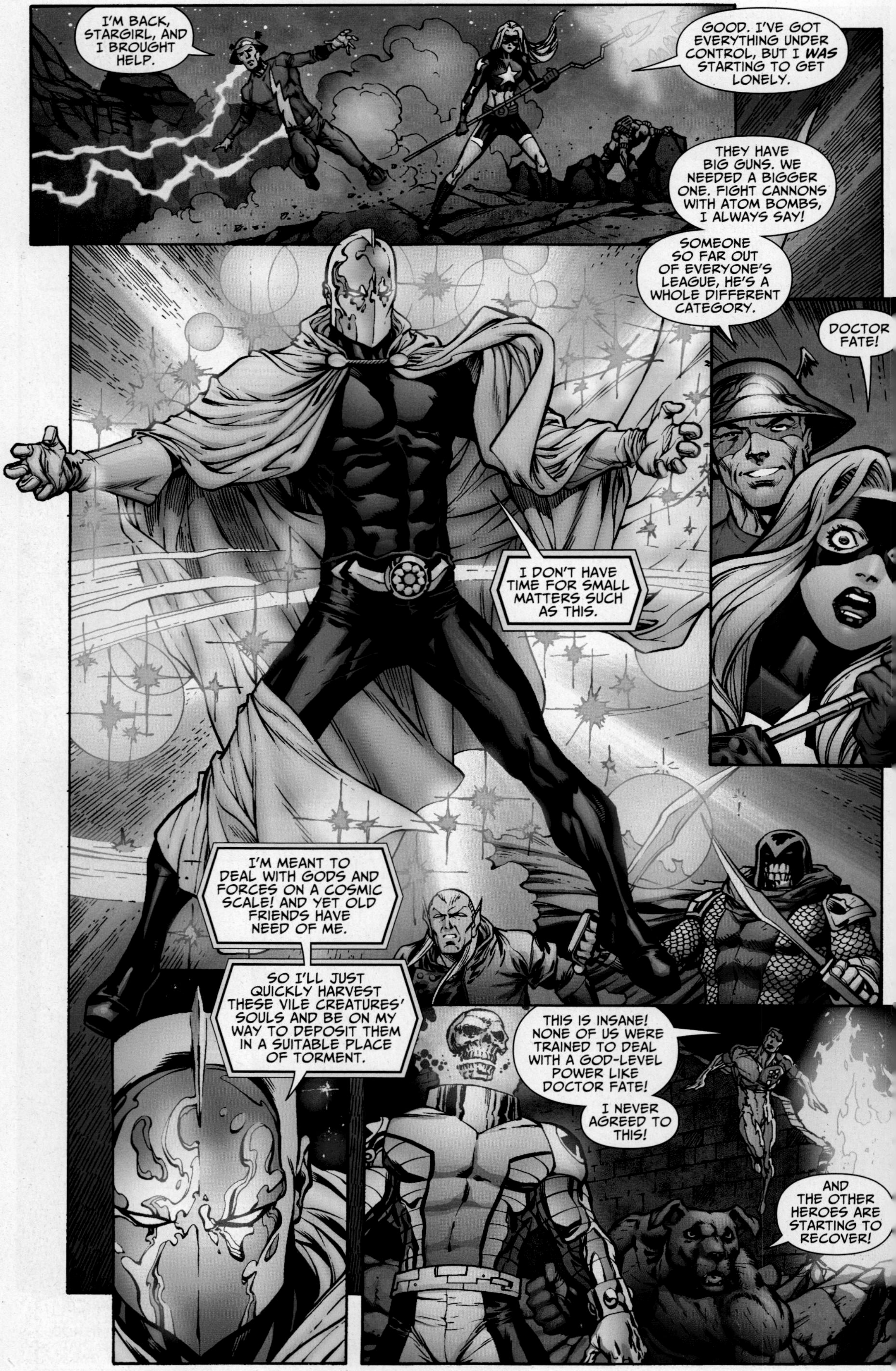
I'M BACK, STARGIRL, AND I BROUGHT HELP.
GOOD. I'VE GOT EVERYTHING UNDER CONTROL, BUT I WAS STARTING TO GET LONELY.
THEY HAVE BIG GUNS. WE NEEDED A BIGGER ONE. FIGHT CANNONS WITH ATOM BOMBS, I ALWAYS SAY!
SOMEONE SO FAR OUT OF EVERYONE'S LEAGUE, HE'S A WHOLE DIFFERENT CATEGORY.
DOCTOR FATE!
I DON'T HAVE TIME FOR SMALL MATTERS SUCH AS THIS.
I'M MEANT TO DEAL WITH GODS AND FORCES ON A COSMIC SCALE! AND YET OLD FRIENDS HAVE NEED OF ME.
SO I'LL JUST QUICKLY HARVEST THESE VILE CREATURES' SOULS AND BE ON MY WAY TO DEPOSIT THEM IN A SUITABLE PLACE OF TORMENT.
THIS IS INSANE! NONE OF US WERE TRAINED TO DEAL WITH A GOD-LEVEL POWER LIKE DOCTOR FATE!
I NEVER AGREED TO THIS!
AND THE OTHER HEROES ARE STARTING TO RECOVER!

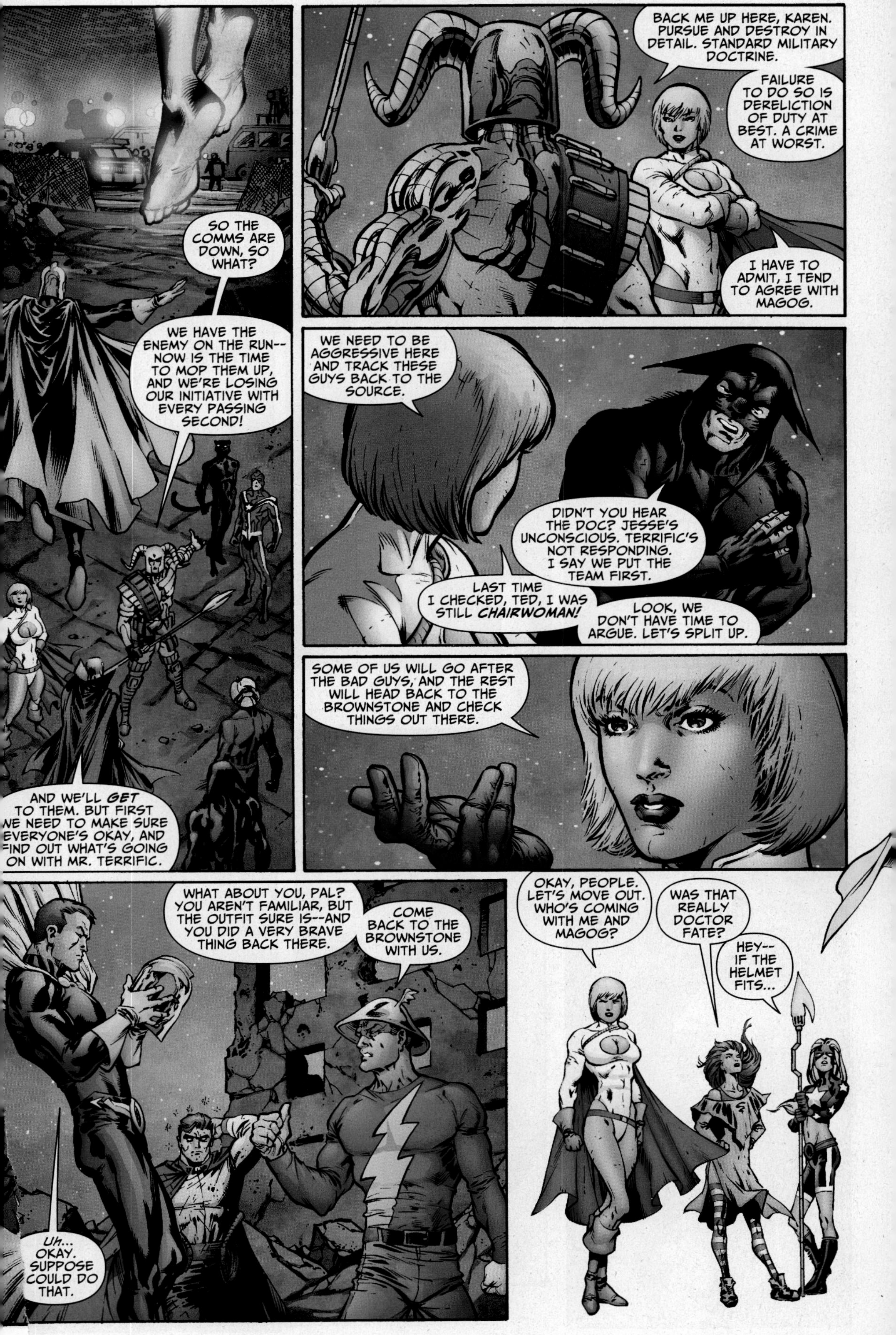
SO THE COMMS ARE DOWN, SO WHAT?
WE HAVE THE ENEMY ON THE RUN--NOW IS THE TIME TO MOP THEM UP, AND WE'RE LOSING OUR INITIATIVE WITH EVERY PASSING SECOND!
AND WE'LL GET TO THEM. BUT FIRST WE NEED TO MAKE SURE EVERYONE'S OKAY, AND FIND OUT WHAT'S GOING ON WITH MR. TERRIFIC.
BACK ME UP HERE, KAREN. PURSUE AND DESTROY IN DETAIL. STANDARD MILITARY DOCTRINE.
FAILURE TO DO SO IS DERELICTION OF DUTY AT BEST. A CRIME AT WORST.
I HAVE TO ADMIT, I TEND TO AGREE WITH MAGOG.
WE NEED TO BE AGGRESSIVE HERE AND TRACK THESE GUYS BACK TO THE SOURCE.
DIDN'T YOU HEAR THE DOC? JESSE'S UNCONSCIOUS. TERRIFIC'S NOT RESPONDING. I SAY WE PUT THE TEAM FIRST.
LAST TIME I CHECKED, TED, I WAS STILL CHAIRWOMAN!
LOOK, WE DON'T HAVE TIME TO ARGUE. LET'S SPLIT UP.
SOME OF US WILL GO AFTER THE BAD GUYS, AND THE REST WILL HEAD BACK TO THE BROWNSTONE AND CHECK THINGS OUT THERE.
WHAT ABOUT YOU, PAL? YOU AREN'T FAMILIAR, BUT THE OUTFIT SURE IS--AND YOU DID A VERY BRAVE THING BACK THERE.
COME BACK TO THE BROWNSTONE WITH US.
Uh... OKAY. SUPPOSE COULD DO THAT.
OKAY, PEOPLE. LET'S MOVE OUT. WHO'S COMING WITH ME AND MAGOG?
WAS THAT REALLY DOCTOR FATE?
HEY-- IF THE HELMET FITS...

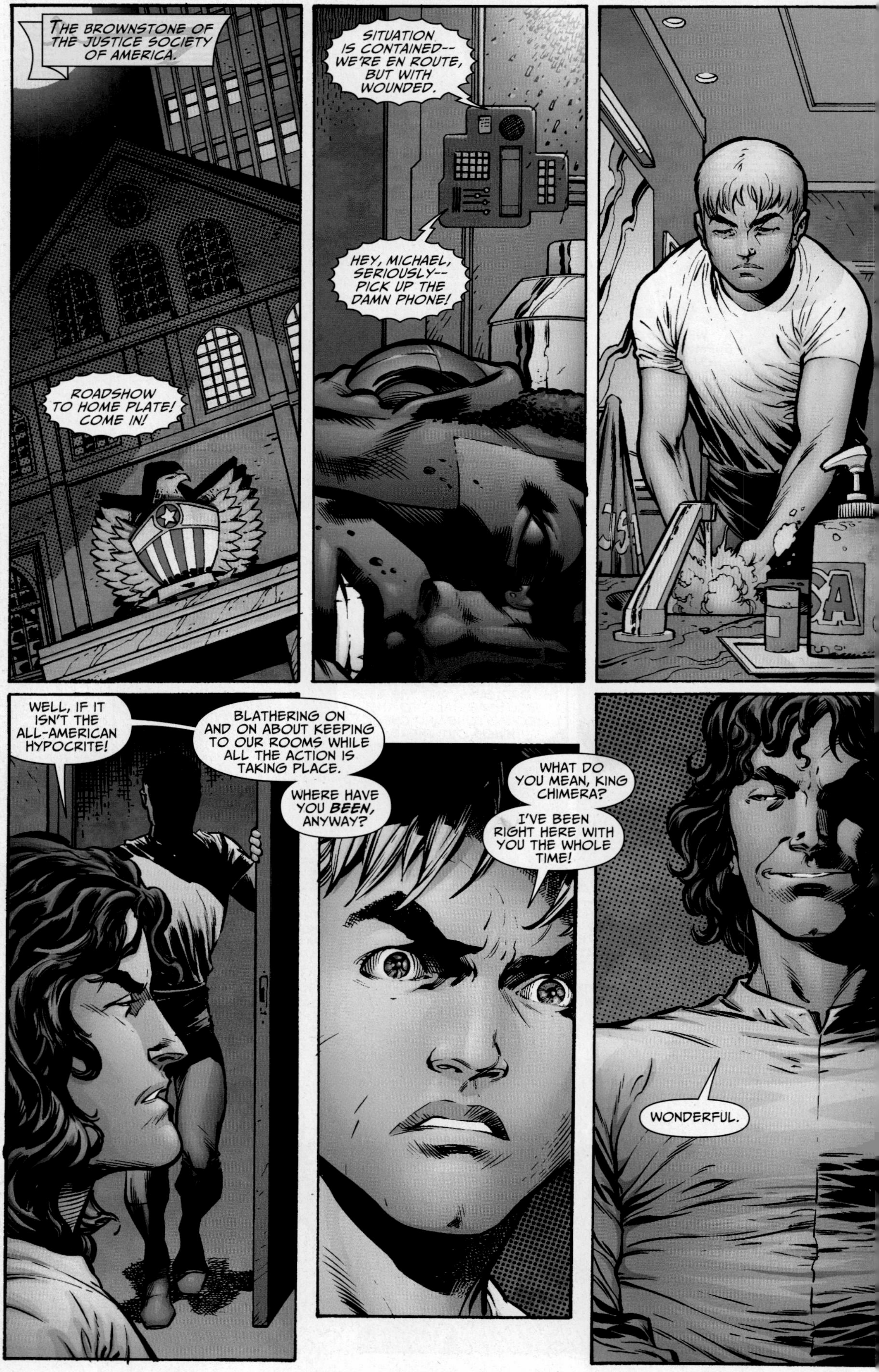
THE BROWNSTONE OF THE JUSTICE SOCIETY OF AMERICA.
ROADSHOW TO HOME PLATE! COME IN!
SITUATION IS CONTAINED-- WE'RE EN ROUTE, BUT WITH WOUNDED.
HEY, MICHAEL, SERIOUSLY-- PICK UP THE DAMN PHONE!
WELL, IF IT ISN'T THE ALL-AMERICAN HYPOCRITE!
BLATHERING ON AND ON ABOUT KEEPING TO OUR ROOMS WHILE ALL THE ACTION IS TAKING PLACE.
WHERE HAVE YOU BEEN, ANYWAY?
WHAT DO YOU MEAN, KING CHIMERA?
I'VE BEEN RIGHT HERE WITH YOU THE WHOLE TIME!
WONDERFUL.

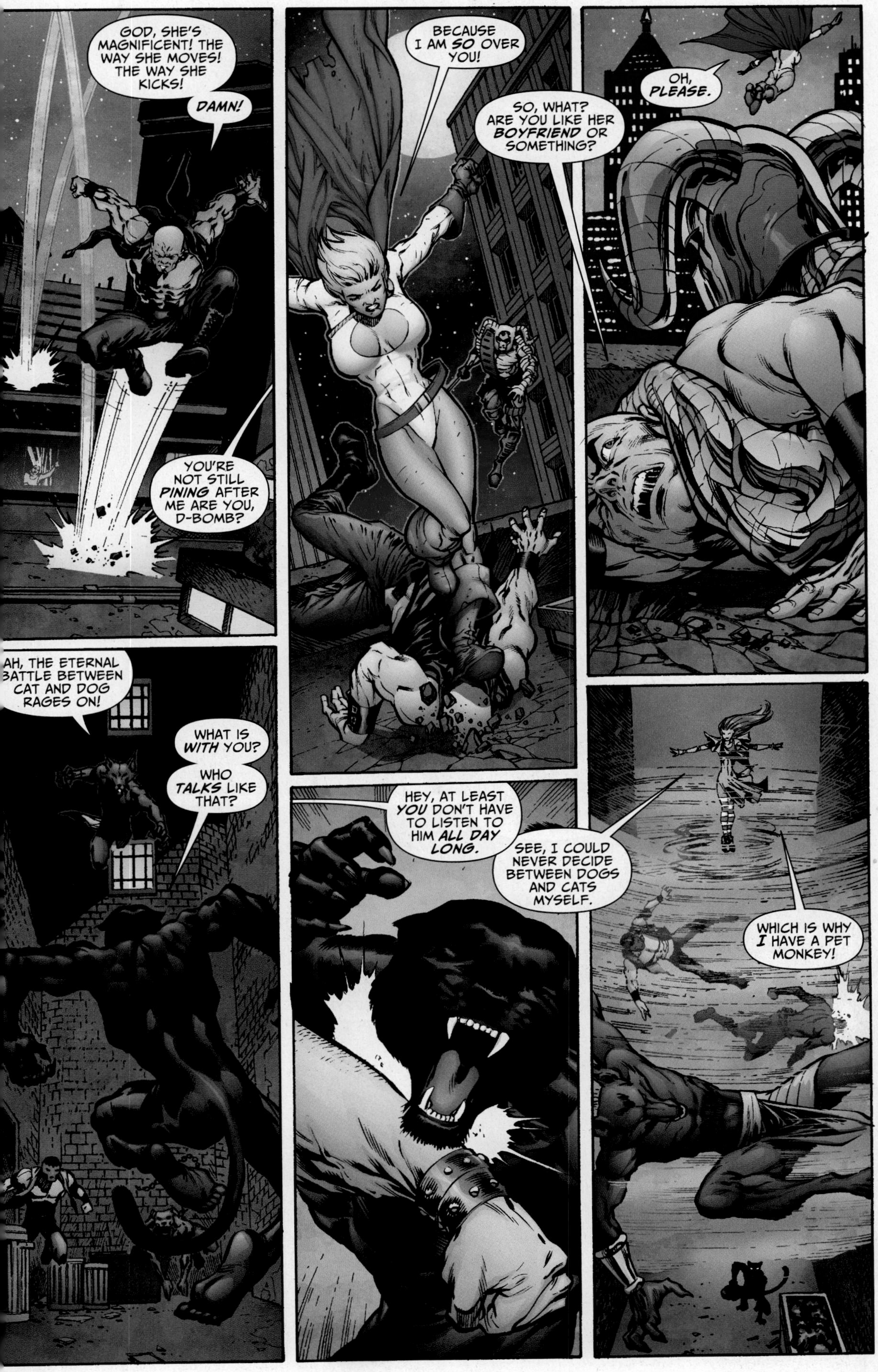
GOD, SHE'S MAGNIFICENT! THE WAY SHE MOVES! THE WAY SHE KICKS!
DAMN!
YOU'RE NOT STILL PINING AFTER ME ARE YOU, D-BOMB?
BECAUSE I AM SO OVER YOU!
SO, WHAT? ARE YOU LIKE HER BOYFRIEND OR SOMETHING?
OH, PLEASE.
AH, THE ETERNAL BATTLE BETWEEN CAT AND DOG RAGES ON!
WHAT IS WITH YOU?
WHO TALKS LIKE THAT?
HEY, AT LEAST YOU DON'T HAVE TO LISTEN TO HIM ALL DAY LONG.
SEE, I COULD NEVER DECIDE BETWEEN DOGS AND CATS MYSELF.
WHICH IS WHY I HAVE A PET MONKEY!

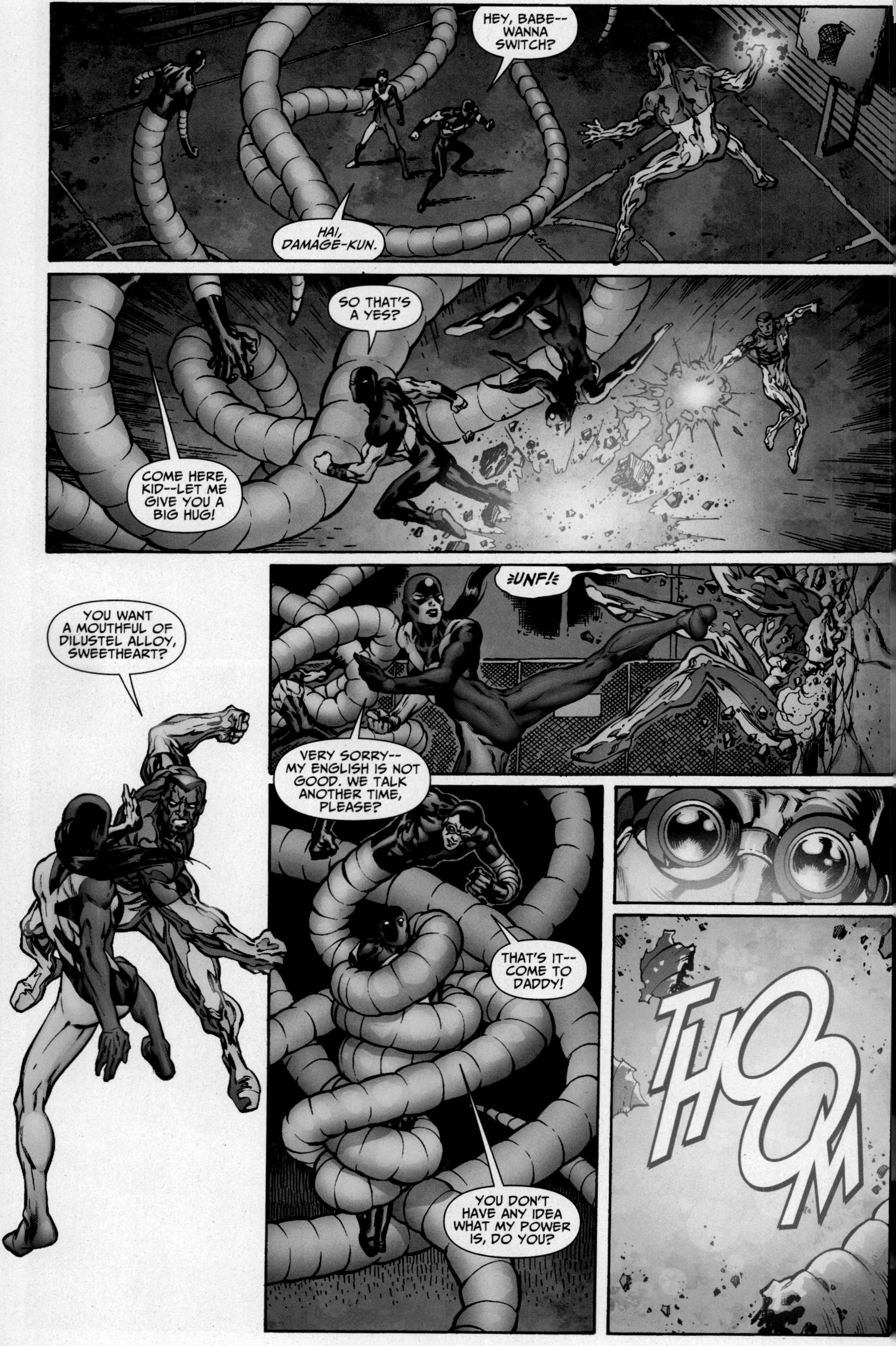
HEY, BABE--WANNA SWITCH?
HAI, DAMAGE-KUN.
SO THAT'S A YES?
COME HERE, KID--LET ME GIVE YOU A BIG HUG!
YOU WANT A MOUTHFUL OF DILUSTEL ALLOY, SWEETHEART?
UNF!
VERY SORRY--MY ENGLISH IS NOT GOOD. WE TALK ANOTHER TIME, PLEASE?
THAT'S IT--COME TO DADDY!
YOU DON'T HAVE ANY IDEA WHAT MY POWER IS, DO YOU?
THOOM

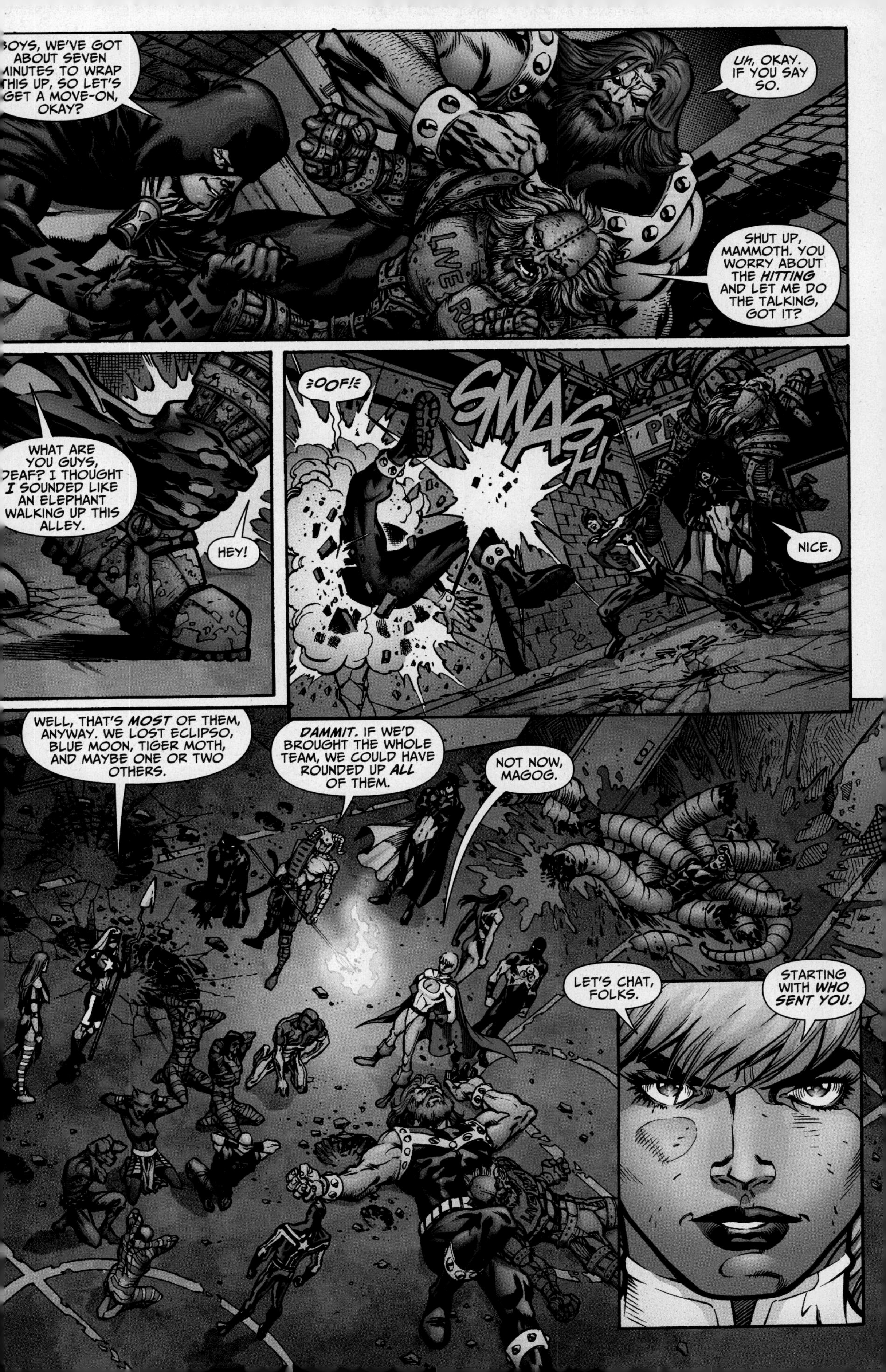

BOYS, WE'VE GOT ABOUT SEVEN MINUTES TO WRAP THIS UP, SO LET'S GET A MOVE-ON, OKAY?
Uh, OKAY. IF YOU SAY SO.
SHUT UP, MAMMOTH. YOU WORRY ABOUT THE *HITTING* AND LET ME DO THE TALKING, GOT IT?
WHAT ARE YOU GUYS, DEAF? I THOUGHT *I* SOUNDED LIKE AN ELEPHANT WALKING UP THIS ALLEY.
HEY!
OOF!
SMASH
NICE.
WELL, THAT'S *MOST* OF THEM, ANYWAY. WE LOST ECLIPSO, BLUE MOON, TIGER MOTH, AND MAYBE ONE OR TWO OTHERS.
DAMMIT. IF WE'D BROUGHT THE WHOLE TEAM, WE COULD HAVE ROUNDED UP *ALL* OF THEM.
NOT NOW, MAGOG.
LET'S CHAT, FOLKS.
STARTING WITH *WHO SENT YOU.*

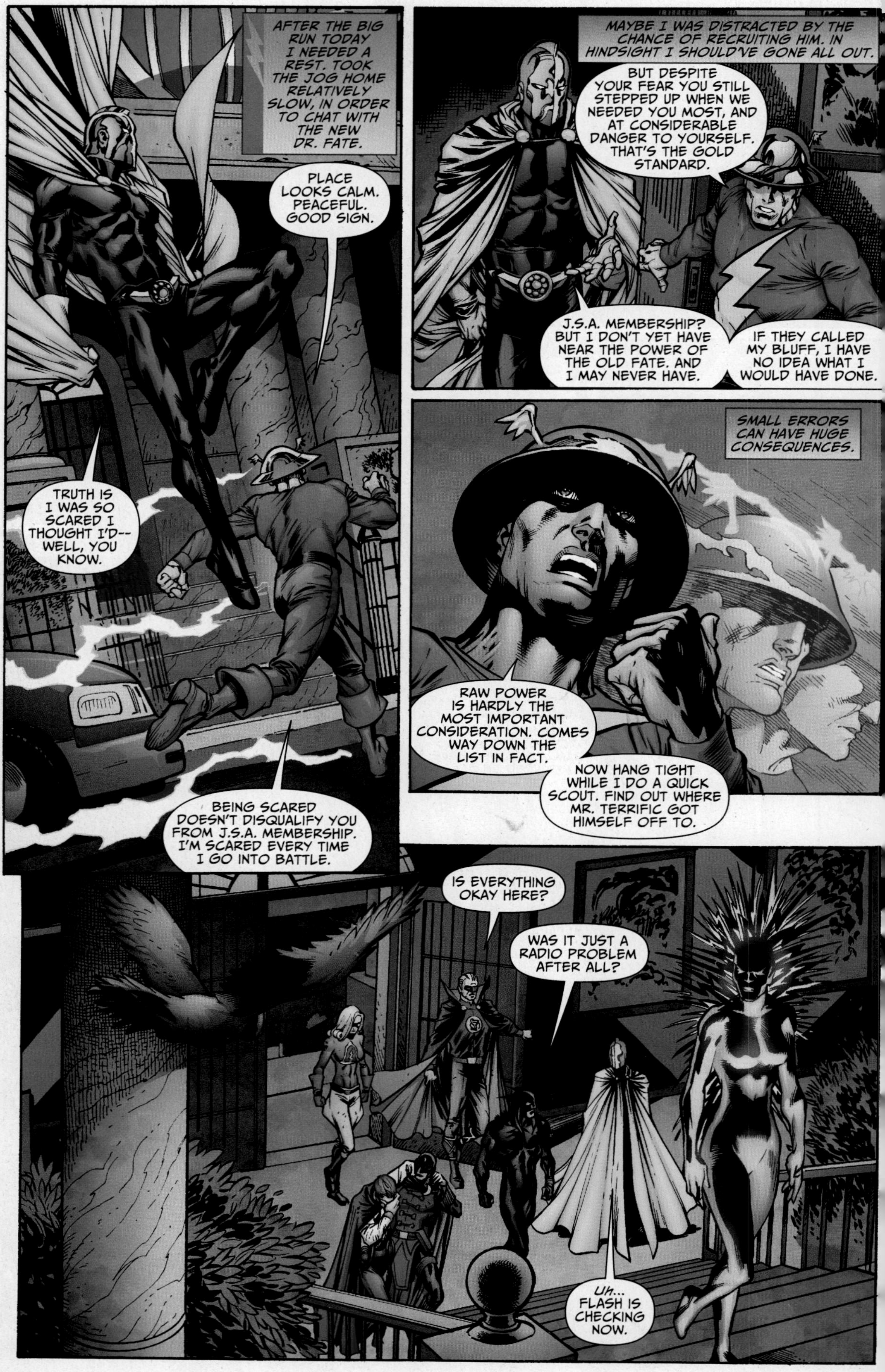

AFTER THE BIG RUN TODAY I NEEDED A REST. TOOK THE JOG HOME RELATIVELY SLOW, IN ORDER TO CHAT WITH THE NEW DR. FATE.
PLACE LOOKS CALM. PEACEFUL. GOOD SIGN.
TRUTH IS I WAS SO SCARED I THOUGHT I'D-- WELL, YOU KNOW.
BEING SCARED DOESN'T DISQUALIFY YOU FROM J.S.A. MEMBERSHIP. I'M SCARED EVERY TIME I GO INTO BATTLE.
MAYBE I WAS DISTRACTED BY THE CHANCE OF RECRUITING HIM. IN HINDSIGHT I SHOULD'VE GONE ALL OUT.
BUT DESPITE YOUR FEAR YOU STILL STEPPED UP WHEN WE NEEDED YOU MOST, AND AT CONSIDERABLE DANGER TO YOURSELF. THAT'S THE GOLD STANDARD.
J.S.A. MEMBERSHIP? BUT I DON'T YET HAVE NEAR THE POWER OF THE OLD FATE. AND I MAY NEVER HAVE.
IF THEY CALLED MY BLUFF, I HAVE NO IDEA WHAT I WOULD HAVE DONE.
SMALL ERRORS CAN HAVE HUGE CONSEQUENCES.
RAW POWER IS HARDLY THE MOST IMPORTANT CONSIDERATION. COMES WAY DOWN THE LIST IN FACT.
NOW HANG TIGHT WHILE I DO A QUICK SCOUT. FIND OUT WHERE MR. TERRIFIC GOT HIMSELF OFF TO.
IS EVERYTHING OKAY HERE?
WAS IT JUST A RADIO PROBLEM AFTER ALL?
Uh... FLASH IS CHECKING NOW.

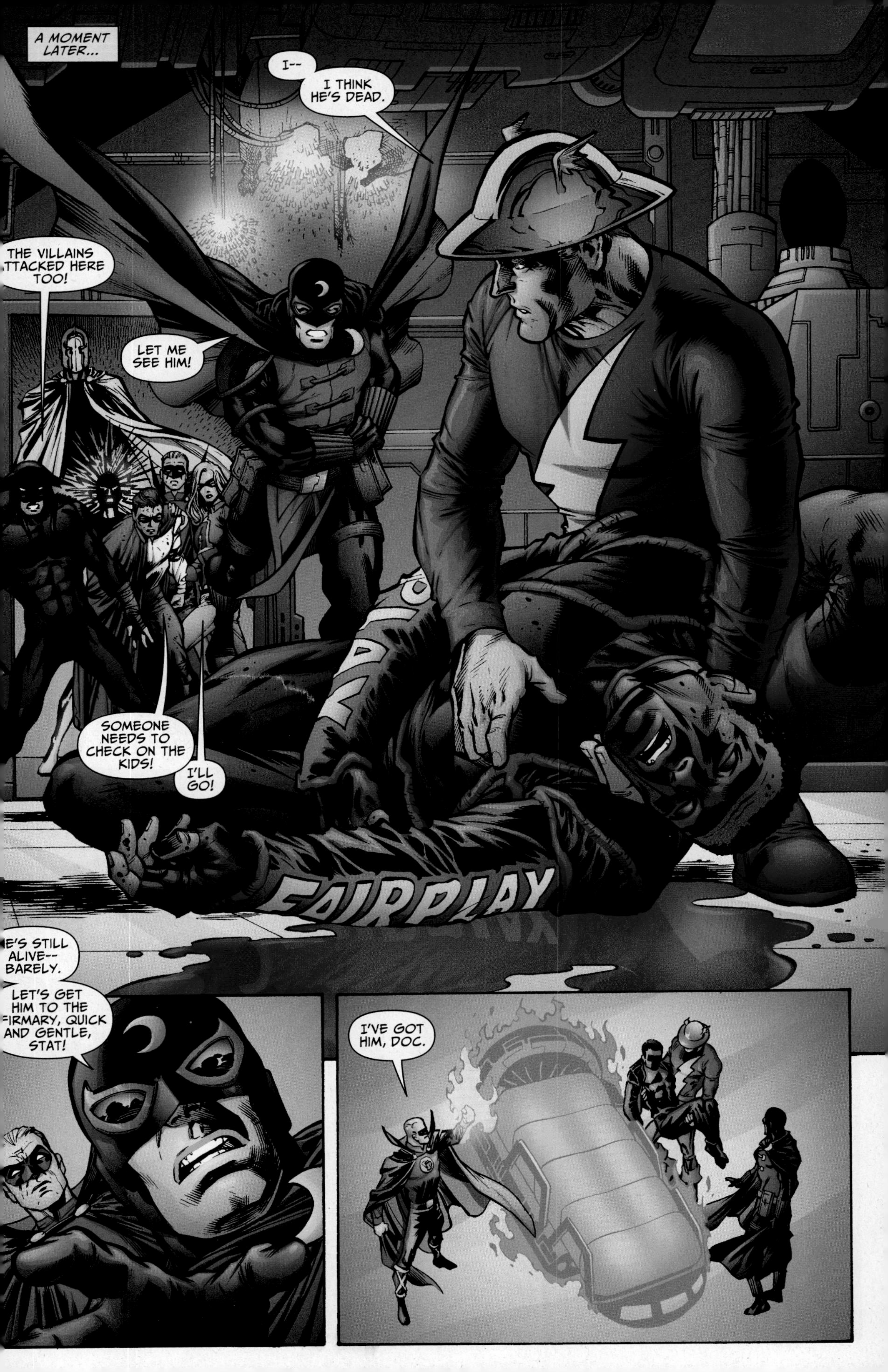

A MOMENT LATER...
I-- I THINK HE'S DEAD.
THE VILLAINS ATTACKED HERE TOO!
LET ME SEE HIM!
SOMEONE NEEDS TO CHECK ON THE KIDS!
I'LL GO!
FAIRPLAY
E'S STILL ALIVE-- BARELY.
LET'S GET HIM TO THE FIRMARY, QUICK AND GENTLE, STAT!
I'VE GOT HIM, DOC.

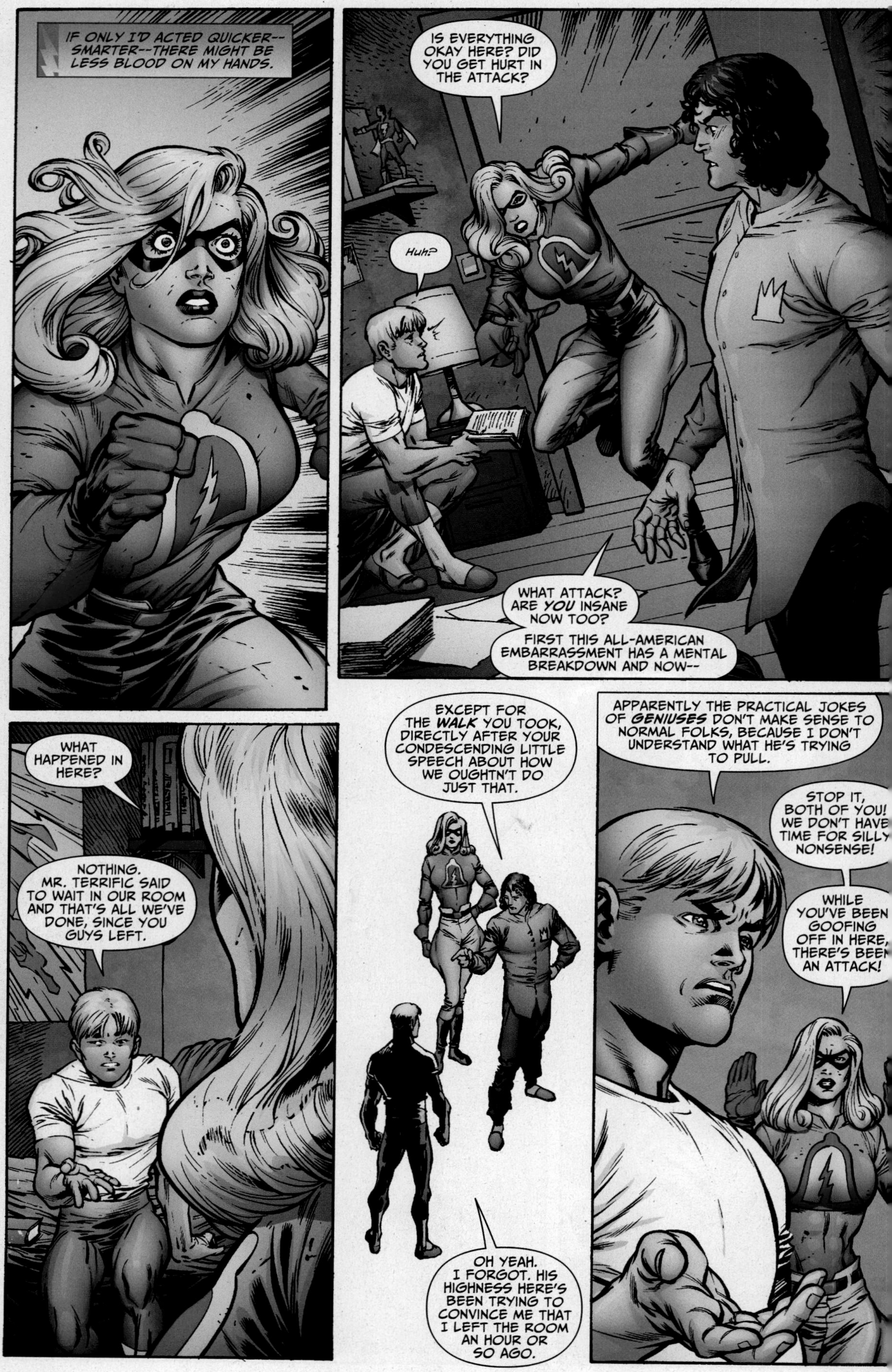
IF ONLY I'D ACTED QUICKER--SMARTER--THERE MIGHT BE LESS BLOOD ON MY HANDS.
IS EVERYTHING OKAY HERE? DID YOU GET HURT IN THE ATTACK?
Huh?
WHAT ATTACK? ARE YOU INSANE NOW TOO?
FIRST THIS ALL-AMERICAN EMBARRASSMENT HAS A MENTAL BREAKDOWN AND NOW--
WHAT HAPPENED IN HERE?
NOTHING. MR. TERRIFIC SAID TO WAIT IN OUR ROOM AND THAT'S ALL WE'VE DONE, SINCE YOU GUYS LEFT.
EXCEPT FOR THE WALK YOU TOOK, DIRECTLY AFTER YOUR CONDESCENDING LITTLE SPEECH ABOUT HOW WE OUGHTN'T DO JUST THAT.
OH YEAH. I FORGOT. HIS HIGHNESS HERE'S BEEN TRYING TO CONVINCE ME THAT I LEFT THE ROOM AN HOUR OR SO AGO.
APPARENTLY THE PRACTICAL JOKES OF GENIUSES DON'T MAKE SENSE TO NORMAL FOLKS, BECAUSE I DON'T UNDERSTAND WHAT HE'S TRYING TO PULL.
STOP IT, BOTH OF YOU! WE DON'T HAVE TIME FOR SILLY NONSENSE!
WHILE YOU'VE BEEN GOOFING OFF IN HERE, THERE'S BEEN AN ATTACK!

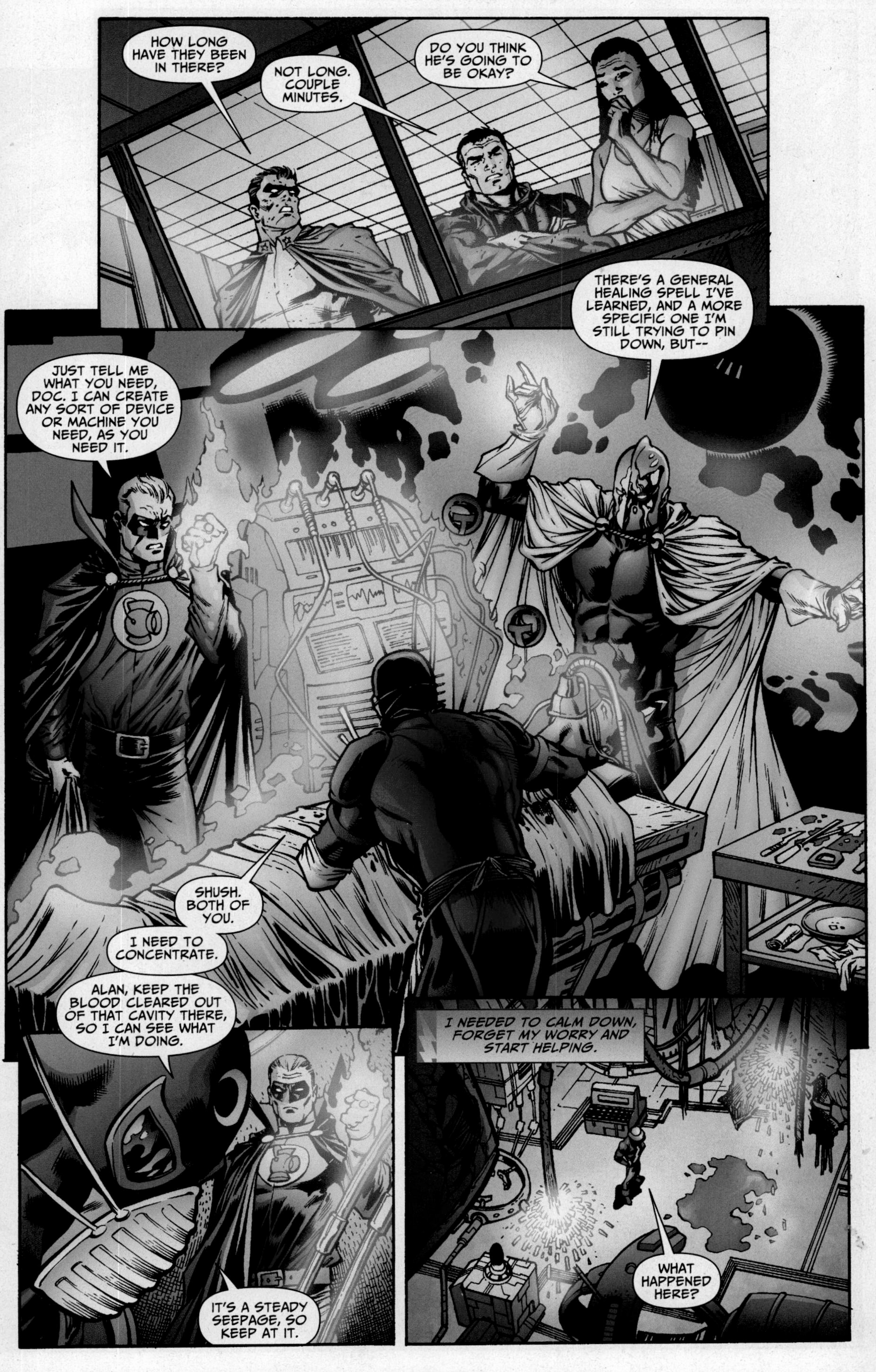
HOW LONG HAVE THEY BEEN IN THERE?
NOT LONG. COUPLE MINUTES.
DO YOU THINK HE'S GOING TO BE OKAY?
THERE'S A GENERAL HEALING SPELL I'VE LEARNED, AND A MORE SPECIFIC ONE I'M STILL TRYING TO PIN DOWN, BUT--
JUST TELL ME WHAT YOU NEED, DOC. I CAN CREATE ANY SORT OF DEVICE OR MACHINE YOU NEED, AS YOU NEED IT.
SHUSH. BOTH OF YOU.
I NEED TO CONCENTRATE.
ALAN, KEEP THE BLOOD CLEARED OUT OF THAT CAVITY THERE, SO I CAN SEE WHAT I'M DOING.
IT'S A STEADY SEEPAGE, SO KEEP AT IT.
I NEEDED TO CALM DOWN, FORGET MY WORRY AND START HELPING.
WHAT HAPPENED HERE?

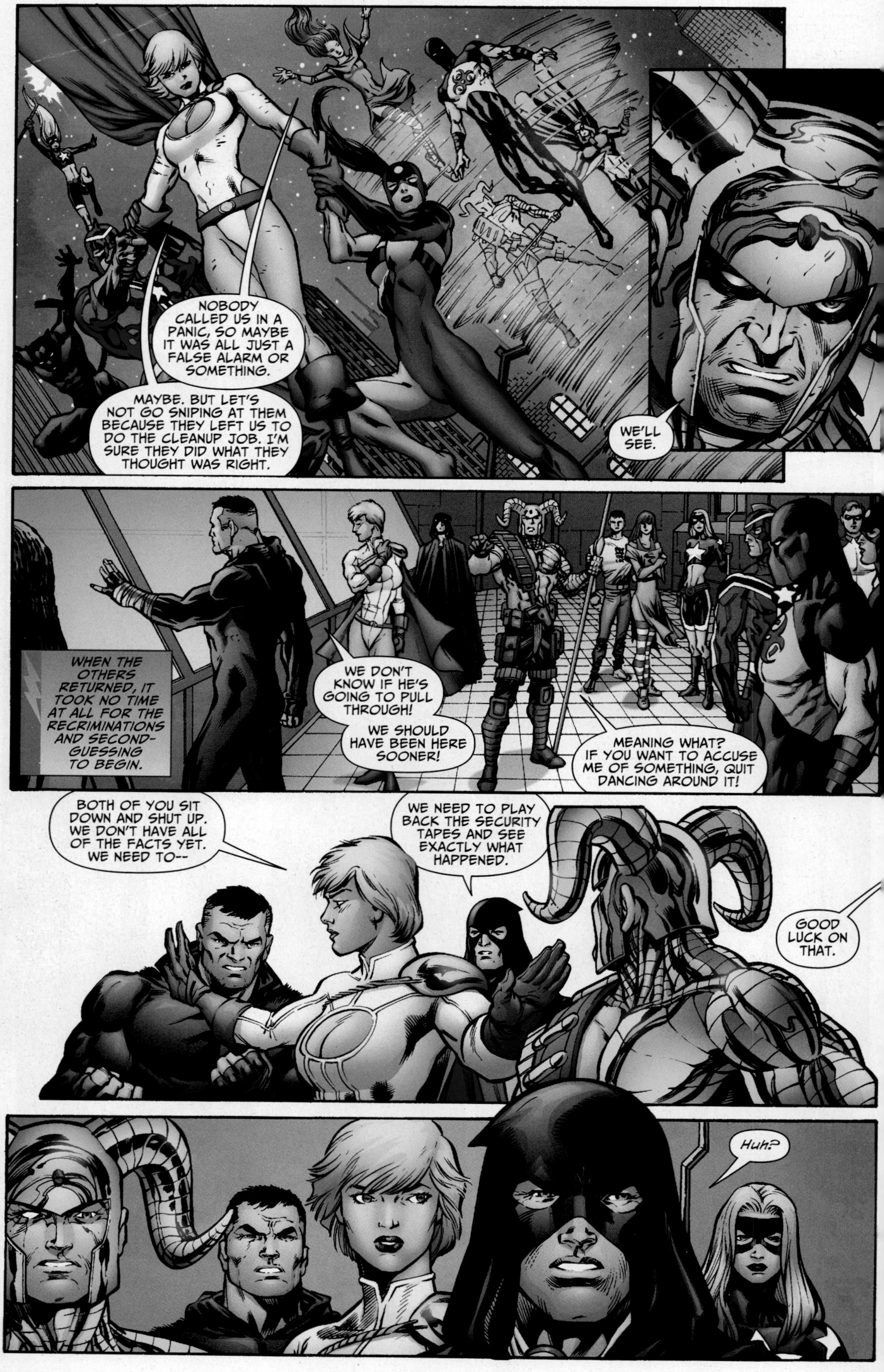
NOBODY CALLED US IN A PANIC, SO MAYBE IT WAS ALL JUST A FALSE ALARM OR SOMETHING.
MAYBE. BUT LET'S NOT GO SNIPING AT THEM BECAUSE THEY LEFT US TO DO THE CLEANUP JOB. I'M SURE THEY DID WHAT THEY THOUGHT WAS RIGHT.
WE'LL SEE.
WHEN THE OTHERS RETURNED, IT TOOK NO TIME AT ALL FOR THE RECRIMINATIONS AND SECOND-GUESSING TO BEGIN.
WE DON'T KNOW IF HE'S GOING TO PULL THROUGH!
WE SHOULD HAVE BEEN HERE SOONER!
MEANING WHAT? IF YOU WANT TO ACCUSE ME OF SOMETHING, QUIT DANCING AROUND IT!
BOTH OF YOU SIT DOWN AND SHUT UP. WE DON'T HAVE ALL OF THE FACTS YET. WE NEED TO--
WE NEED TO PLAY BACK THE SECURITY TAPES AND SEE EXACTLY WHAT HAPPENED.
GOOD LUCK ON THAT.
Huh?

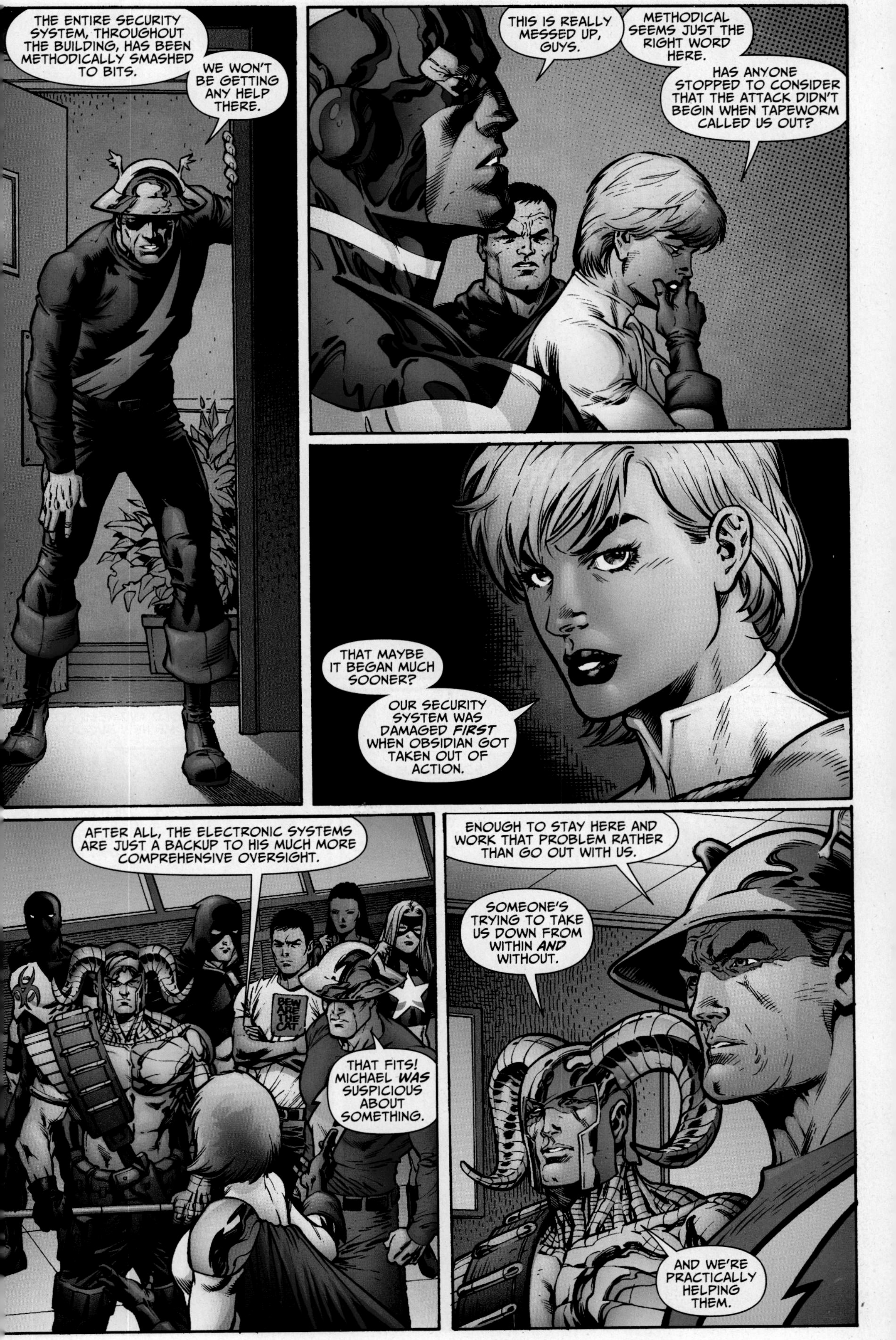
THE ENTIRE SECURITY SYSTEM, THROUGHOUT THE BUILDING, HAS BEEN METHODICALLY SMASHED TO BITS.
WE WON'T BE GETTING ANY HELP THERE.
THIS IS REALLY MESSED UP, GUYS.
METHODICAL SEEMS JUST THE RIGHT WORD HERE.
HAS ANYONE STOPPED TO CONSIDER THAT THE ATTACK DIDN'T BEGIN WHEN TAPEWORM CALLED US OUT?
THAT MAYBE IT BEGAN MUCH SOONER?
OUR SECURITY SYSTEM WAS DAMAGED *FIRST* WHEN OBSIDIAN GOT TAKEN OUT OF ACTION.
AFTER ALL, THE ELECTRONIC SYSTEMS ARE JUST A BACKUP TO HIS MUCH MORE COMPREHENSIVE OVERSIGHT.
THAT FITS! MICHAEL *WAS* SUSPICIOUS ABOUT SOMETHING.
ENOUGH TO STAY HERE AND WORK THAT PROBLEM RATHER THAN GO OUT WITH US.
SOMEONE'S TRYING TO TAKE US DOWN FROM WITHIN *AND* WITHOUT.
AND WE'RE PRACTICALLY HELPING THEM.

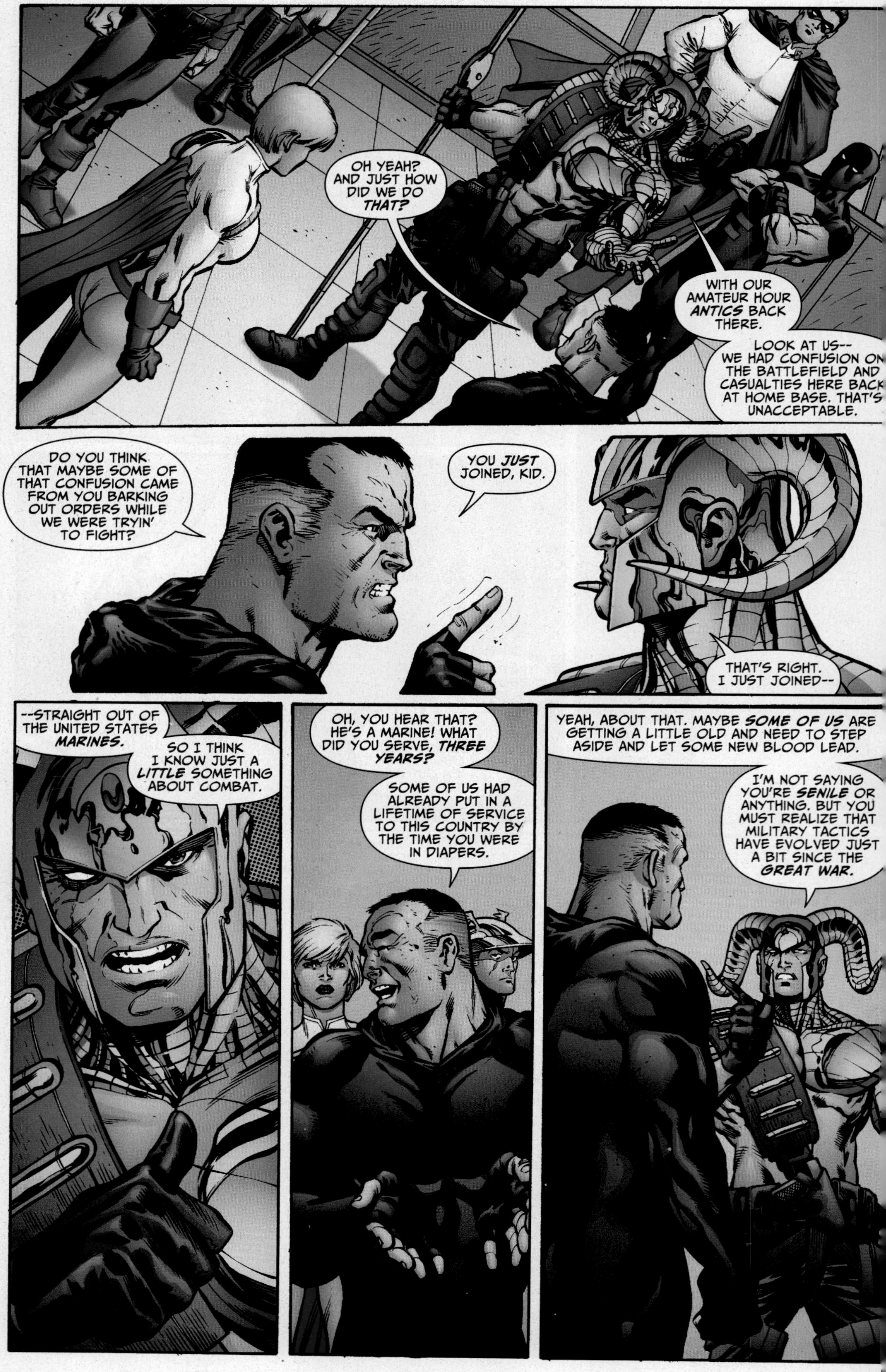
OH YEAH? AND JUST HOW DID WE DO THAT?
WITH OUR AMATEUR HOUR ANTICS BACK THERE.
LOOK AT US-- WE HAD CONFUSION ON THE BATTLEFIELD AND CASUALTIES HERE BACK AT HOME BASE. THAT'S UNACCEPTABLE.
DO YOU THINK THAT MAYBE SOME OF THAT CONFUSION CAME FROM YOU BARKING OUT ORDERS WHILE WE WERE TRYIN' TO FIGHT?
YOU JUST JOINED, KID.
THAT'S RIGHT. I JUST JOINED--
--STRAIGHT OUT OF THE UNITED STATES MARINES.
SO I THINK I KNOW JUST A LITTLE SOMETHING ABOUT COMBAT.
OH, YOU HEAR THAT? HE'S A MARINE! WHAT DID YOU SERVE, THREE YEARS?
SOME OF US HAD ALREADY PUT IN A LIFETIME OF SERVICE TO THIS COUNTRY BY THE TIME YOU WERE IN DIAPERS.
YEAH, ABOUT THAT. MAYBE SOME OF US ARE GETTING A LITTLE OLD AND NEED TO STEP ASIDE AND LET SOME NEW BLOOD LEAD.
I'M NOT SAYING YOU'RE SENILE OR ANYTHING. BUT YOU MUST REALIZE THAT MILITARY TACTICS HAVE EVOLVED JUST A BIT SINCE THE GREAT WAR.

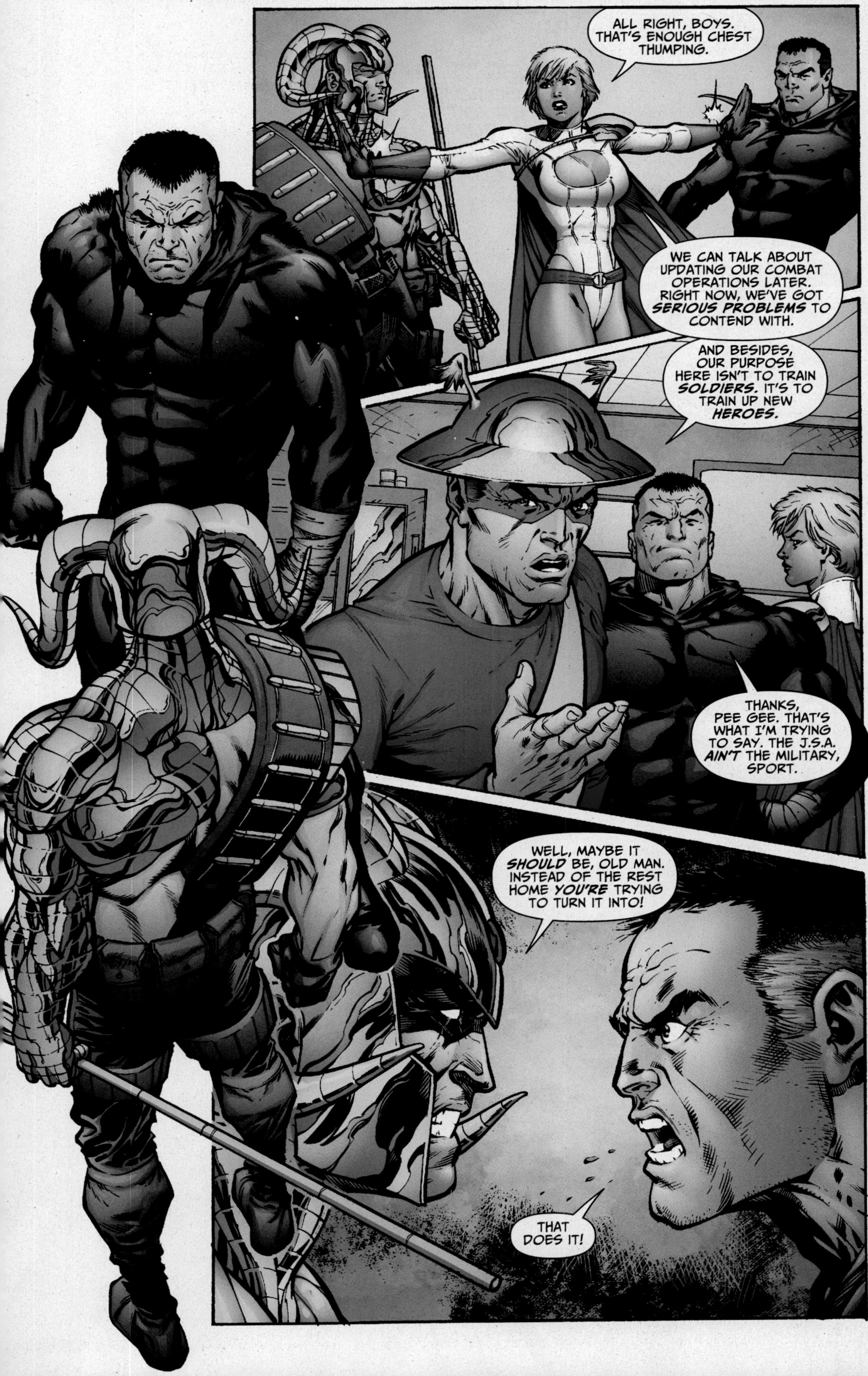
ALL RIGHT, BOYS. THAT'S ENOUGH CHEST THUMPING.
WE CAN TALK ABOUT UPDATING OUR COMBAT OPERATIONS LATER. RIGHT NOW, WE'VE GOT SERIOUS PROBLEMS TO CONTEND WITH.
AND BESIDES, OUR PURPOSE HERE ISN'T TO TRAIN SOLDIERS. IT'S TO TRAIN UP NEW HEROES.
THANKS, PEE GEE. THAT'S WHAT I'M TRYING TO SAY. THE J.S.A. AIN'T THE MILITARY, SPORT.
WELL, MAYBE IT SHOULD BE, OLD MAN. INSTEAD OF THE REST HOME YOU'RE TRYING TO TURN IT INTO!
THAT DOES IT!

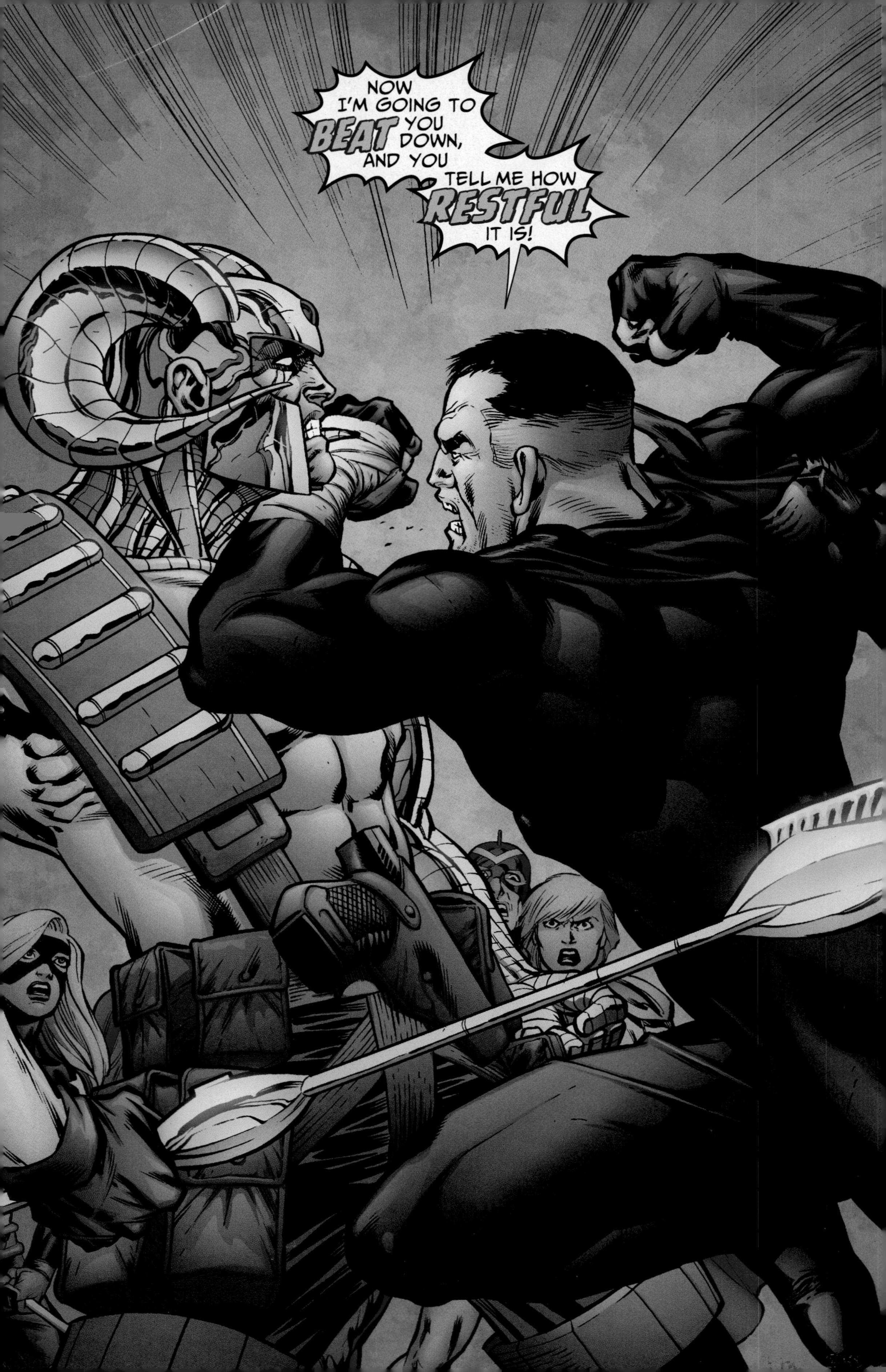
NOW I'M GOING TO BEAT YOU DOWN, AND YOU TELL ME HOW RESTFUL IT IS!

 **THE BAD SEED Part Three**

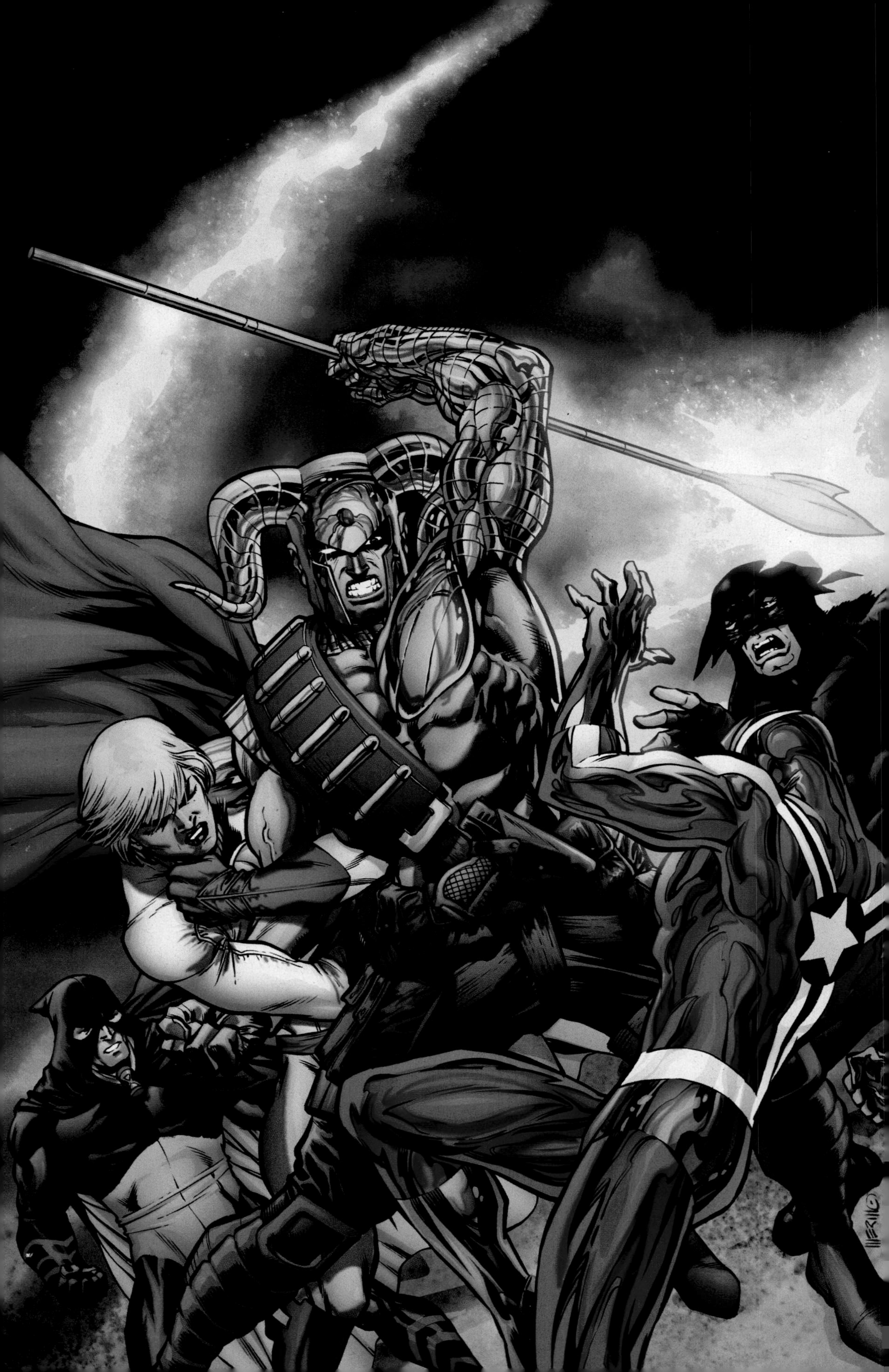

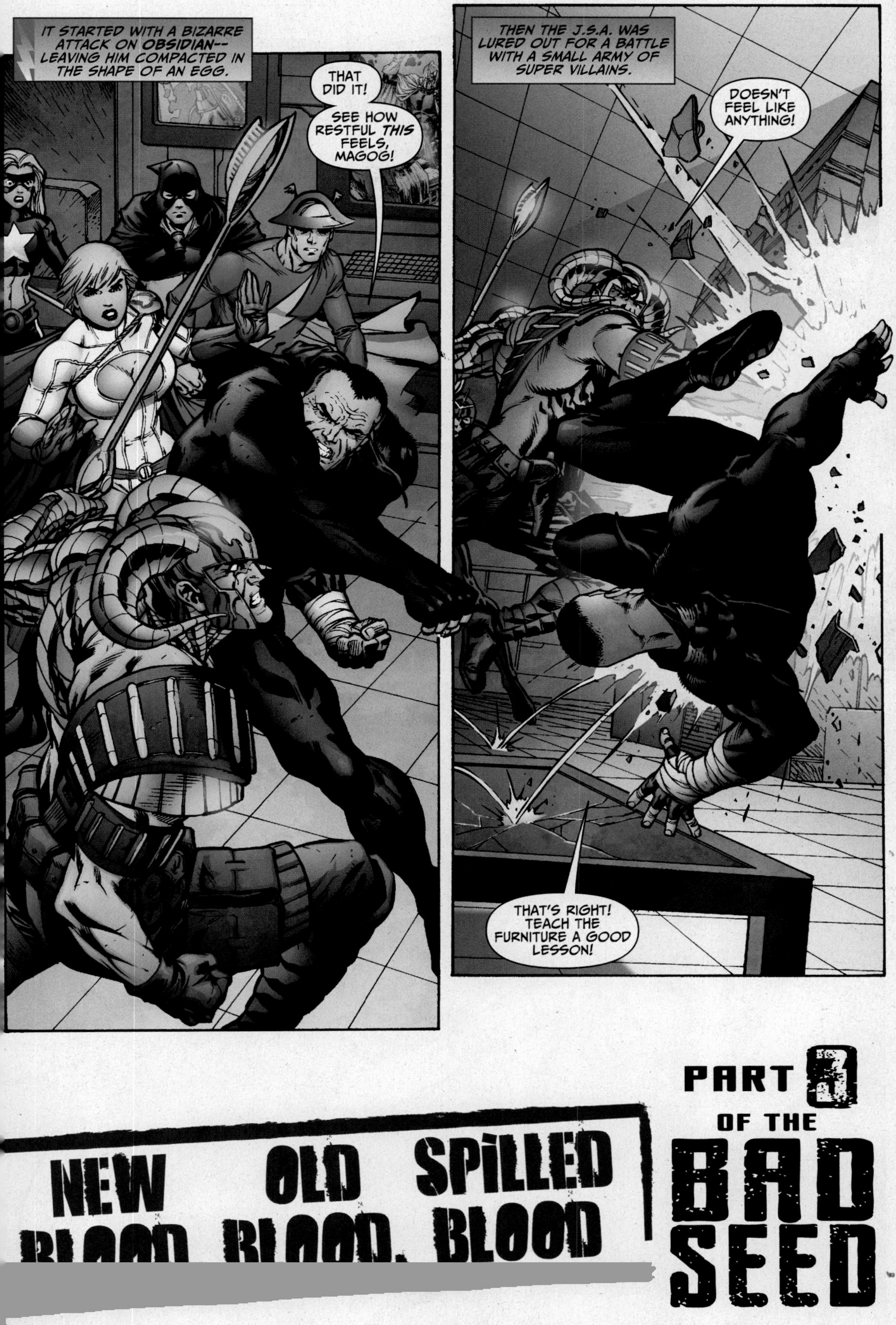
IT STARTED WITH A BIZARRE ATTACK ON OBSIDIAN-- LEAVING HIM COMPACTED IN THE SHAPE OF AN EGG.
THAT DID IT!
SEE HOW RESTFUL *THIS* FEELS, MAGOG!
THEN THE J.S.A. WAS LURED OUT FOR A BATTLE WITH A SMALL ARMY OF SUPER VILLAINS.
DOESN'T FEEL LIKE ANYTHING!
THAT'S RIGHT! TEACH THE FURNITURE A GOOD LESSON!

NEW BLOOD, OLD BLOOD, SPILLED BLOOD

PART 3 OF THE BAD SEED

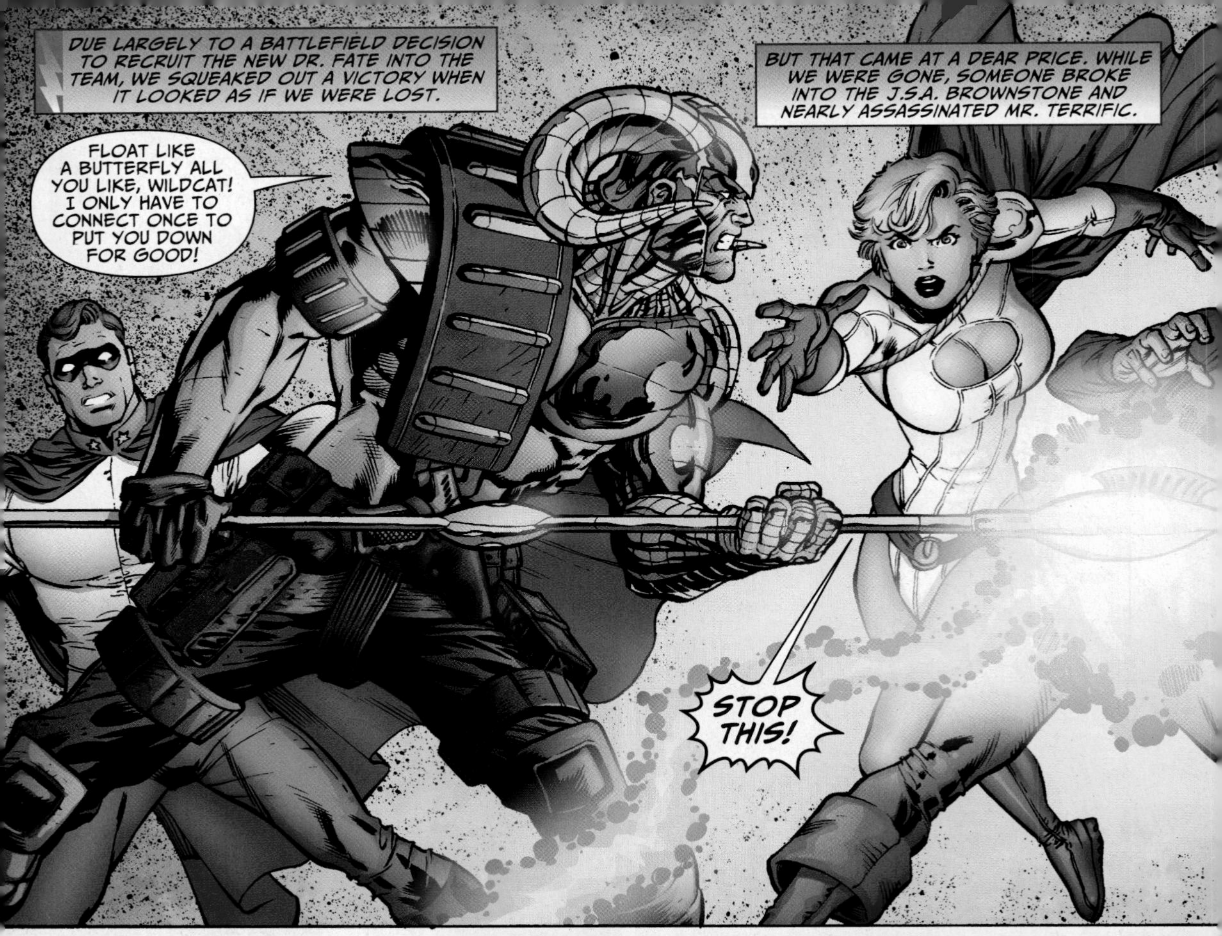
DUE LARGELY TO A BATTLEFIELD DECISION TO RECRUIT THE NEW DR. FATE INTO THE TEAM, WE SQUEAKED OUT A VICTORY WHEN IT LOOKED AS IF WE WERE LOST.
BUT THAT CAME AT A DEAR PRICE. WHILE WE WERE GONE, SOMEONE BROKE INTO THE J.S.A. BROWNSTONE AND NEARLY ASSASSINATED MR. TERRIFIC.
FLOAT LIKE A BUTTERFLY ALL YOU LIKE, WILDCAT! I ONLY HAVE TO CONNECT ONCE TO PUT YOU DOWN FOR GOOD!
STOP THIS!
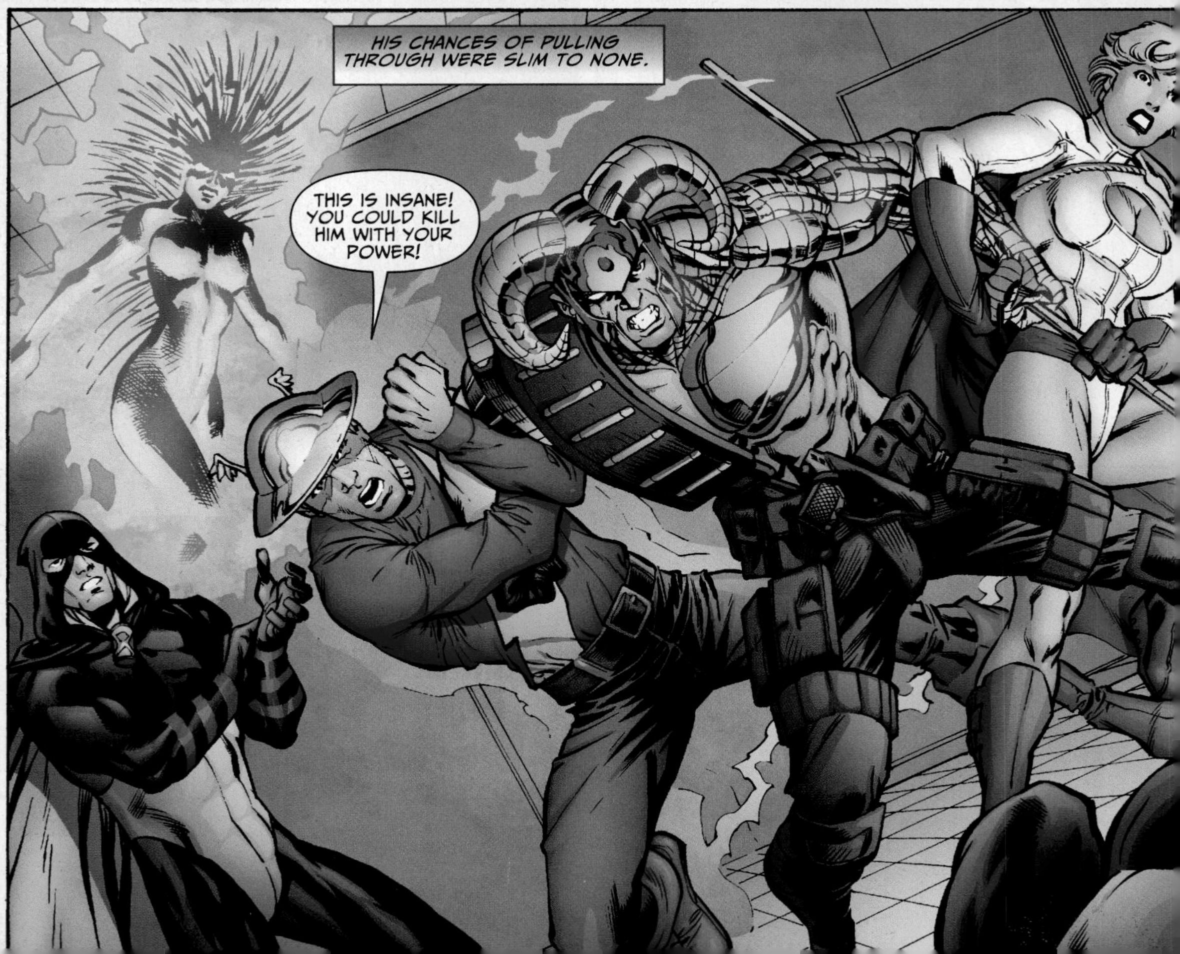
HIS CHANCES OF PULLING THROUGH WERE SLIM TO NONE.
THIS IS INSANE! YOU COULD KILL HIM WITH YOUR POWER!

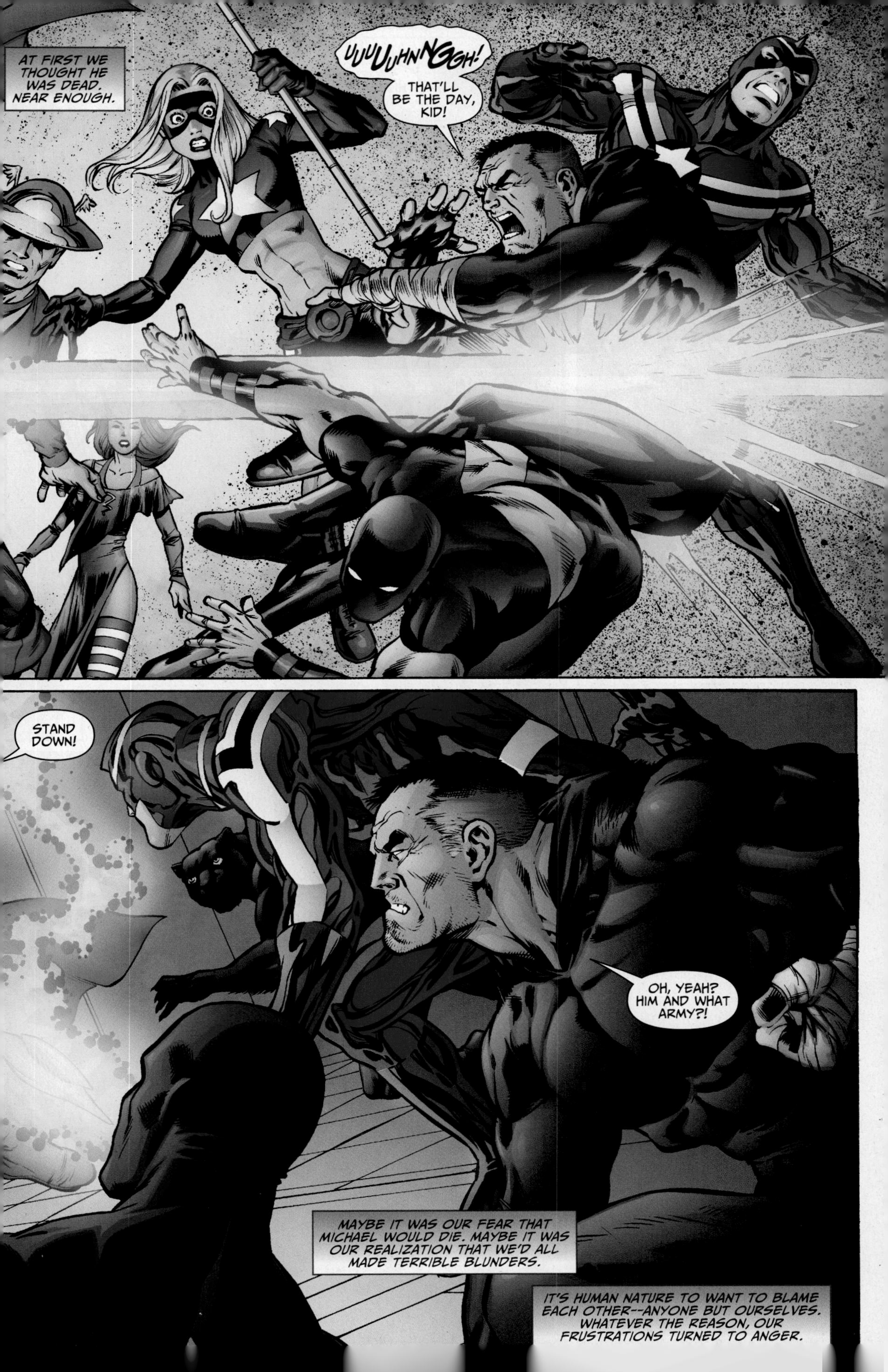
AT FIRST WE THOUGHT HE WAS DEAD. NEAR ENOUGH.
UUUUUHNNGGH!
THAT'LL BE THE DAY, KID!
STAND DOWN!
OH, YEAH? HIM AND WHAT ARMY?!
MAYBE IT WAS OUR FEAR THAT MICHAEL WOULD DIE. MAYBE IT WAS OUR REALIZATION THAT WE'D ALL MADE TERRIBLE BLUNDERS.
IT'S HUMAN NATURE TO WANT TO BLAME EACH OTHER--ANYONE BUT OURSELVES. WHATEVER THE REASON, OUR FRUSTRATIONS TURNED TO ANGER.

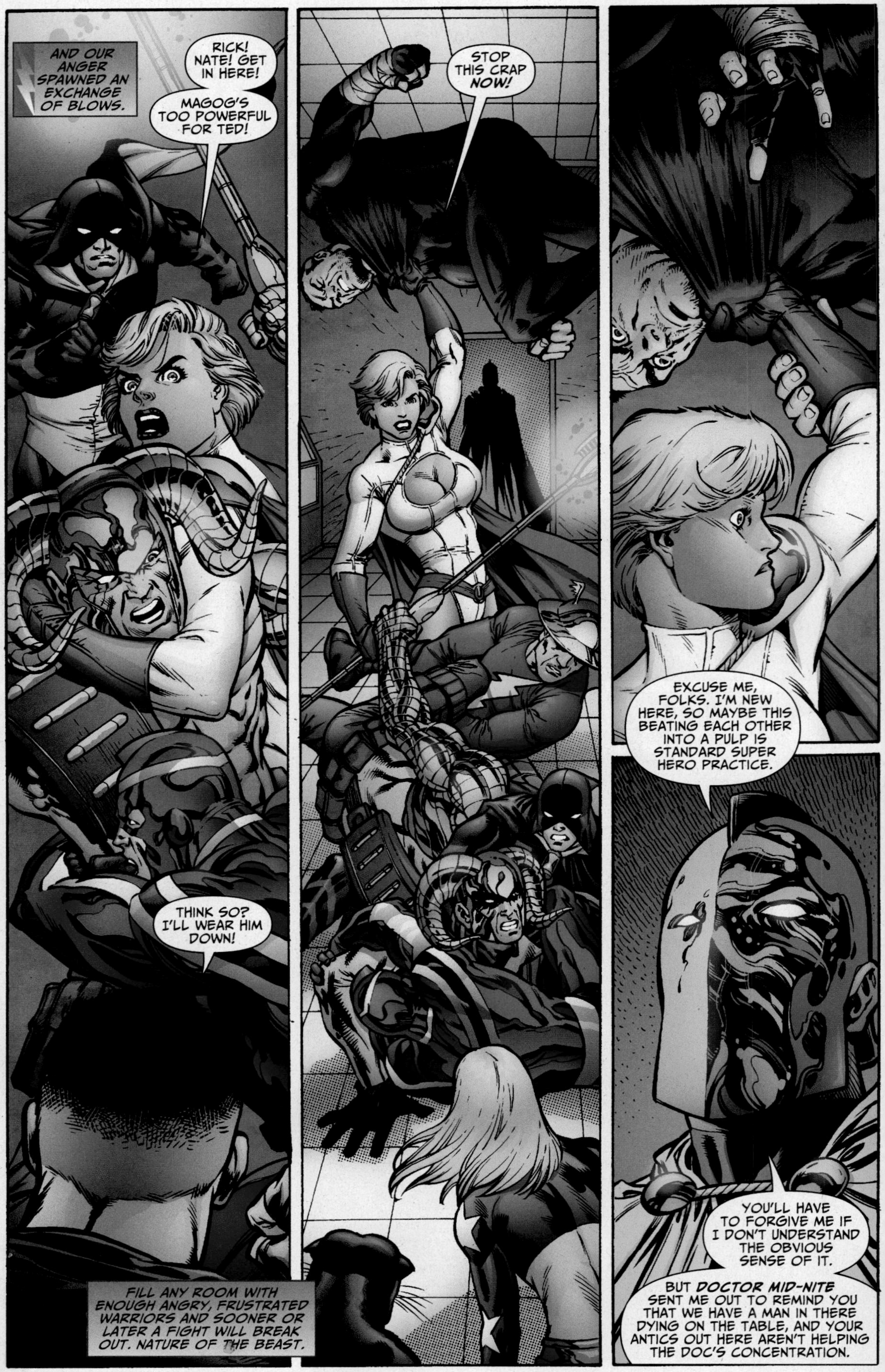

AND OUR ANGER SPAWNED AN EXCHANGE OF BLOWS.
RICK! NATE! GET IN HERE!
MAGOG'S TOO POWERFUL FOR TED!
THINK SO? I'LL WEAR HIM DOWN!
FILL ANY ROOM WITH ENOUGH ANGRY, FRUSTRATED WARRIORS AND SOONER OR LATER A FIGHT WILL BREAK OUT. NATURE OF THE BEAST.
STOP THIS CRAP NOW!
EXCUSE ME, FOLKS. I'M NEW HERE, SO MAYBE THIS BEATING EACH OTHER INTO A PULP IS STANDARD SUPER HERO PRACTICE.
YOU'LL HAVE TO FORGIVE ME IF I DON'T UNDERSTAND THE OBVIOUS SENSE OF IT.
BUT DOCTOR MID-NITE SENT ME OUT TO REMIND YOU THAT WE HAVE A MAN IN THERE DYING ON THE TABLE, AND YOUR ANTICS OUT HERE AREN'T HELPING THE DOC'S CONCENTRATION.

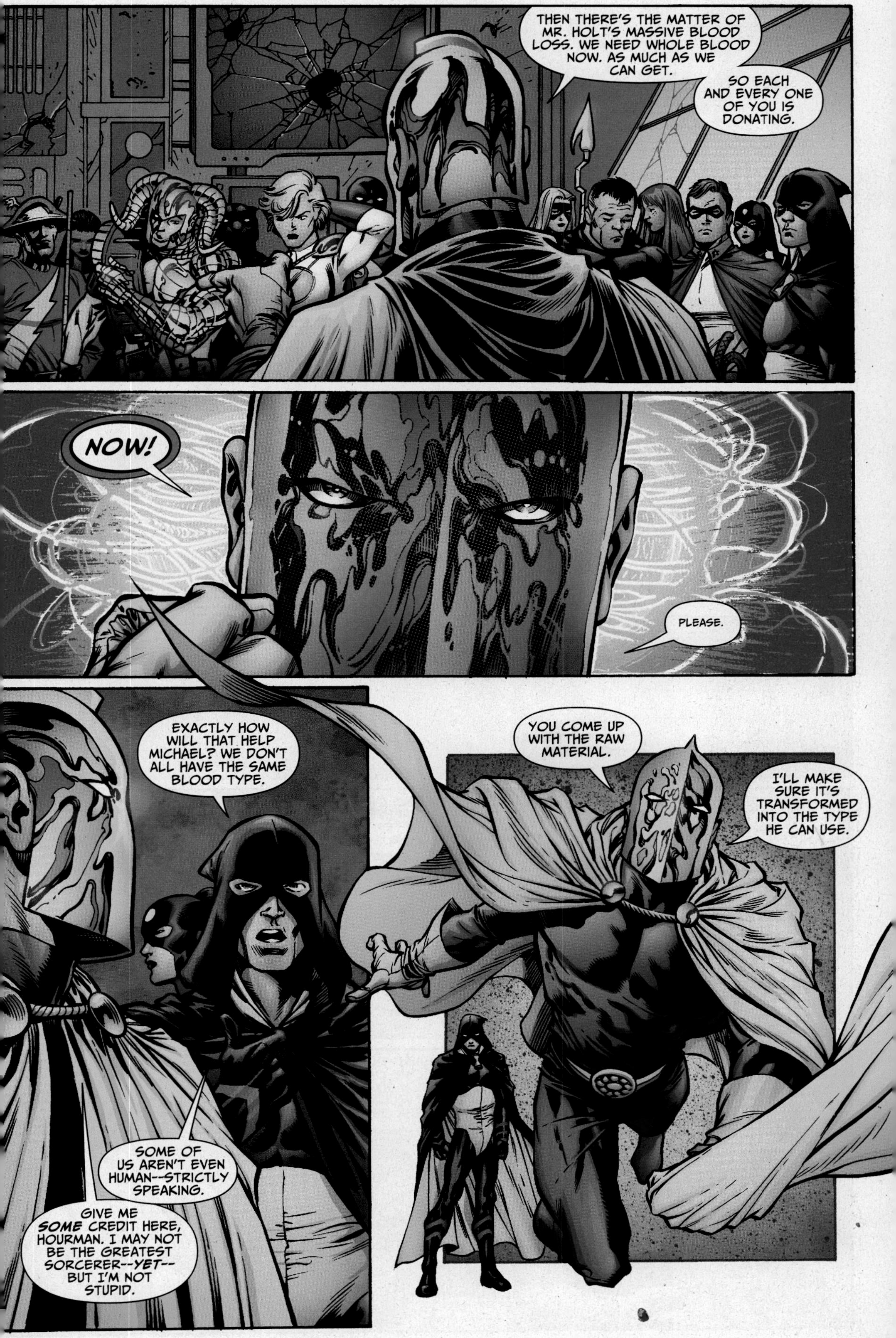
THEN THERE'S THE MATTER OF MR. HOLT'S MASSIVE BLOOD LOSS. WE NEED WHOLE BLOOD NOW. AS MUCH AS WE CAN GET.
SO EACH AND EVERY ONE OF YOU IS DONATING.
NOW!
PLEASE.
EXACTLY HOW WILL THAT HELP MICHAEL? WE DON'T ALL HAVE THE SAME BLOOD TYPE.
SOME OF US AREN'T EVEN HUMAN--STRICTLY SPEAKING.
GIVE ME SOME CREDIT HERE, HOURMAN. I MAY NOT BE THE GREATEST SORCERER--YET--BUT I'M NOT STUPID.
YOU COME UP WITH THE RAW MATERIAL.
I'LL MAKE SURE IT'S TRANSFORMED INTO THE TYPE HE CAN USE.

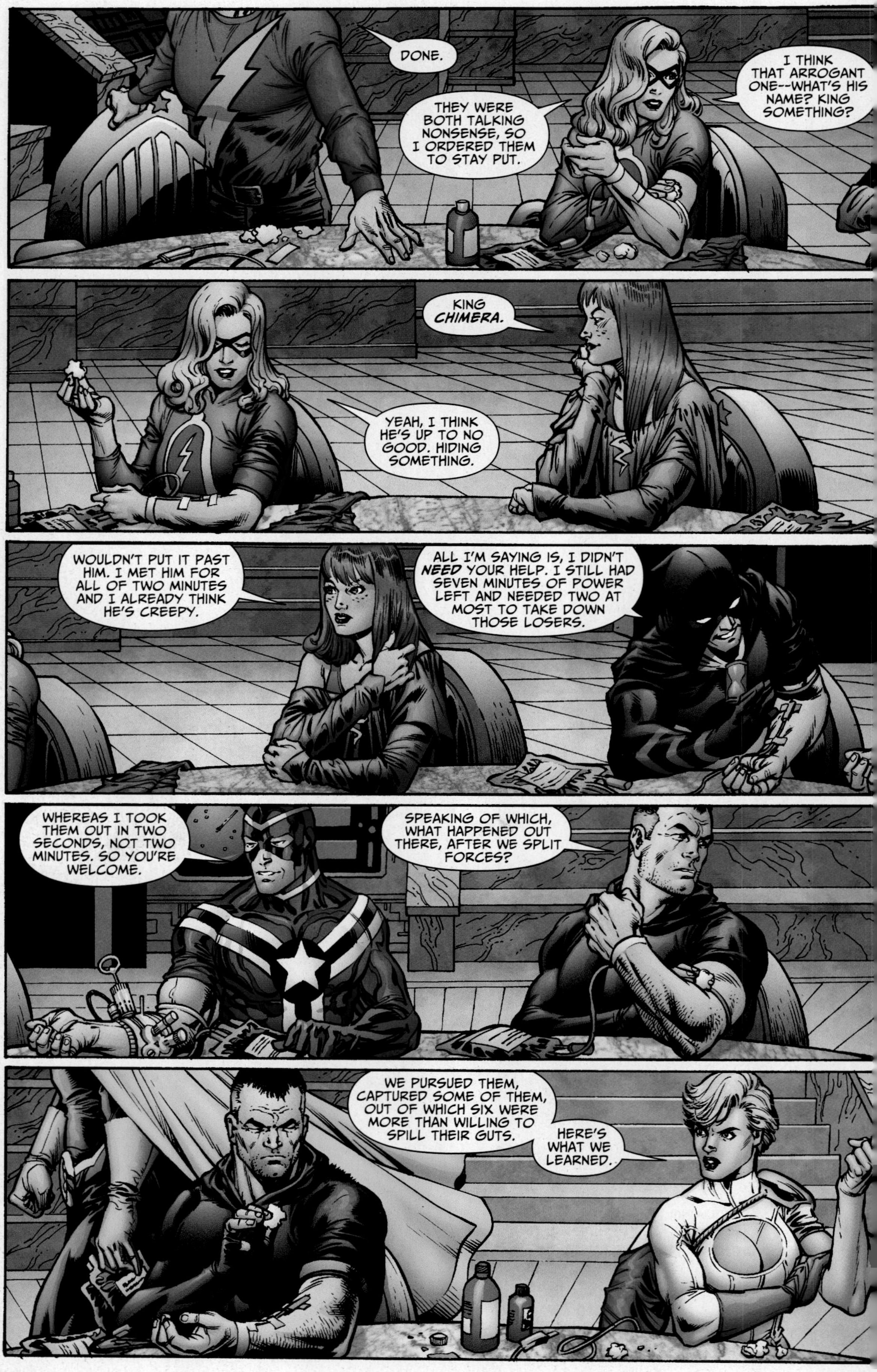
DONE.
THEY WERE BOTH TALKING NONSENSE, SO I ORDERED THEM TO STAY PUT.
I THINK THAT ARROGANT ONE--WHAT'S HIS NAME? KING SOMETHING?
KING *CHIMERA.*
YEAH, I THINK HE'S UP TO NO GOOD. HIDING SOMETHING.
WOULDN'T PUT IT PAST HIM. I MET HIM FOR ALL OF TWO MINUTES AND I ALREADY THINK HE'S CREEPY.
ALL I'M SAYING IS, I DIDN'T ***NEED*** YOUR HELP. I STILL HAD SEVEN MINUTES OF POWER LEFT AND NEEDED TWO AT MOST TO TAKE DOWN THOSE LOSERS.
WHEREAS I TOOK THEM OUT IN TWO SECONDS, NOT TWO MINUTES. SO YOU'RE WELCOME.
SPEAKING OF WHICH, WHAT HAPPENED OUT THERE, AFTER WE SPLIT FORCES?
WE PURSUED THEM, CAPTURED SOME OF THEM, OUT OF WHICH SIX WERE MORE THAN WILLING TO SPILL THEIR GUTS.
HERE'S WHAT WE LEARNED.

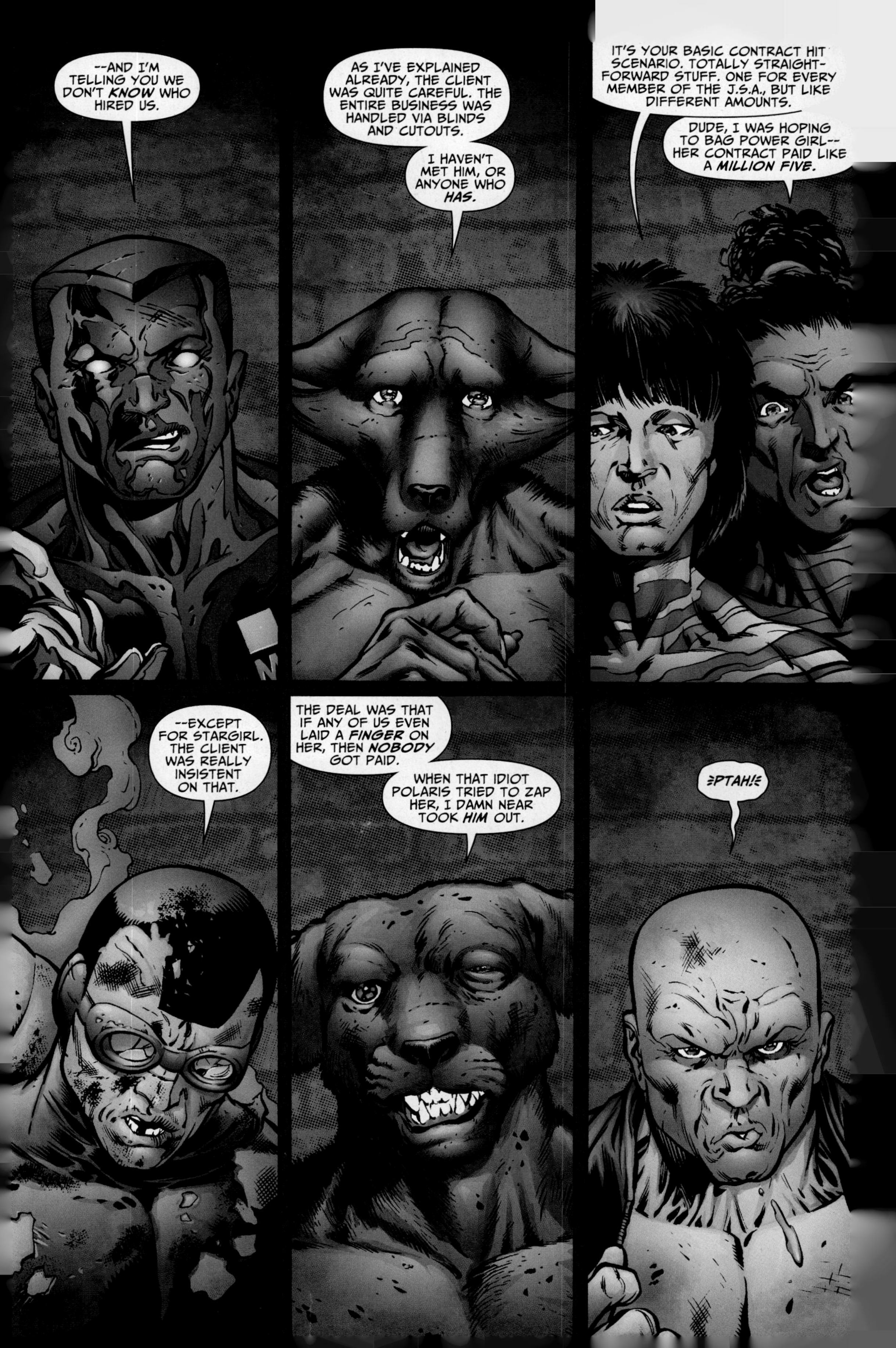
--AND I'M TELLING YOU WE DON'T KNOW WHO HIRED US.
AS I'VE EXPLAINED ALREADY, THE CLIENT WAS QUITE CAREFUL. THE ENTIRE BUSINESS WAS HANDLED VIA BLINDS AND CUTOUTS.
I HAVEN'T MET HIM, OR ANYONE WHO HAS.
IT'S YOUR BASIC CONTRACT HIT SCENARIO. TOTALLY STRAIGHT-FORWARD STUFF. ONE FOR EVERY MEMBER OF THE J.S.A., BUT LIKE DIFFERENT AMOUNTS.
DUDE, I WAS HOPING TO BAG POWER GIRL--HER CONTRACT PAID LIKE A MILLION FIVE.
--EXCEPT FOR STARGIRL. THE CLIENT WAS REALLY INSISTENT ON THAT.
THE DEAL WAS THAT IF ANY OF US EVEN LAID A FINGER ON HER, THEN NOBODY GOT PAID.
WHEN THAT IDIOT POLARIS TRIED TO ZAP HER, I DAMN NEAR TOOK HIM OUT.
PTAH!

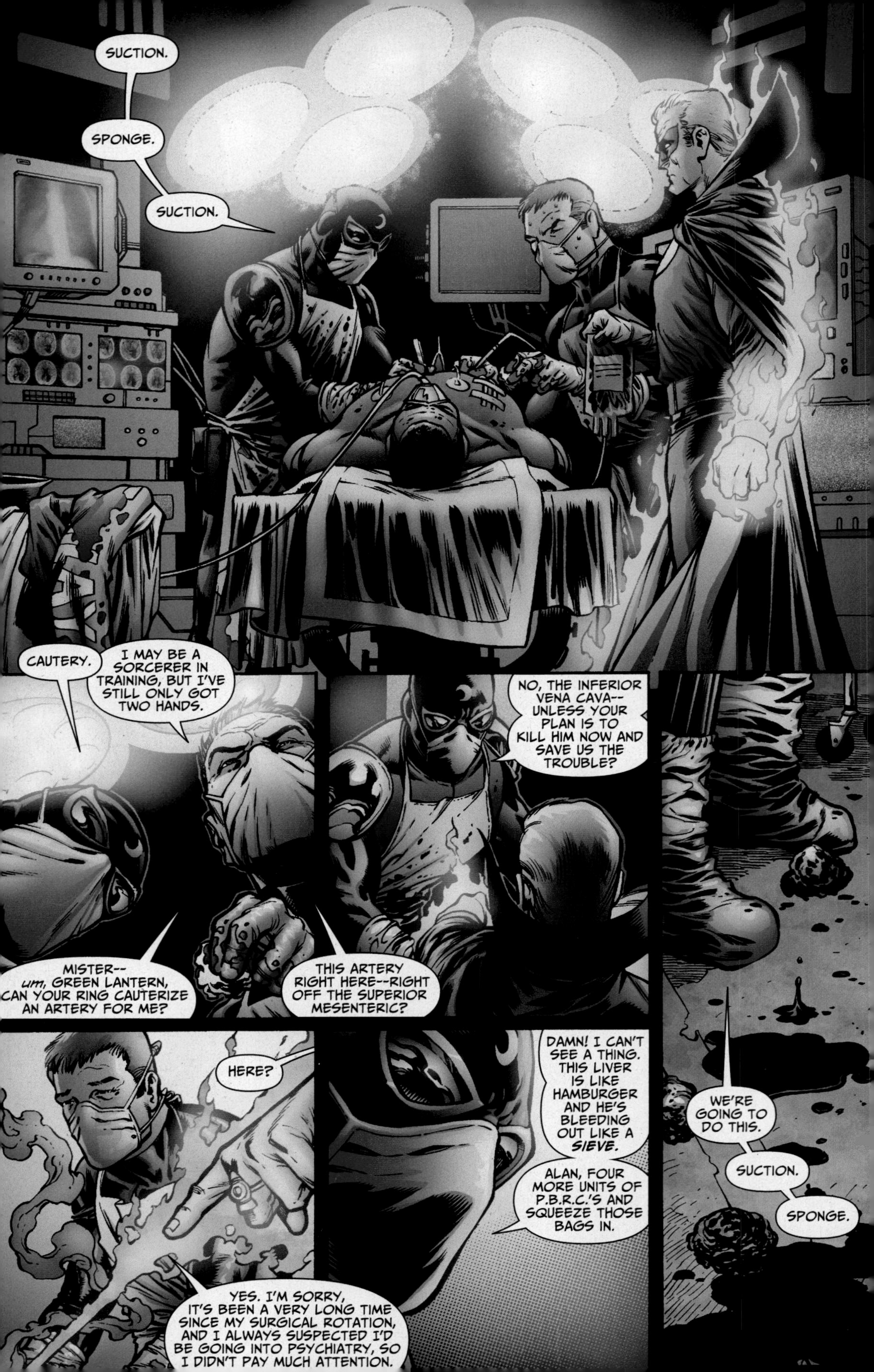
SUCTION.
SPONGE.
SUCTION.
CAUTERY.
I MAY BE A SORCERER IN TRAINING, BUT I'VE STILL ONLY GOT TWO HANDS.
MISTER-- *um*, GREEN LANTERN, CAN YOUR RING CAUTERIZE AN ARTERY FOR ME?
THIS ARTERY RIGHT HERE--RIGHT OFF THE SUPERIOR MESENTERIC?
NO, THE INFERIOR VENA CAVA-- UNLESS YOUR PLAN IS TO KILL HIM NOW AND SAVE US THE TROUBLE?
HERE?
YES. I'M SORRY, IT'S BEEN A VERY LONG TIME SINCE MY SURGICAL ROTATION, AND I ALWAYS SUSPECTED I'D BE GOING INTO PSYCHIATRY, SO I DIDN'T PAY MUCH ATTENTION.
DAMN! I CAN'T SEE A THING. THIS LIVER IS LIKE HAMBURGER AND HE'S BLEEDING OUT LIKE A *SIEVE.*
ALAN, FOUR MORE UNITS OF P.B.R.C.'S AND SQUEEZE THOSE BAGS IN.
WE'RE GOING TO DO THIS.
SUCTION.
SPONGE.

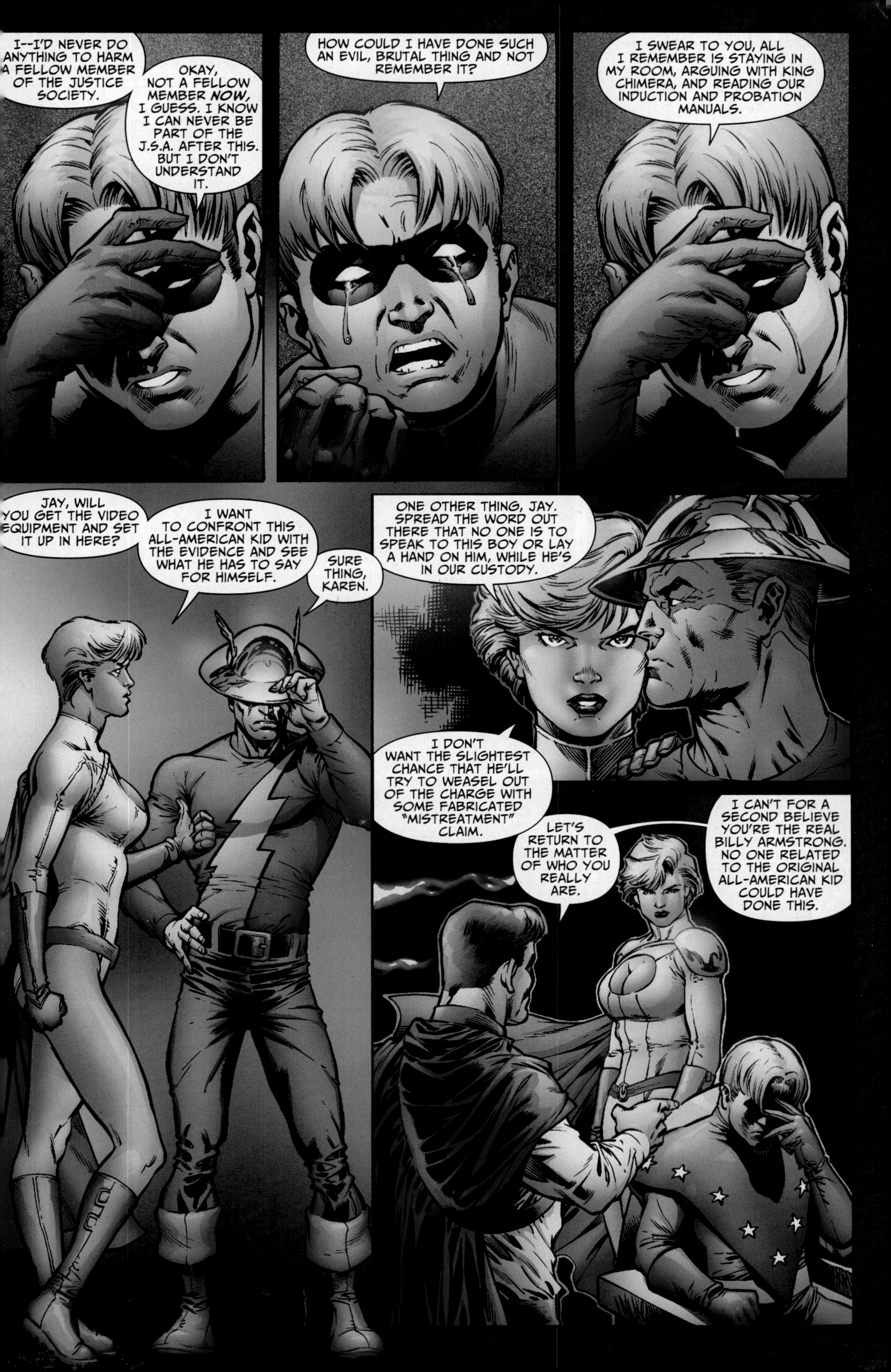

I--I'D NEVER DO ANYTHING TO HARM A FELLOW MEMBER OF THE JUSTICE SOCIETY.
OKAY, NOT A FELLOW MEMBER *NOW*, I GUESS. I KNOW I CAN NEVER BE PART OF THE J.S.A. AFTER THIS. BUT I DON'T UNDERSTAND IT.
HOW COULD I HAVE DONE SUCH AN EVIL, BRUTAL THING AND NOT REMEMBER IT?
I SWEAR TO YOU, ALL I REMEMBER IS STAYING IN MY ROOM, ARGUING WITH KING CHIMERA, AND READING OUR INDUCTION AND PROBATION MANUALS.
JAY, WILL YOU GET THE VIDEO EQUIPMENT AND SET IT UP IN HERE?
I WANT TO CONFRONT THIS ALL-AMERICAN KID WITH THE EVIDENCE AND SEE WHAT HE HAS TO SAY FOR HIMSELF.
SURE THING, KAREN.
ONE OTHER THING, JAY. SPREAD THE WORD OUT THERE THAT NO ONE IS TO SPEAK TO THIS BOY OR LAY A HAND ON HIM, WHILE HE'S IN OUR CUSTODY.
I DON'T WANT THE SLIGHTEST CHANCE THAT HE'LL TRY TO WEASEL OUT OF THE CHARGE WITH SOME FABRICATED "MISTREATMENT" CLAIM.
LET'S RETURN TO THE MATTER OF WHO YOU REALLY ARE.
I CAN'T FOR A SECOND BELIEVE YOU'RE THE REAL BILLY ARMSTRONG. NO ONE RELATED TO THE ORIGINAL ALL-AMERICAN KID COULD HAVE DONE THIS.

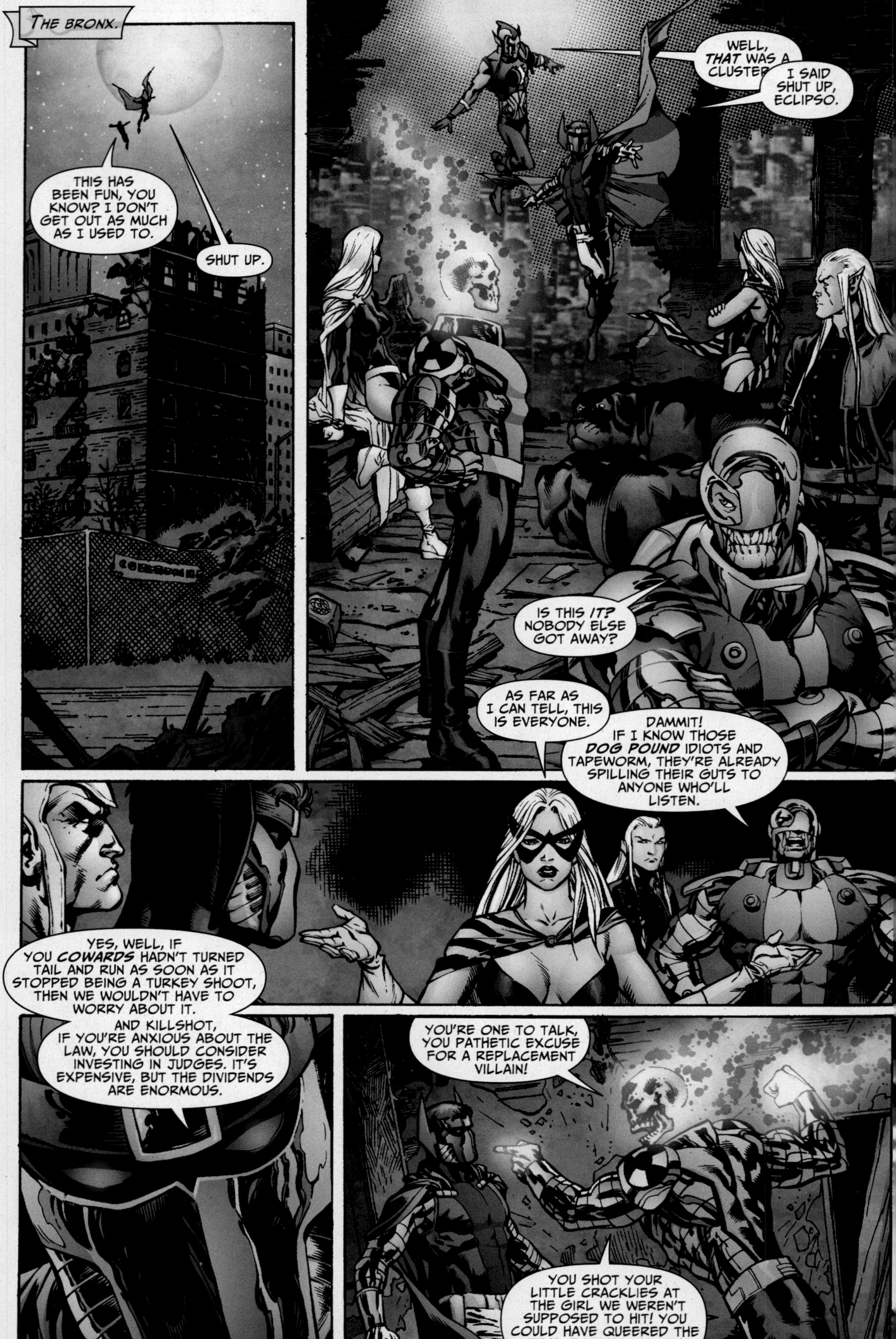
THE BRONX.
THIS HAS BEEN FUN, YOU KNOW? I DON'T GET OUT AS MUCH AS I USED TO.
SHUT UP.
WELL, THAT WAS A CLUSTER
I SAID SHUT UP, ECLIPSO.
IS THIS IT? NOBODY ELSE GOT AWAY?
AS FAR AS I CAN TELL, THIS IS EVERYONE.
DAMMIT! IF I KNOW THOSE DOG POUND IDIOTS AND TAPEWORM, THEY'RE ALREADY SPILLING THEIR GUTS TO ANYONE WHO'LL LISTEN.
YES, WELL, IF YOU COWARDS HADN'T TURNED TAIL AND RUN AS SOON AS IT STOPPED BEING A TURKEY SHOOT, THEN WE WOULDN'T HAVE TO WORRY ABOUT IT.
AND KILLSHOT, IF YOU'RE ANXIOUS ABOUT THE LAW, YOU SHOULD CONSIDER INVESTING IN JUDGES. IT'S EXPENSIVE, BUT THE DIVIDENDS ARE ENORMOUS.
YOU'RE ONE TO TALK, YOU PATHETIC EXCUSE FOR A REPLACEMENT VILLAIN!
YOU SHOT YOUR LITTLE CRACKLIES AT THE GIRL WE WEREN'T SUPPOSED TO HIT! YOU COULD HAVE QUEERED THE DEAL FOR ALL OF US!

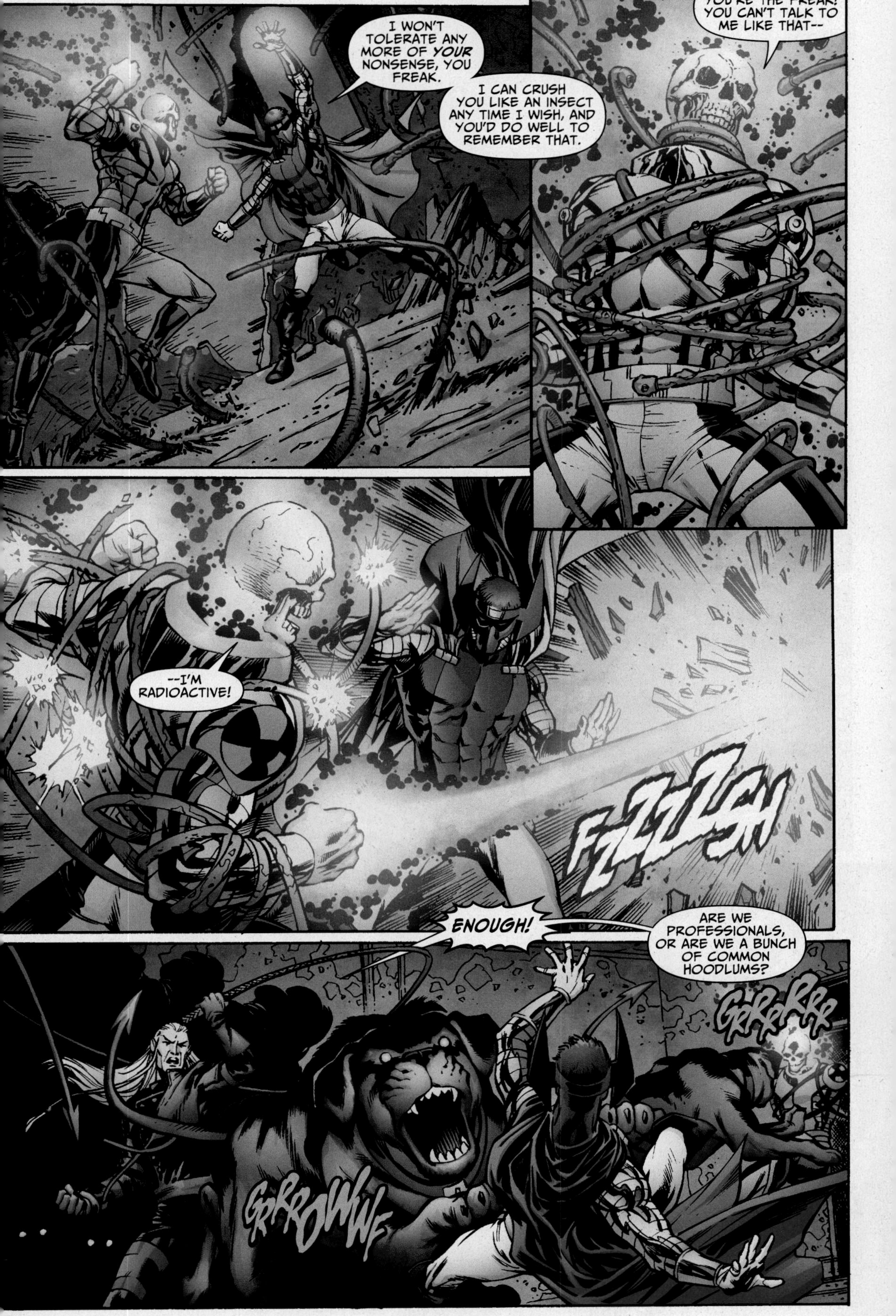
I WON'T TOLERATE ANY MORE OF *YOUR* NONSENSE, YOU FREAK.
I CAN CRUSH YOU LIKE AN INSECT ANY TIME I WISH, AND YOU'D DO WELL TO REMEMBER THAT.
YOU'RE THE FREAK! YOU CAN'T TALK TO ME LIKE THAT--
--I'M RADIOACTIVE!
FZZZTCH
ENOUGH!
ARE WE PROFESSIONALS, OR ARE WE A BUNCH OF COMMON HOODLUMS?
GRRRRRR
GRRROWWF

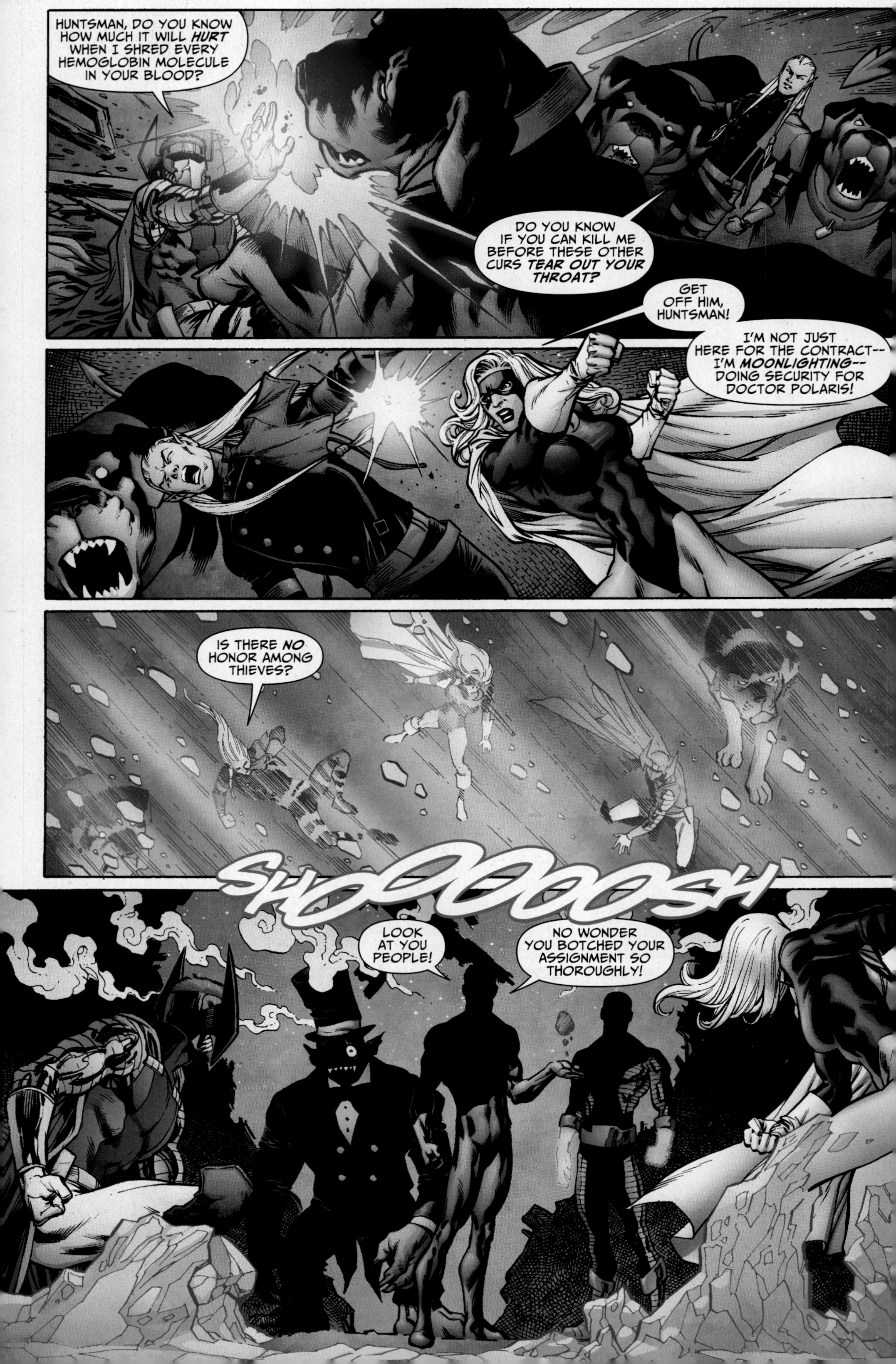
HUNTSMAN, DO YOU KNOW HOW MUCH IT WILL HURT WHEN I SHRED EVERY HEMOGLOBIN MOLECULE IN YOUR BLOOD?
DO YOU KNOW IF YOU CAN KILL ME BEFORE THESE OTHER CURS TEAR OUT YOUR THROAT?
GET OFF HIM, HUNTSMAN!
I'M NOT JUST HERE FOR THE CONTRACT-- I'M MOONLIGHTING-- DOING SECURITY FOR DOCTOR POLARIS!
IS THERE NO HONOR AMONG THIEVES?
SHOOOOOSH
LOOK AT YOU PEOPLE!
NO WONDER YOU BOTCHED YOUR ASSIGNMENT SO THOROUGHLY!

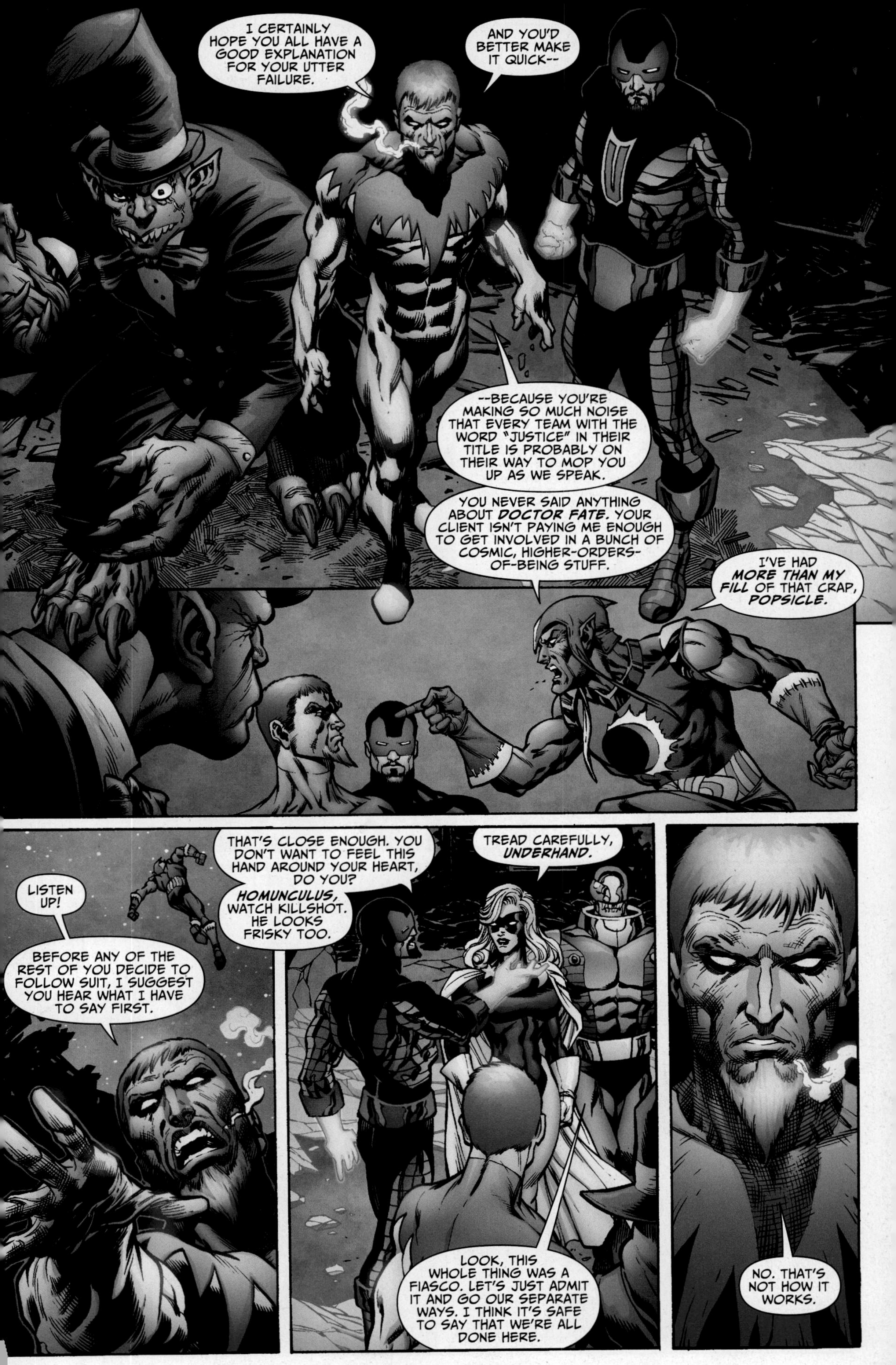

I CERTAINLY HOPE YOU ALL HAVE A GOOD EXPLANATION FOR YOUR UTTER FAILURE.
AND YOU'D BETTER MAKE IT QUICK--
--BECAUSE YOU'RE MAKING SO MUCH NOISE THAT EVERY TEAM WITH THE WORD "JUSTICE" IN THEIR TITLE IS PROBABLY ON THEIR WAY TO MOP YOU UP AS WE SPEAK.
YOU NEVER SAID ANYTHING ABOUT **DOCTOR FATE.** YOUR CLIENT ISN'T PAYING ME ENOUGH TO GET INVOLVED IN A BUNCH OF COSMIC, HIGHER-ORDERS-OF-BEING STUFF.
I'VE HAD **MORE THAN MY FILL** OF THAT CRAP, **POPSICLE.**
LISTEN UP!
BEFORE ANY OF THE REST OF YOU DECIDE TO FOLLOW SUIT, I SUGGEST YOU HEAR WHAT I HAVE TO SAY FIRST.
THAT'S CLOSE ENOUGH. YOU DON'T WANT TO FEEL THIS HAND AROUND YOUR HEART, DO YOU?
HOMUNCULUS, WATCH KILLSHOT. HE LOOKS FRISKY TOO.
TREAD CAREFULLY, **UNDERHAND.**
LOOK, THIS WHOLE THING WAS A FIASCO. LET'S JUST ADMIT IT AND GO OUR SEPARATE WAYS. I THINK IT'S SAFE TO SAY THAT WE'RE ALL DONE HERE.
NO. THAT'S NOT HOW IT WORKS.

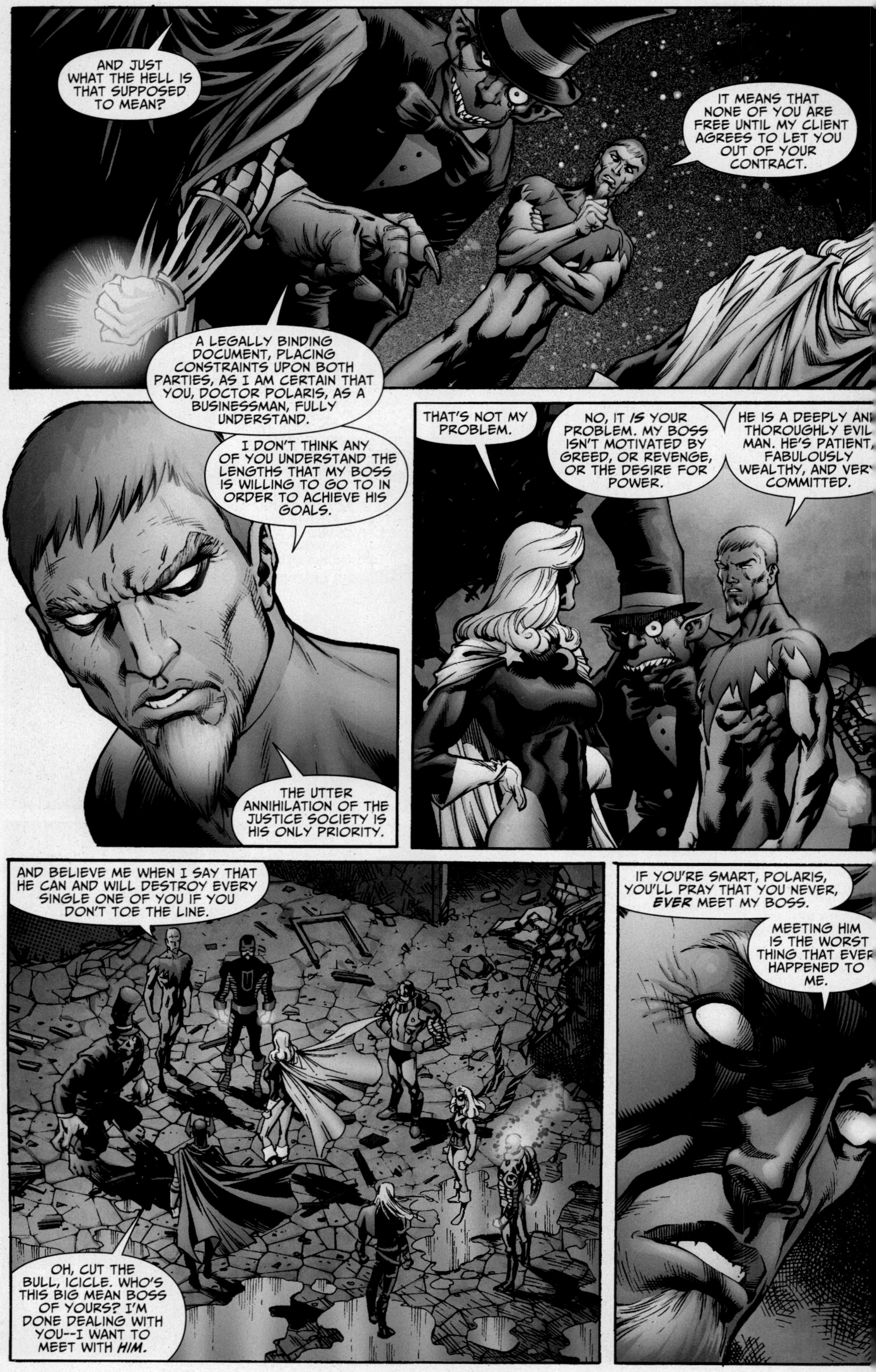
AND JUST WHAT THE HELL IS THAT SUPPOSED TO MEAN?
IT MEANS THAT NONE OF YOU ARE FREE UNTIL MY CLIENT AGREES TO LET YOU OUT OF YOUR CONTRACT.
A LEGALLY BINDING DOCUMENT, PLACING CONSTRAINTS UPON BOTH PARTIES, AS I AM CERTAIN THAT YOU, DOCTOR POLARIS, AS A BUSINESSMAN, FULLY UNDERSTAND.
I DON'T THINK ANY OF YOU UNDERSTAND THE LENGTHS THAT MY BOSS IS WILLING TO GO TO IN ORDER TO ACHIEVE HIS GOALS.
THE UTTER ANNIHILATION OF THE JUSTICE SOCIETY IS HIS ONLY PRIORITY.
THAT'S NOT MY PROBLEM.
NO, IT *IS* YOUR PROBLEM. MY BOSS ISN'T MOTIVATED BY GREED, OR REVENGE, OR THE DESIRE FOR POWER.
HE IS A DEEPLY AN THOROUGHLY EVIL MAN. HE'S PATIENT, FABULOUSLY WEALTHY, AND VER COMMITTED.
AND BELIEVE ME WHEN I SAY THAT HE CAN AND WILL DESTROY EVERY SINGLE ONE OF YOU IF YOU DON'T TOE THE LINE.
OH, CUT THE BULL, ICICLE. WHO'S THIS BIG MEAN BOSS OF YOURS? I'M DONE DEALING WITH YOU--I WANT TO MEET WITH ***HIM.***
IF YOU'RE SMART, POLARIS, YOU'LL PRAY THAT YOU NEVER, ***EVER*** MEET MY BOSS.
MEETING HIM IS THE WORST THING THAT EVE HAPPENED TO ME.

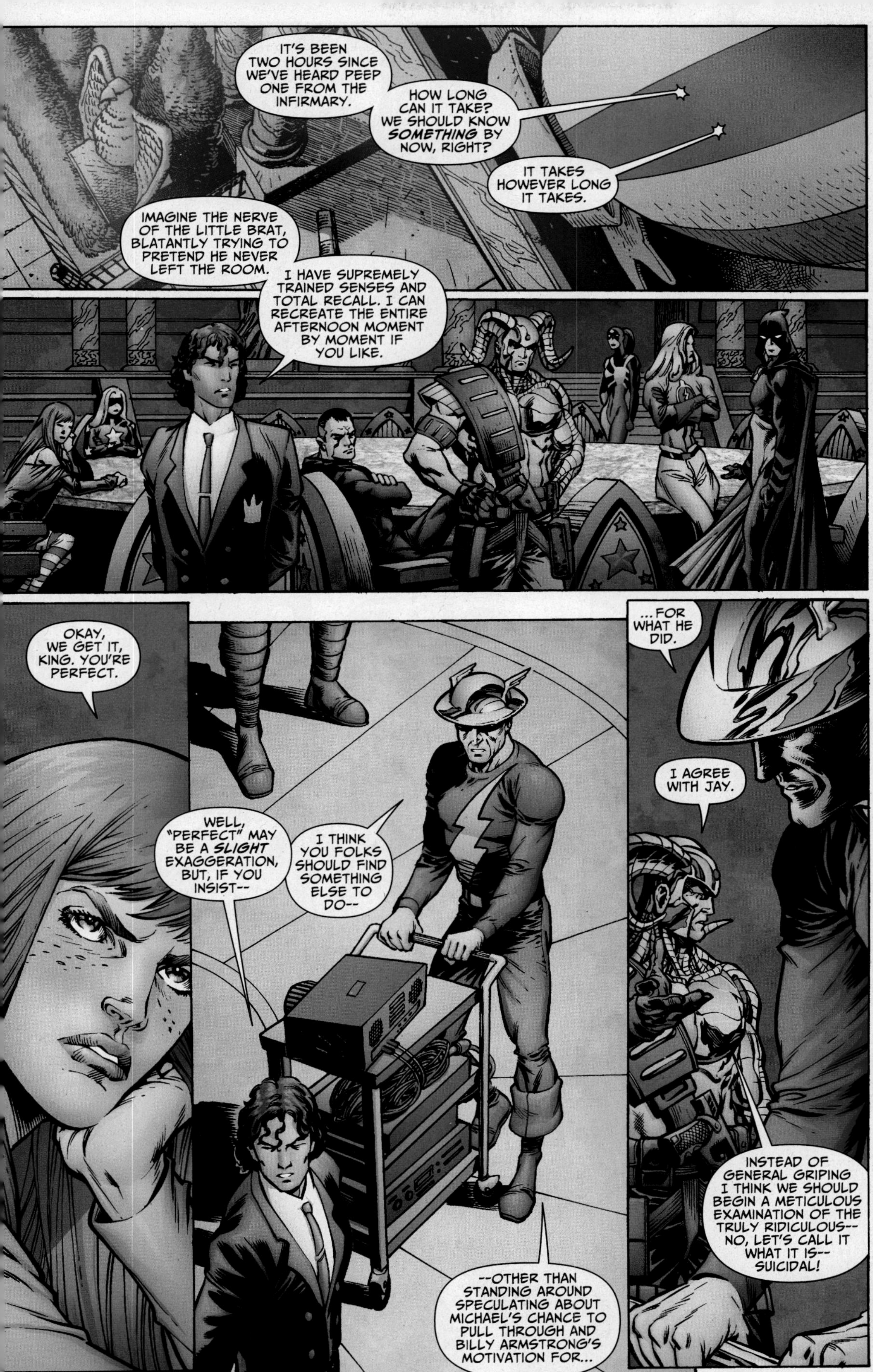
IT'S BEEN TWO HOURS SINCE WE'VE HEARD PEEP ONE FROM THE INFIRMARY.
HOW LONG CAN IT TAKE? WE SHOULD KNOW SOMETHING BY NOW, RIGHT?
IT TAKES HOWEVER LONG IT TAKES.
IMAGINE THE NERVE OF THE LITTLE BRAT, BLATANTLY TRYING TO PRETEND HE NEVER LEFT THE ROOM.
I HAVE SUPREMELY TRAINED SENSES AND TOTAL RECALL. I CAN RECREATE THE ENTIRE AFTERNOON MOMENT BY MOMENT IF YOU LIKE.
OKAY, WE GET IT, KING. YOU'RE PERFECT.
WELL, "PERFECT" MAY BE A SLIGHT EXAGGERATION, BUT, IF YOU INSIST--
I THINK YOU FOLKS SHOULD FIND SOMETHING ELSE TO DO--
--OTHER THAN STANDING AROUND SPECULATING ABOUT MICHAEL'S CHANCE TO PULL THROUGH AND BILLY ARMSTRONG'S MOTIVATION FOR...
...FOR WHAT HE DID.
I AGREE WITH JAY.
INSTEAD OF GENERAL GRIPING I THINK WE SHOULD BEGIN A METICULOUS EXAMINATION OF THE TRULY RIDICULOUS-- NO, LET'S CALL IT WHAT IT IS-- SUICIDAL!

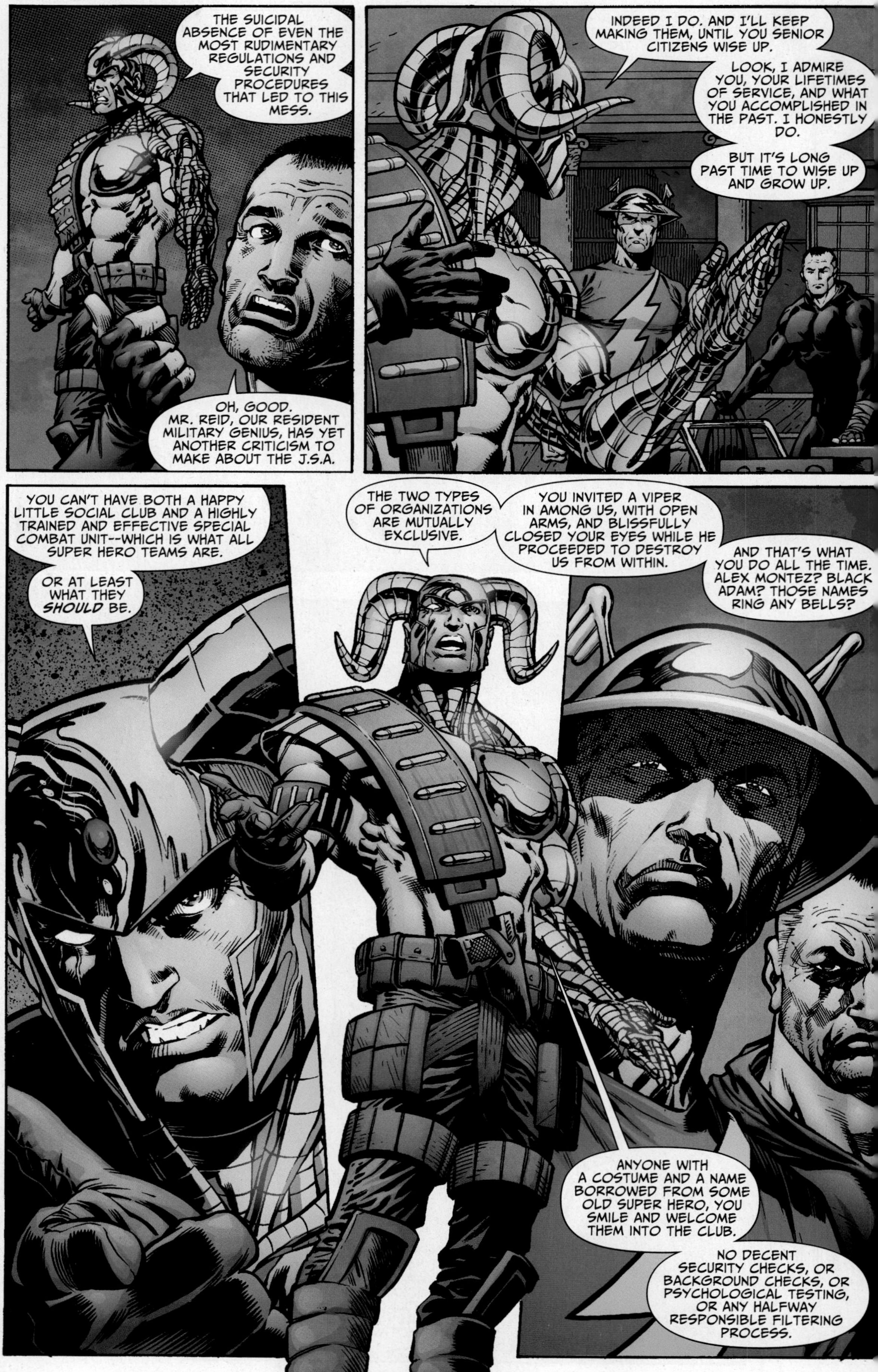
THE SUICIDAL ABSENCE OF EVEN THE MOST RUDIMENTARY REGULATIONS AND SECURITY PROCEDURES THAT LED TO THIS MESS.
OH, GOOD. MR. REID, OUR RESIDENT MILITARY GENIUS, HAS YET ANOTHER CRITICISM TO MAKE ABOUT THE J.S.A.
INDEED I DO. AND I'LL KEEP MAKING THEM, UNTIL YOU SENIOR CITIZENS WISE UP.
LOOK, I ADMIRE YOU, YOUR LIFETIMES OF SERVICE, AND WHAT YOU ACCOMPLISHED IN THE PAST. I HONESTLY DO.
BUT IT'S LONG PAST TIME TO WISE UP AND GROW UP.
YOU CAN'T HAVE BOTH A HAPPY LITTLE SOCIAL CLUB AND A HIGHLY TRAINED AND EFFECTIVE SPECIAL COMBAT UNIT--WHICH IS WHAT ALL SUPER HERO TEAMS ARE.
OR AT LEAST WHAT THEY *SHOULD* BE.
THE TWO TYPES OF ORGANIZATIONS ARE MUTUALLY EXCLUSIVE.
YOU INVITED A VIPER IN AMONG US, WITH OPEN ARMS, AND BLISSFULLY CLOSED YOUR EYES WHILE HE PROCEEDED TO DESTROY US FROM WITHIN.
AND THAT'S WHAT YOU DO ALL THE TIME. ALEX MONTEZ? BLACK ADAM? THOSE NAMES RING ANY BELLS?
ANYONE WITH A COSTUME AND A NAME BORROWED FROM SOME OLD SUPER HERO, YOU SMILE AND WELCOME THEM INTO THE CLUB.
NO DECENT SECURITY CHECKS, OR BACKGROUND CHECKS, OR PSYCHOLOGICAL TESTING, OR ANY HALFWAY RESPONSIBLE FILTERING PROCESS.

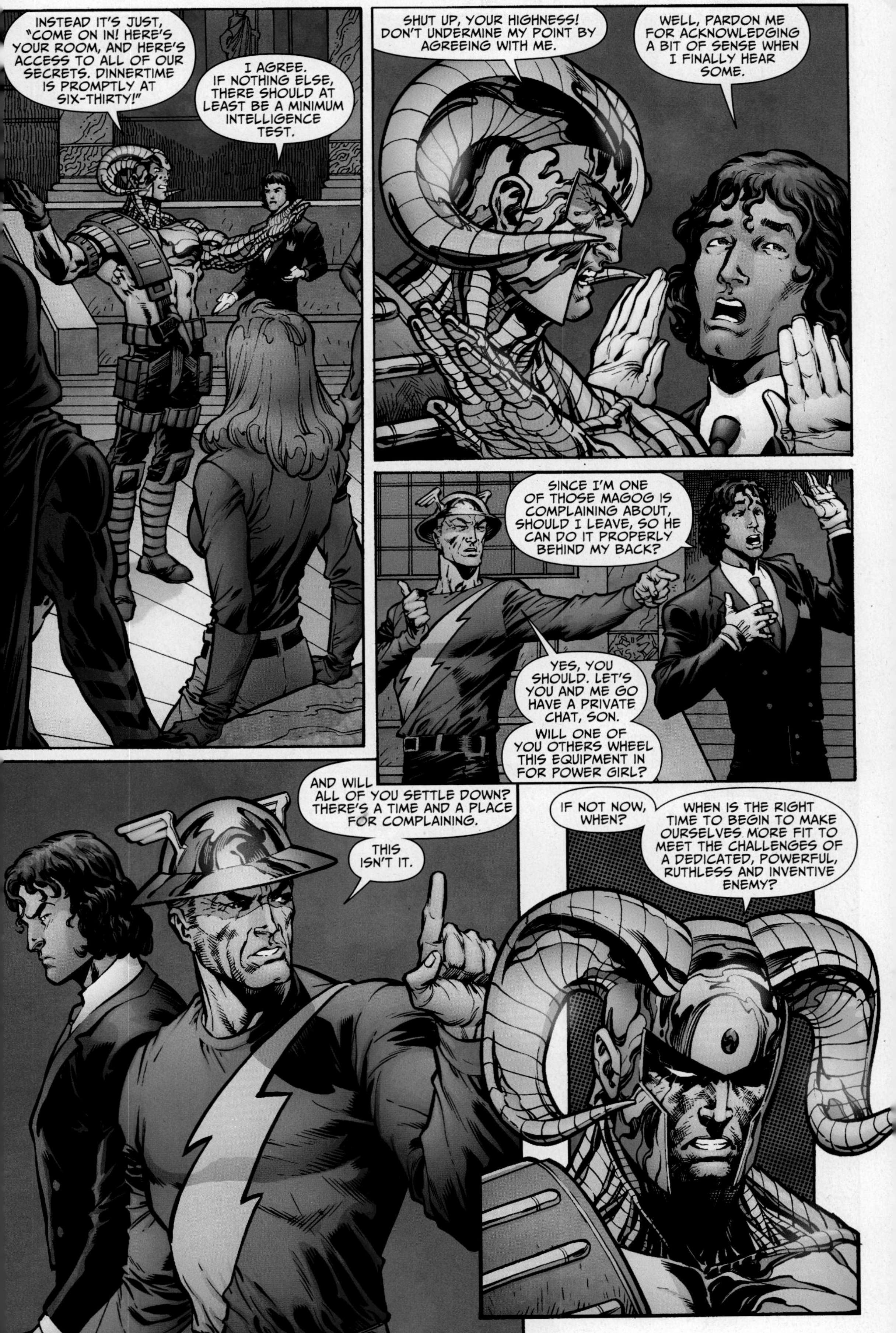
INSTEAD IT'S JUST, "COME ON IN! HERE'S YOUR ROOM, AND HERE'S ACCESS TO ALL OF OUR SECRETS. DINNERTIME IS PROMPTLY AT SIX-THIRTY!"
I AGREE. IF NOTHING ELSE, THERE SHOULD AT LEAST BE A MINIMUM INTELLIGENCE TEST.
SHUT UP, YOUR HIGHNESS! DON'T UNDERMINE MY POINT BY AGREEING WITH ME.
WELL, PARDON ME FOR ACKNOWLEDGING A BIT OF SENSE WHEN I FINALLY HEAR SOME.
SINCE I'M ONE OF THOSE MAGOG IS COMPLAINING ABOUT, SHOULD I LEAVE, SO HE CAN DO IT PROPERLY BEHIND MY BACK?
YES, YOU SHOULD. LET'S YOU AND ME GO HAVE A PRIVATE CHAT, SON.
WILL ONE OF YOU OTHERS WHEEL THIS EQUIPMENT IN FOR POWER GIRL?
AND WILL ALL OF YOU SETTLE DOWN? THERE'S A TIME AND A PLACE FOR COMPLAINING.
THIS ISN'T IT.
IF NOT NOW, WHEN?
WHEN IS THE RIGHT TIME TO BEGIN TO MAKE OURSELVES MORE FIT TO MEET THE CHALLENGES OF A DEDICATED, POWERFUL, RUTHLESS AND INVENTIVE ENEMY?

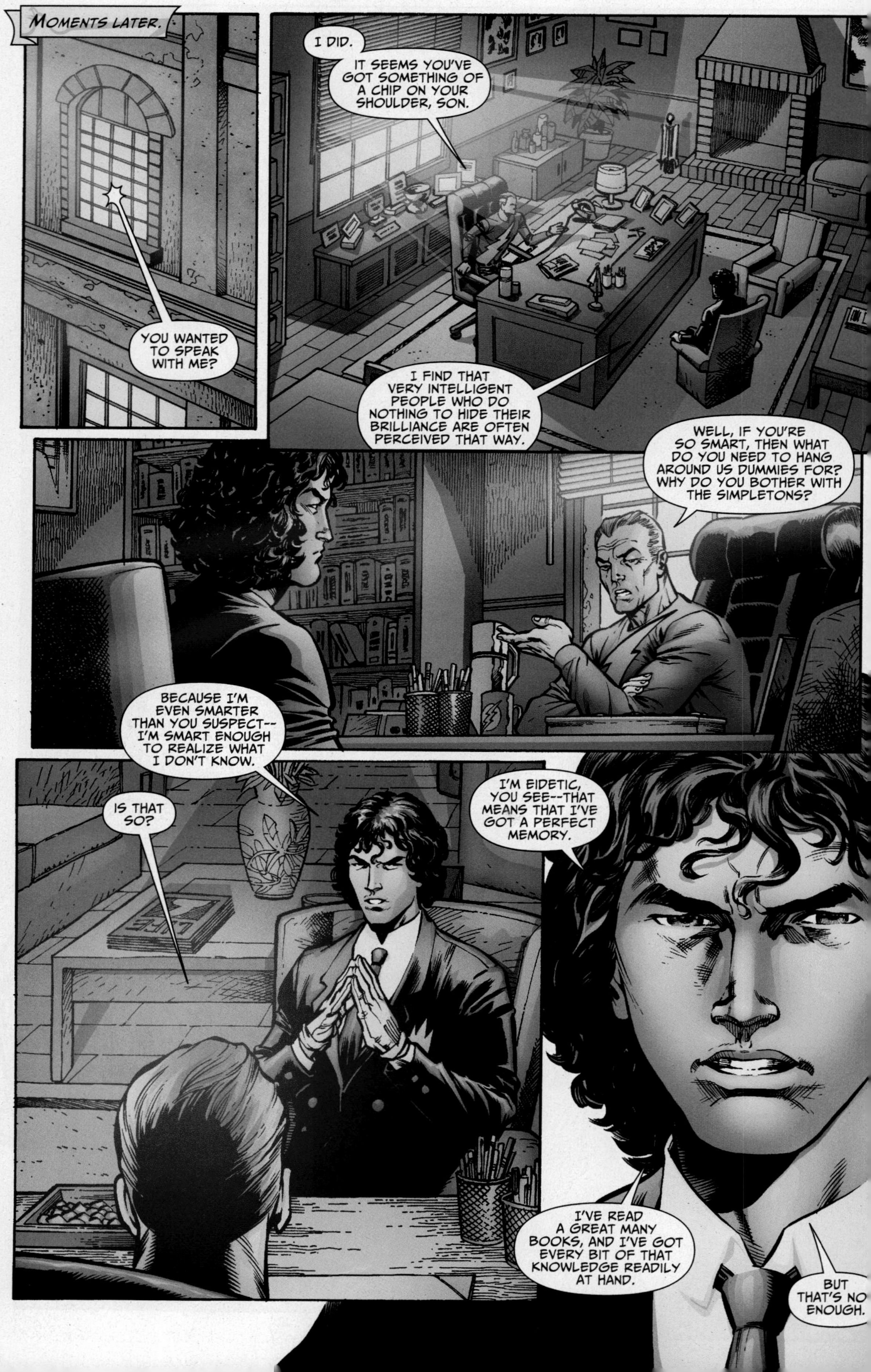
MOMENTS LATER.
YOU WANTED TO SPEAK WITH ME?
I DID.
IT SEEMS YOU'VE GOT SOMETHING OF A CHIP ON YOUR SHOULDER, SON.
I FIND THAT VERY INTELLIGENT PEOPLE WHO DO NOTHING TO HIDE THEIR BRILLIANCE ARE OFTEN PERCEIVED THAT WAY.
WELL, IF YOU'RE SO SMART, THEN WHAT DO YOU NEED TO HANG AROUND US DUMMIES FOR? WHY DO YOU BOTHER WITH THE SIMPLETONS?
BECAUSE I'M EVEN SMARTER THAN YOU SUSPECT-- I'M SMART ENOUGH TO REALIZE WHAT I DON'T KNOW.
IS THAT SO?
I'M EIDETIC, YOU SEE--THAT MEANS THAT I'VE GOT A PERFECT MEMORY.
I'VE READ A GREAT MANY BOOKS, AND I'VE GOT EVERY BIT OF THAT KNOWLEDGE READILY AT HAND.
BUT THAT'S NO ENOUGH.

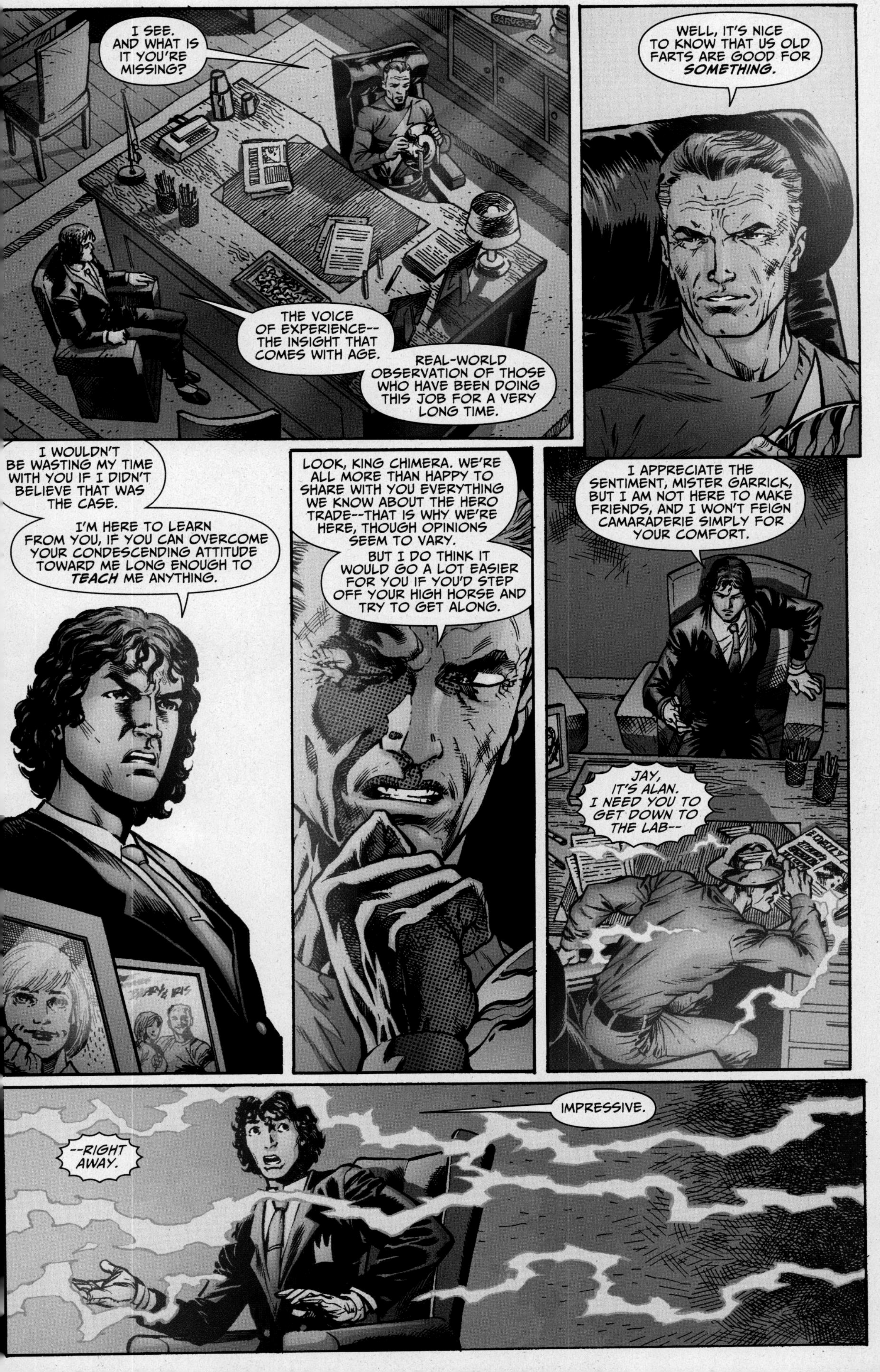
I SEE. AND WHAT IS IT YOU'RE MISSING?
THE VOICE OF EXPERIENCE-- THE INSIGHT THAT COMES WITH AGE.
REAL-WORLD OBSERVATION OF THOSE WHO HAVE BEEN DOING THIS JOB FOR A VERY LONG TIME.
WELL, IT'S NICE TO KNOW THAT US OLD FARTS ARE GOOD FOR *SOMETHING.*
I WOULDN'T BE WASTING MY TIME WITH YOU IF I DIDN'T BELIEVE THAT WAS THE CASE.
I'M HERE TO LEARN FROM YOU, IF YOU CAN OVERCOME YOUR CONDESCENDING ATTITUDE TOWARD ME LONG ENOUGH TO *TEACH* ME ANYTHING.
LOOK, KING CHIMERA. WE'RE ALL MORE THAN HAPPY TO SHARE WITH YOU EVERYTHING WE KNOW ABOUT THE HERO TRADE--THAT IS WHY WE'RE HERE, THOUGH OPINIONS SEEM TO VARY.
BUT I DO THINK IT WOULD GO A LOT EASIER FOR YOU IF YOU'D STEP OFF YOUR HIGH HORSE AND TRY TO GET ALONG.
I APPRECIATE THE SENTIMENT, MISTER GARRICK, BUT I AM NOT HERE TO MAKE FRIENDS, AND I WON'T FEIGN CAMARADERIE SIMPLY FOR YOUR COMFORT.
JAY, IT'S ALAN. I NEED YOU TO GET DOWN TO THE LAB--
--RIGHT AWAY.
IMPRESSIVE.

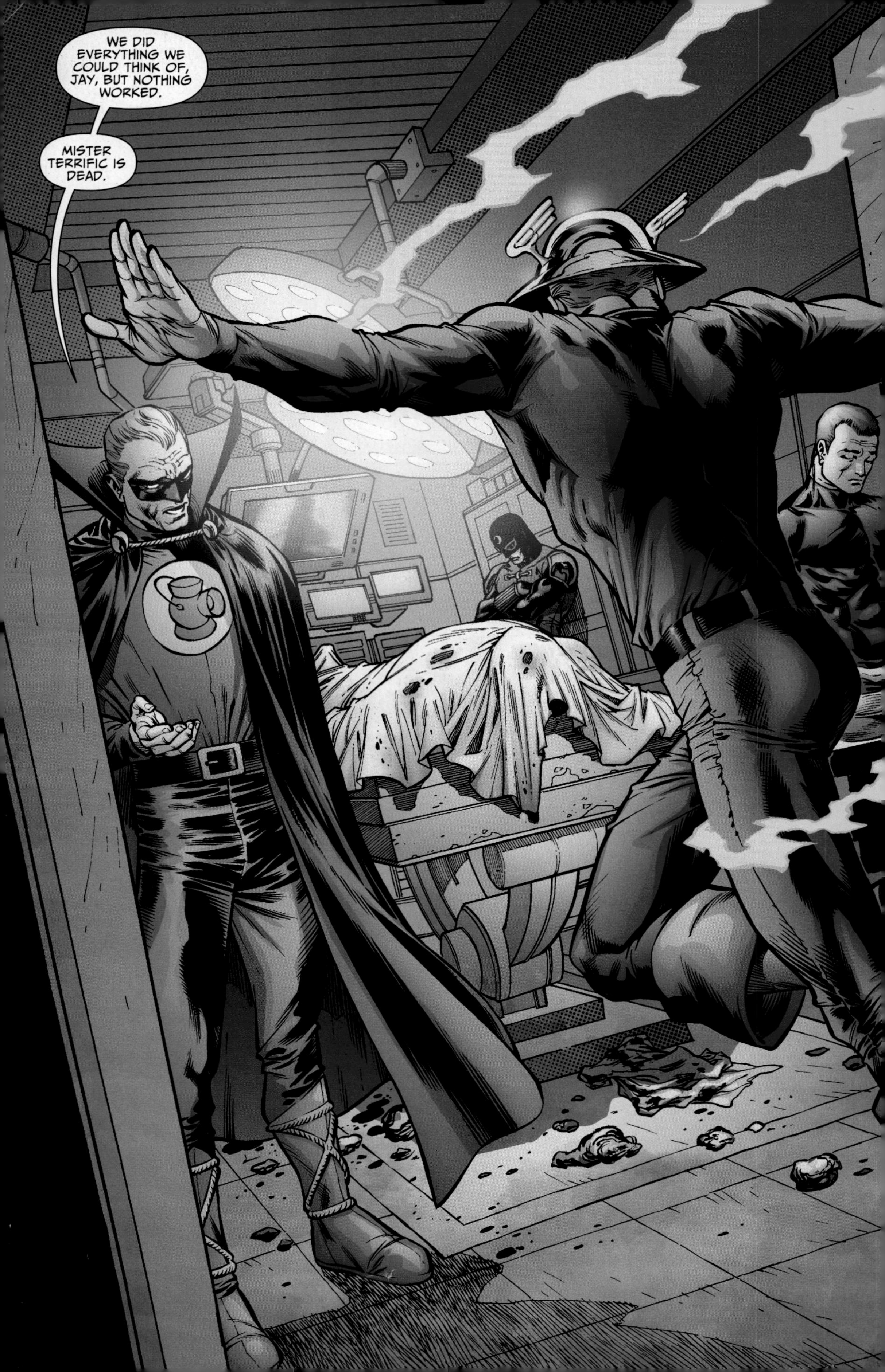
WE DID EVERYTHING WE COULD THINK OF, JAY, BUT NOTHING WORKED.
MISTER TERRIFIC IS DEAD.

THE BAD SEED Part Four

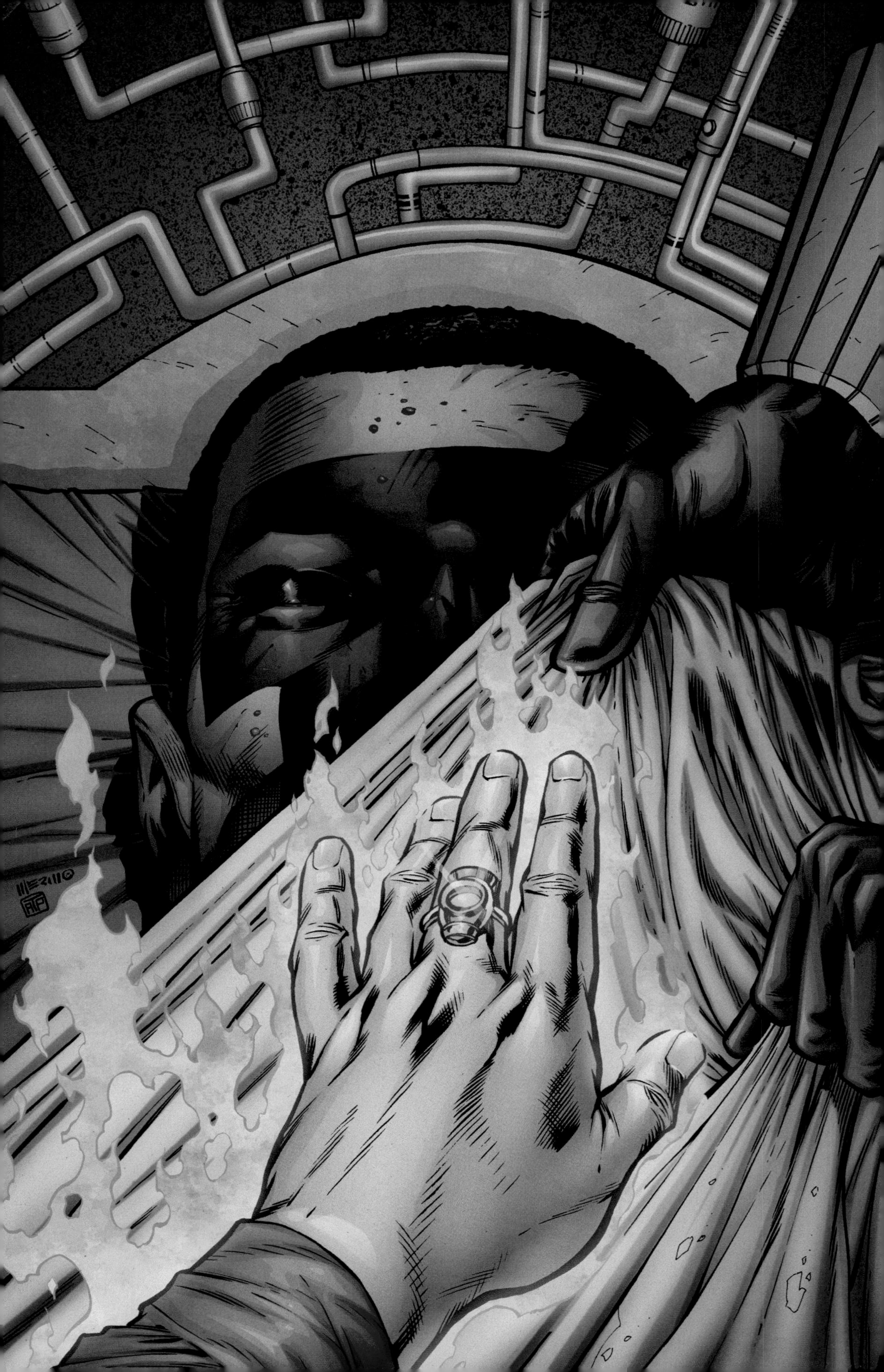

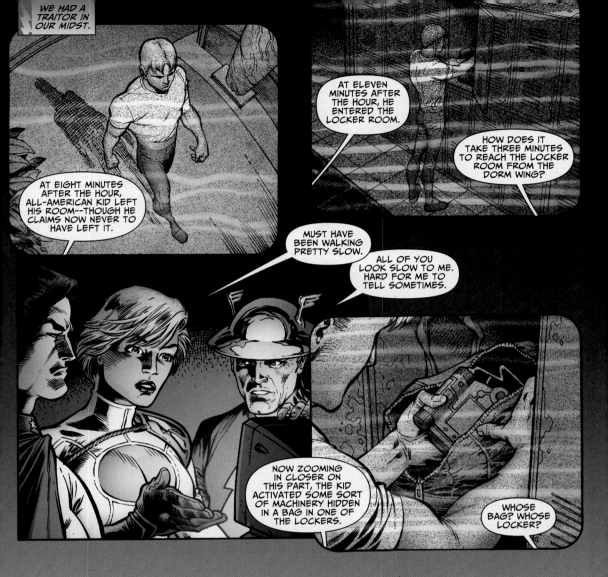

WE HAD A TRAITOR IN OUR MIDST.

AT EIGHT MINUTES AFTER THE HOUR, ALL-AMERICAN KID LEFT HIS ROOM--THOUGH HE CLAIMS NOW NEVER TO HAVE LEFT IT.

AT ELEVEN MINUTES AFTER THE HOUR, HE ENTERED THE LOCKER ROOM.

HOW DOES IT TAKE THREE MINUTES TO REACH THE LOCKER ROOM FROM THE DORM WING?

MUST HAVE BEEN WALKING PRETTY SLOW.

ALL OF YOU LOOK SLOW TO ME. HARD FOR ME TO TELL SOMETIMES.

NOW ZOOMING IN CLOSER ON THIS PART, THE KID ACTIVATED SOME SORT OF MACHINERY HIDDEN IN A BAG IN ONE OF THE LOCKERS.

WHOSE BAG? WHOSE LOCKER?

THE WORTH OF A HERO

PART 4 OF THE BAD SEED

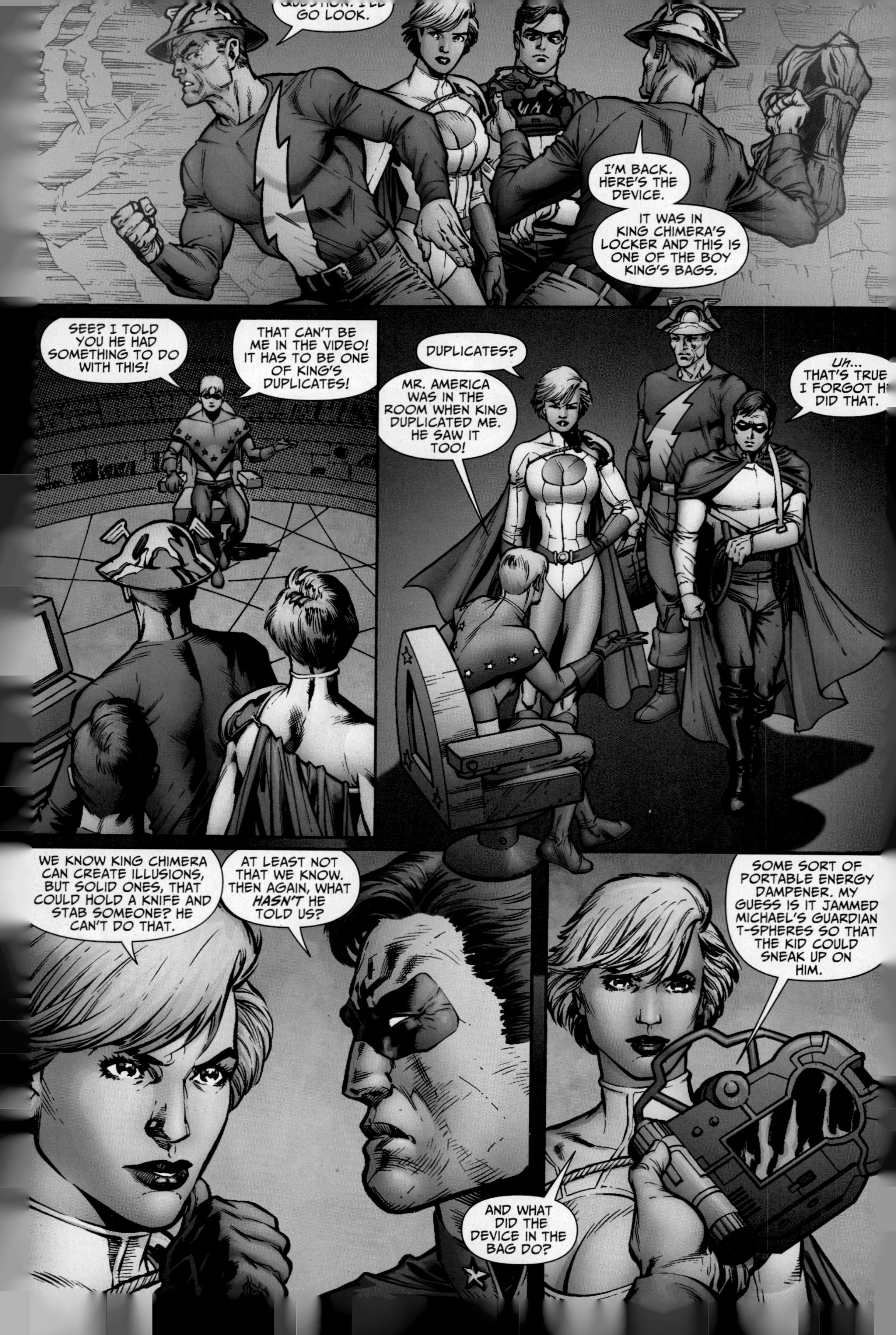
GO LOOK.
I'M BACK. HERE'S THE DEVICE.
IT WAS IN KING CHIMERA'S LOCKER AND THIS IS ONE OF THE BOY KING'S BAGS.
SEE? I TOLD YOU HE HAD SOMETHING TO DO WITH THIS!
THAT CAN'T BE ME IN THE VIDEO! IT HAS TO BE ONE OF KING'S DUPLICATES!
DUPLICATES?
MR. AMERICA WAS IN THE ROOM WHEN KING DUPLICATED ME. HE SAW IT TOO!
Uh... THAT'S TRUE I FORGOT DID THAT.
WE KNOW KING CHIMERA CAN CREATE ILLUSIONS, BUT SOLID ONES, THAT COULD HOLD A KNIFE AND STAB SOMEONE? HE CAN'T DO THAT.
AT LEAST NOT THAT WE KNOW. THEN AGAIN, WHAT ***HASN'T*** HE TOLD US?
AND WHAT DID THE DEVICE IN THE BAG DO?
SOME SORT OF PORTABLE ENERGY DAMPENER. MY GUESS IS IT JAMMED MICHAEL'S GUARDIAN T-SPHERES SO THAT THE KID COULD SNEAK UP ON HIM.

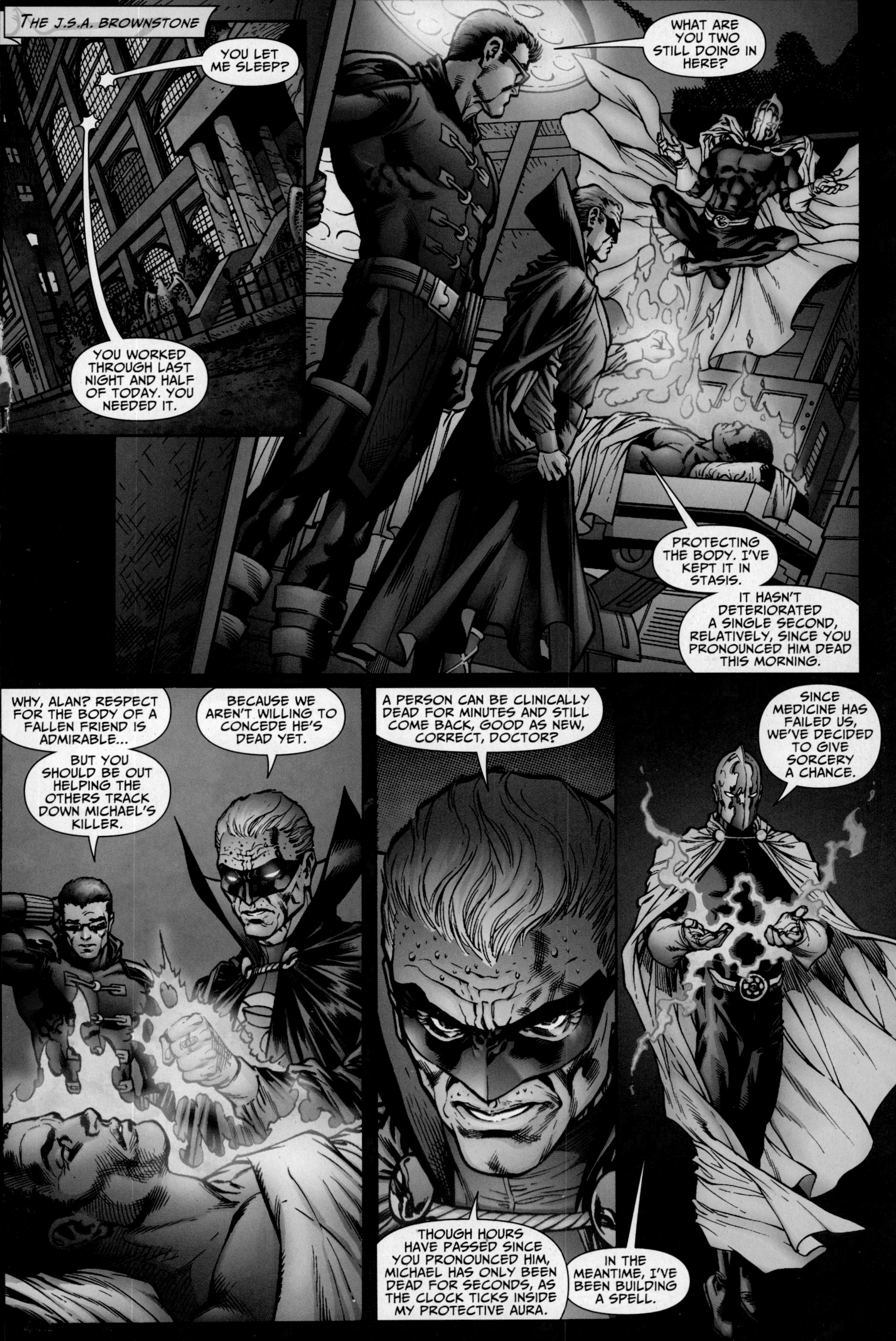
THE J.S.A. BROWNSTONE
YOU LET ME SLEEP?
YOU WORKED THROUGH LAST NIGHT AND HALF OF TODAY. YOU NEEDED IT.
WHAT ARE YOU TWO STILL DOING IN HERE?
PROTECTING THE BODY. I'VE KEPT IT IN STASIS.
IT HASN'T DETERIORATED A SINGLE SECOND, RELATIVELY, SINCE YOU PRONOUNCED HIM DEAD THIS MORNING.
WHY, ALAN? RESPECT FOR THE BODY OF A FALLEN FRIEND IS ADMIRABLE...
BUT YOU SHOULD BE OUT HELPING THE OTHERS TRACK DOWN MICHAEL'S KILLER.
BECAUSE WE AREN'T WILLING TO CONCEDE HE'S DEAD YET.
A PERSON CAN BE CLINICALLY DEAD FOR MINUTES AND STILL COME BACK, GOOD AS NEW, CORRECT, DOCTOR?
THOUGH HOURS HAVE PASSED SINCE YOU PRONOUNCED HIM, MICHAEL HAS ONLY BEEN DEAD FOR SECONDS, AS THE CLOCK TICKS INSIDE MY PROTECTIVE AURA.
SINCE MEDICINE HAS FAILED US, WE'VE DECIDED TO GIVE SORCERY A CHANCE.
IN THE MEANTIME, I'VE BEEN BUILDING A SPELL.

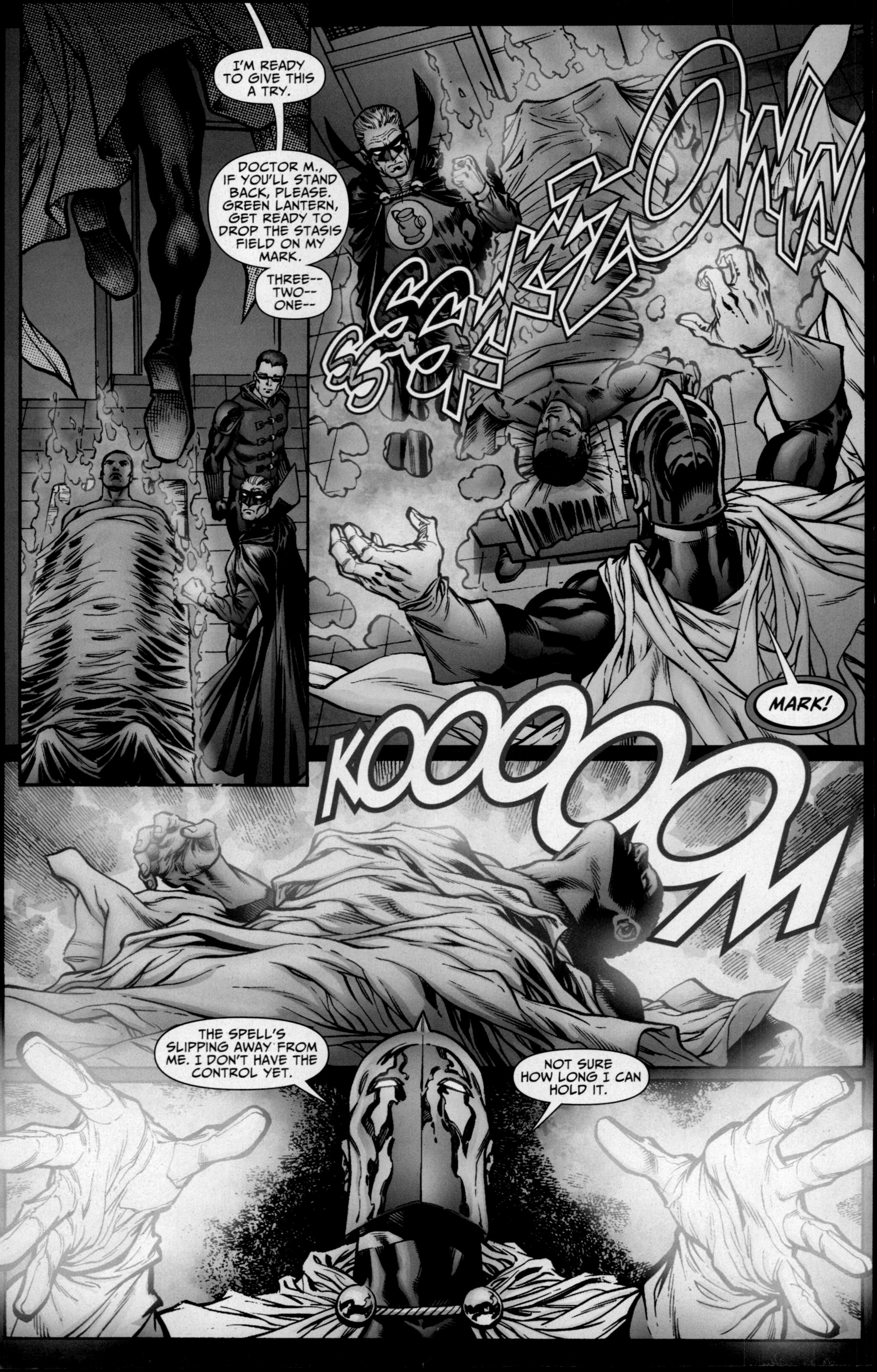
I'M READY TO GIVE THIS A TRY.
DOCTOR M., IF YOU'LL STAND BACK, PLEASE. GREEN LANTERN, GET READY TO DROP THE STASIS FIELD ON MY MARK.
THREE-- TWO-- ONE--
SSSKKZZOWWW
MARK!
KOOOOOOM
THE SPELL'S SLIPPING AWAY FROM ME. I DON'T HAVE THE CONTROL YET.
NOT SURE HOW LONG I CAN HOLD IT.

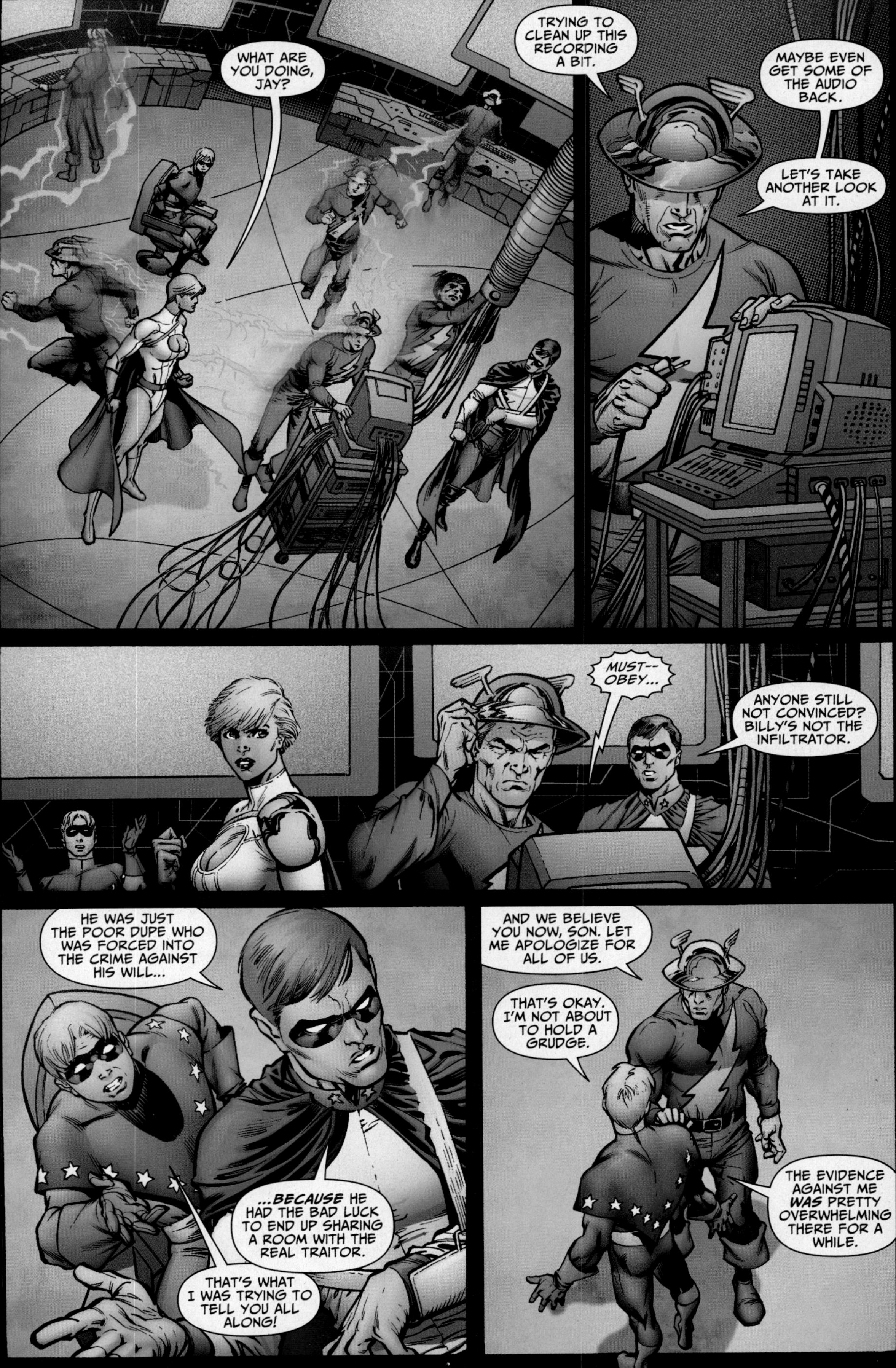
WHAT ARE YOU DOING, JAY?
TRYING TO CLEAN UP THIS RECORDING A BIT.
MAYBE EVEN GET SOME OF THE AUDIO BACK.
LET'S TAKE ANOTHER LOOK AT IT.
MUST-- OBEY...
ANYONE STILL NOT CONVINCED? BILLY'S NOT THE INFILTRATOR.
HE WAS JUST THE POOR DUPE WHO WAS FORCED INTO THE CRIME AGAINST HIS WILL...
...BECAUSE HE HAD THE BAD LUCK TO END UP SHARING A ROOM WITH THE REAL TRAITOR.
THAT'S WHAT I WAS TRYING TO TELL YOU ALL ALONG!
AND WE BELIEVE YOU NOW, SON. LET ME APOLOGIZE FOR ALL OF US.
THAT'S OKAY. I'M NOT ABOUT TO HOLD A GRUDGE.
THE EVIDENCE AGAINST ME WAS PRETTY OVERWHELMING THERE FOR A WHILE.

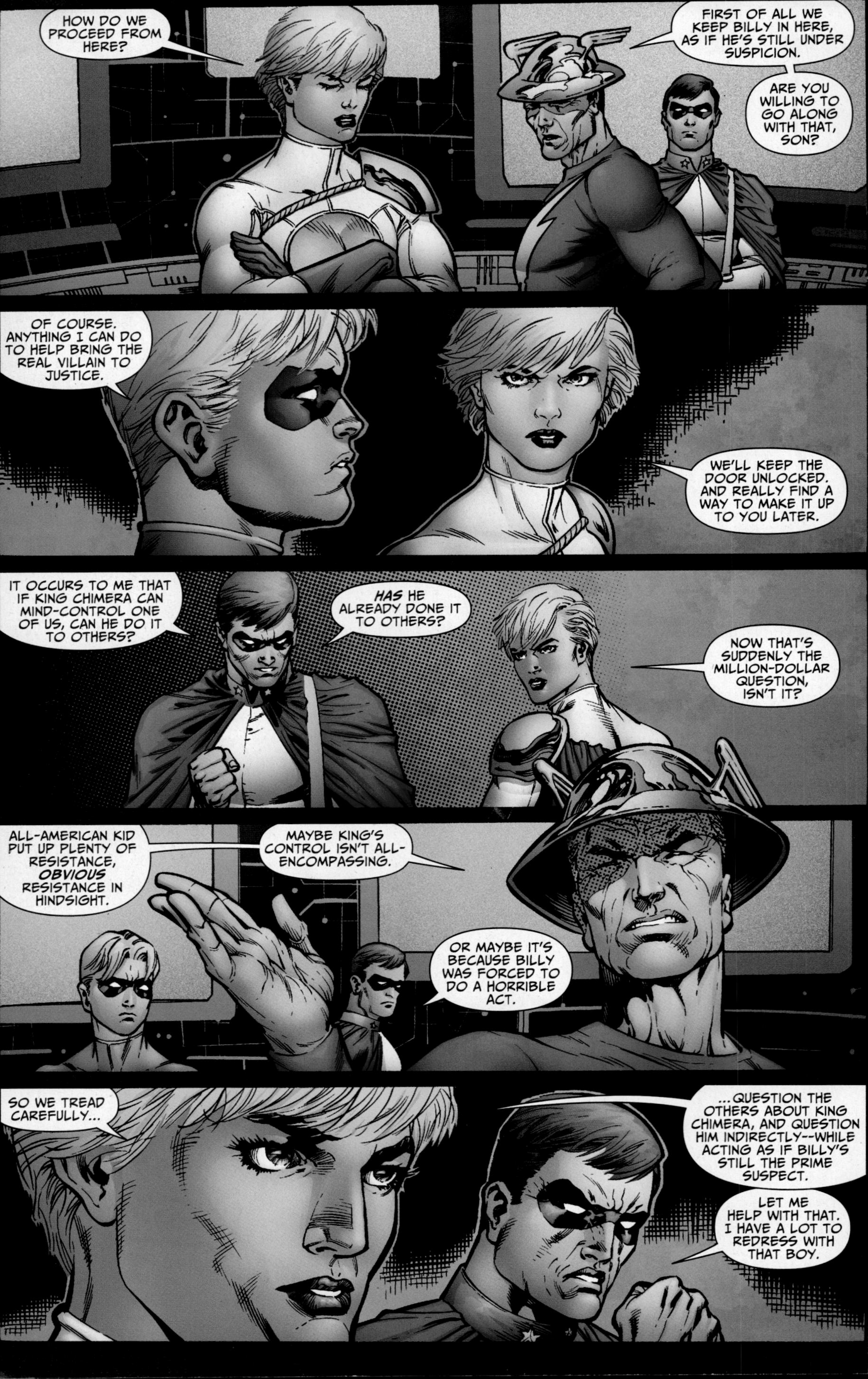
HOW DO WE PROCEED FROM HERE?
FIRST OF ALL WE KEEP BILLY IN HERE, AS IF HE'S STILL UNDER SUSPICION.
ARE YOU WILLING TO GO ALONG WITH THAT, SON?
OF COURSE. ANYTHING I CAN DO TO HELP BRING THE REAL VILLAIN TO JUSTICE.
WE'LL KEEP THE DOOR UNLOCKED. AND REALLY FIND A WAY TO MAKE IT UP TO YOU LATER.
IT OCCURS TO ME THAT IF KING CHIMERA CAN MIND-CONTROL ONE OF US, CAN HE DO IT TO OTHERS?
HAS HE ALREADY DONE IT TO OTHERS?
NOW THAT'S SUDDENLY THE MILLION-DOLLAR QUESTION, ISN'T IT?
ALL-AMERICAN KID PUT UP PLENTY OF RESISTANCE, *OBVIOUS* RESISTANCE IN HINDSIGHT.
MAYBE KING'S CONTROL ISN'T ALL-ENCOMPASSING.
OR MAYBE IT'S BECAUSE BILLY WAS FORCED TO DO A HORRIBLE ACT.
SO WE TREAD CAREFULLY...
...QUESTION THE OTHERS ABOUT KING CHIMERA, AND QUESTION HIM INDIRECTLY--WHILE ACTING AS IF BILLY'S STILL THE PRIME SUSPECT.
LET ME HELP WITH THAT. I HAVE A LOT TO REDRESS WITH THAT BOY.

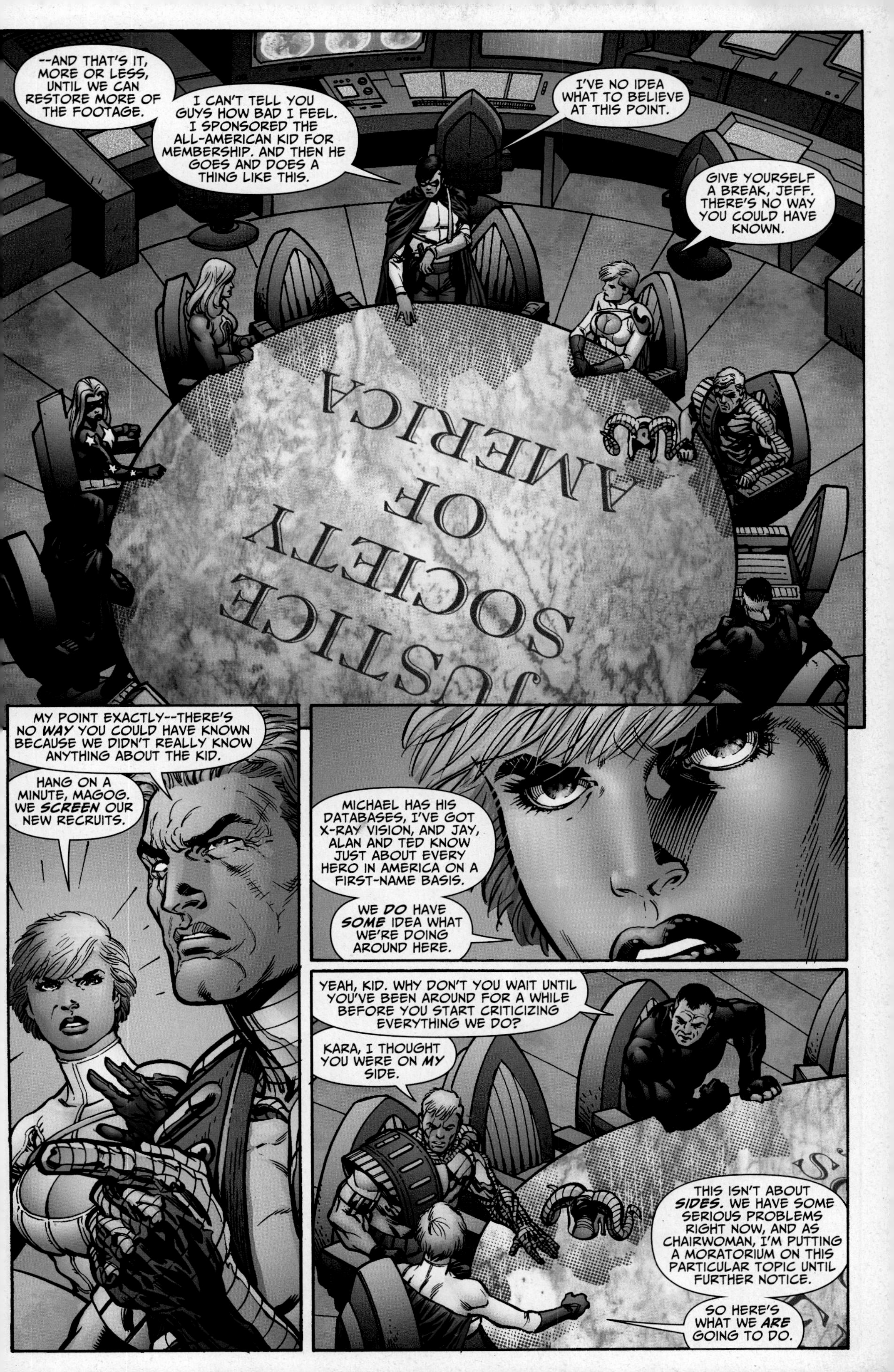
--AND THAT'S IT, MORE OR LESS, UNTIL WE CAN RESTORE MORE OF THE FOOTAGE.
I CAN'T TELL YOU GUYS HOW BAD I FEEL. I SPONSORED THE ALL-AMERICAN KID FOR MEMBERSHIP. AND THEN HE GOES AND DOES A THING LIKE THIS.
I'VE NO IDEA WHAT TO BELIEVE AT THIS POINT.
GIVE YOURSELF A BREAK, JEFF. THERE'S NO WAY YOU COULD HAVE KNOWN.
JUSTICE SOCIETY OF AMERICA
MY POINT EXACTLY--THERE'S NO *WAY* YOU COULD HAVE KNOWN BECAUSE WE DIDN'T REALLY KNOW ANYTHING ABOUT THE KID.
HANG ON A MINUTE, MAGOG. WE *SCREEN* OUR NEW RECRUITS.
MICHAEL HAS HIS DATABASES, I'VE GOT X-RAY VISION, AND JAY, ALAN AND TED KNOW JUST ABOUT EVERY HERO IN AMERICA ON A FIRST-NAME BASIS.
WE *DO* HAVE *SOME* IDEA WHAT WE'RE DOING AROUND HERE.
YEAH, KID. WHY DON'T YOU WAIT UNTIL YOU'VE BEEN AROUND FOR A WHILE BEFORE YOU START CRITICIZING EVERYTHING WE DO?
KARA, I THOUGHT YOU WERE ON *MY* SIDE.
THIS ISN'T ABOUT *SIDES.* WE HAVE SOME SERIOUS PROBLEMS RIGHT NOW, AND AS CHAIRWOMAN, I'M PUTTING A MORATORIUM ON THIS PARTICULAR TOPIC UNTIL FURTHER NOTICE.
SO HERE'S WHAT WE *ARE* GOING TO DO.

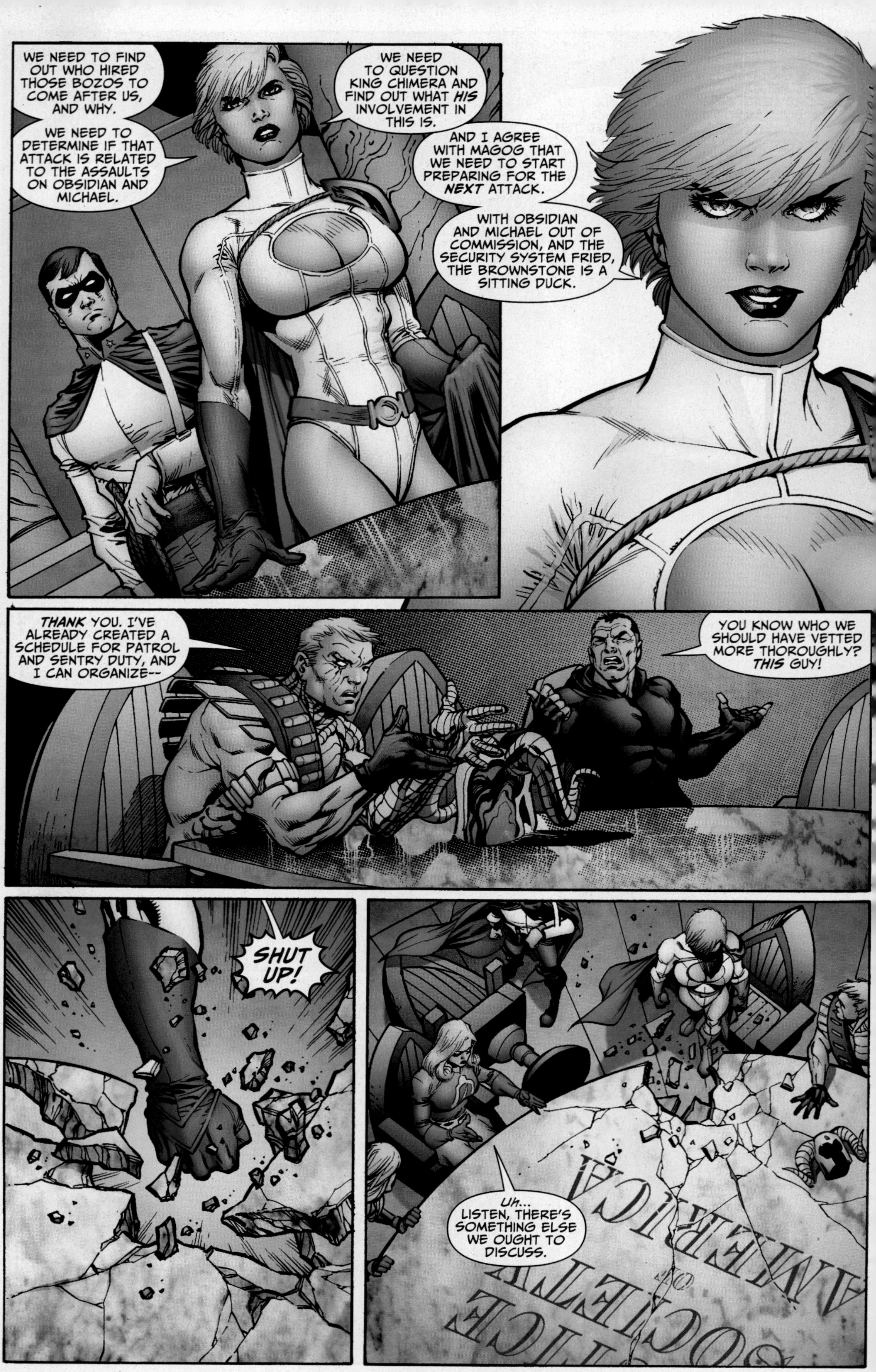
WE NEED TO FIND OUT WHO HIRED THOSE BOZOS TO COME AFTER US, AND WHY.
WE NEED TO DETERMINE IF THAT ATTACK IS RELATED TO THE ASSAULTS ON OBSIDIAN AND MICHAEL.
WE NEED TO QUESTION KING CHIMERA AND FIND OUT WHAT *HIS* INVOLVEMENT IN THIS IS.
AND I AGREE WITH MAGOG THAT WE NEED TO START PREPARING FOR THE *NEXT* ATTACK.
WITH OBSIDIAN AND MICHAEL OUT OF COMMISSION, AND THE SECURITY SYSTEM FRIED, THE BROWNSTONE IS A SITTING DUCK.
THANK YOU. I'VE ALREADY CREATED A SCHEDULE FOR PATROL AND SENTRY DUTY, AND I CAN ORGANIZE--
YOU KNOW WHO WE SHOULD HAVE VETTED MORE THOROUGHLY? *THIS* GUY!
SHUT UP!
Uh... LISTEN, THERE'S SOMETHING ELSE WE OUGHT TO DISCUSS.

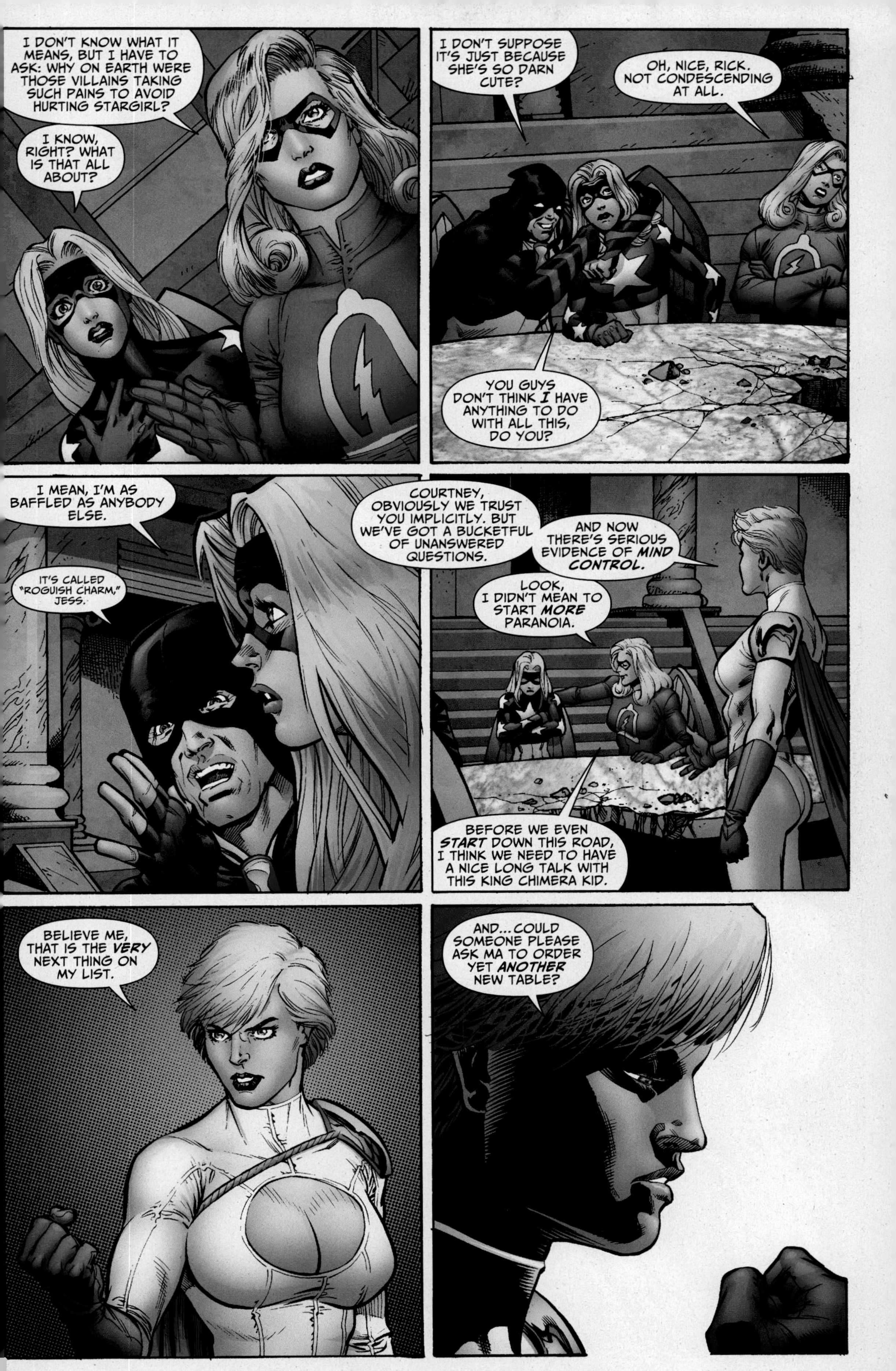
I DON'T KNOW WHAT IT MEANS, BUT I HAVE TO ASK: WHY ON EARTH WERE THOSE VILLAINS TAKING SUCH PAINS TO AVOID HURTING STARGIRL?
I KNOW, RIGHT? WHAT IS THAT ALL ABOUT?
I DON'T SUPPOSE IT'S JUST BECAUSE SHE'S SO DARN CUTE?
OH, NICE, RICK. NOT CONDESCENDING AT ALL.
YOU GUYS DON'T THINK I HAVE ANYTHING TO DO WITH ALL THIS, DO YOU?
I MEAN, I'M AS BAFFLED AS ANYBODY ELSE.
IT'S CALLED "ROGUISH CHARM," JESS.
COURTNEY, OBVIOUSLY WE TRUST YOU IMPLICITLY. BUT WE'VE GOT A BUCKETFUL OF UNANSWERED QUESTIONS.
AND NOW THERE'S SERIOUS EVIDENCE OF MIND CONTROL.
LOOK, I DIDN'T MEAN TO START MORE PARANOIA.
BEFORE WE EVEN START DOWN THIS ROAD, I THINK WE NEED TO HAVE A NICE LONG TALK WITH THIS KING CHIMERA KID.
BELIEVE ME, THAT IS THE VERY NEXT THING ON MY LIST.
AND...COULD SOMEONE PLEASE ASK MA TO ORDER YET ANOTHER NEW TABLE?

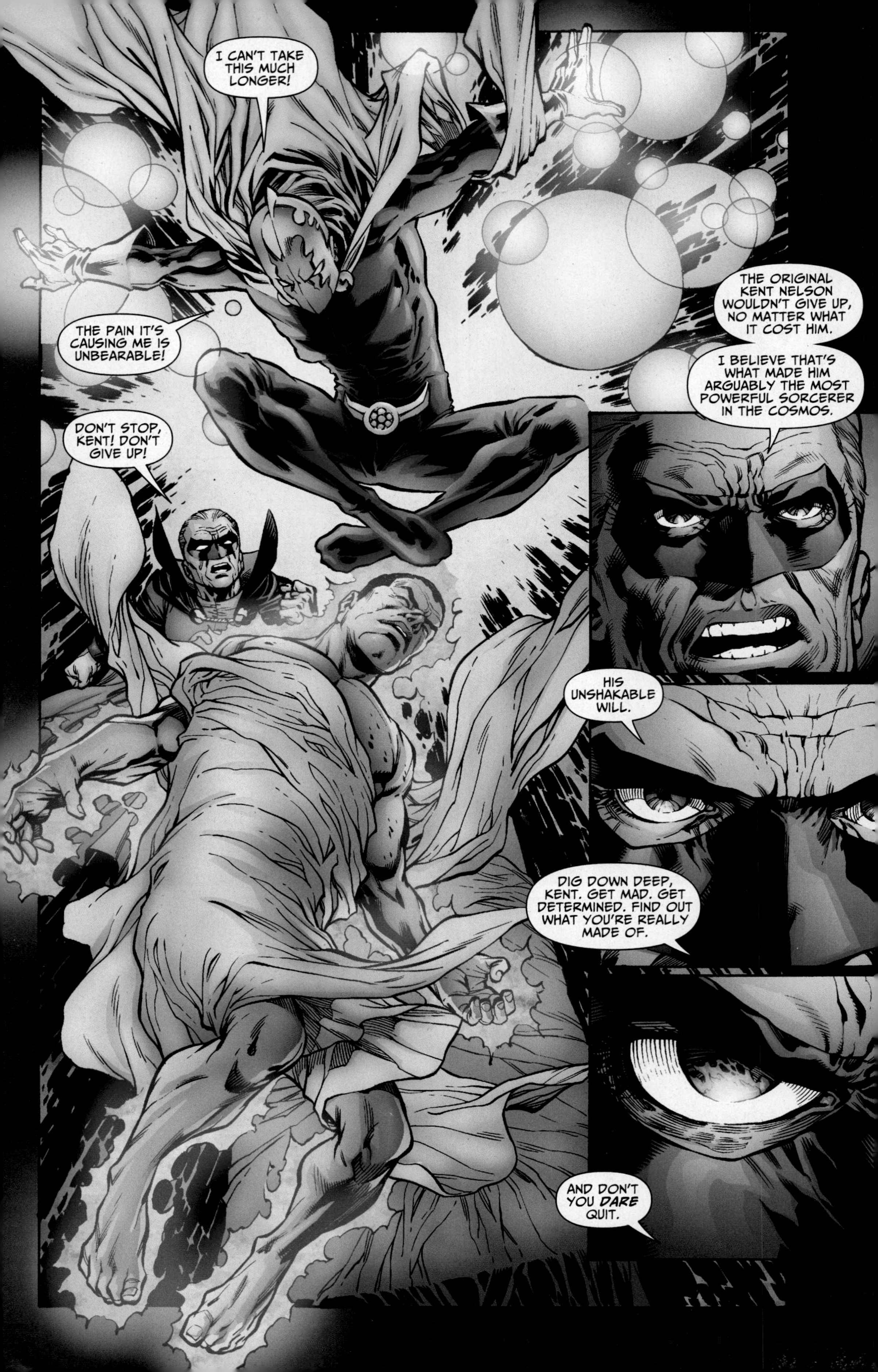
I CAN'T TAKE THIS MUCH LONGER!
THE PAIN IT'S CAUSING ME IS UNBEARABLE!
DON'T STOP, KENT! DON'T GIVE UP!
THE ORIGINAL KENT NELSON WOULDN'T GIVE UP, NO MATTER WHAT IT COST HIM.
I BELIEVE THAT'S WHAT MADE HIM ARGUABLY THE MOST POWERFUL SORCERER IN THE COSMOS.
HIS UNSHAKABLE WILL.
DIG DOWN DEEP, KENT. GET MAD. GET DETERMINED. FIND OUT WHAT YOU'RE REALLY MADE OF.
AND DON'T YOU *DARE* QUIT.

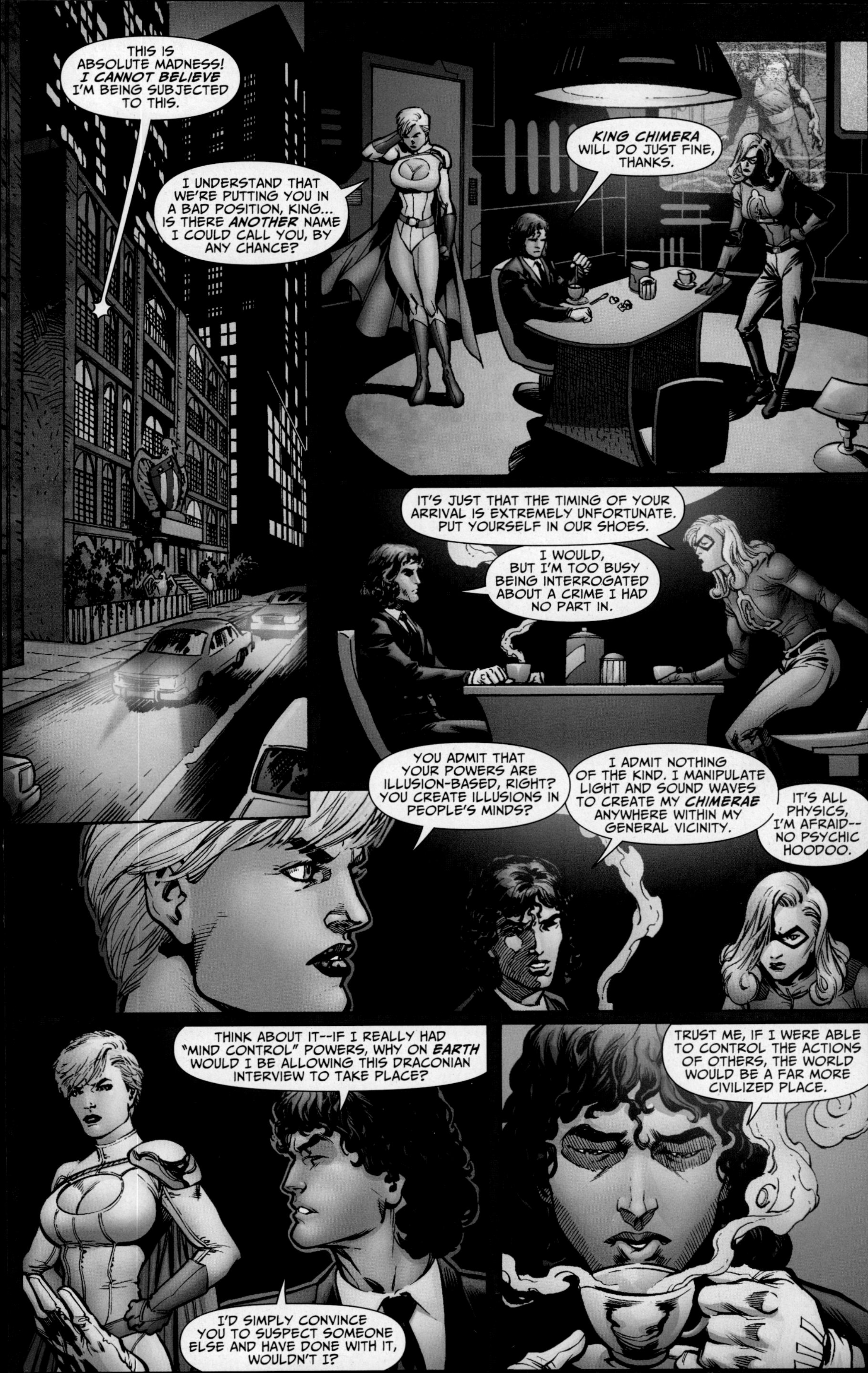
THIS IS ABSOLUTE MADNESS! *I CANNOT BELIEVE* I'M BEING SUBJECTED TO THIS.
I UNDERSTAND THAT WE'RE PUTTING YOU IN A BAD POSITION, KING... IS THERE *ANOTHER* NAME I COULD CALL YOU, BY ANY CHANCE?
KING CHIMERA WILL DO JUST FINE, THANKS.
IT'S JUST THAT THE TIMING OF YOUR ARRIVAL IS EXTREMELY UNFORTUNATE. PUT YOURSELF IN OUR SHOES.
I WOULD, BUT I'M TOO BUSY BEING INTERROGATED ABOUT A CRIME I HAD NO PART IN.
YOU ADMIT THAT YOUR POWERS ARE ILLUSION-BASED, RIGHT? YOU CREATE ILLUSIONS IN PEOPLE'S MINDS?
I ADMIT NOTHING OF THE KIND. I MANIPULATE LIGHT AND SOUND WAVES TO CREATE MY *CHIMERAE* ANYWHERE WITHIN MY GENERAL VICINITY.
IT'S ALL PHYSICS, I'M AFRAID--NO PSYCHIC HOODOO.
THINK ABOUT IT--IF I REALLY HAD "MIND CONTROL" POWERS, WHY ON *EARTH* WOULD I BE ALLOWING THIS DRACONIAN INTERVIEW TO TAKE PLACE?
I'D SIMPLY CONVINCE YOU TO SUSPECT SOMEONE ELSE AND HAVE DONE WITH IT, WOULDN'T I?
TRUST ME, IF I WERE ABLE TO CONTROL THE ACTIONS OF OTHERS, THE WORLD WOULD BE A FAR MORE CIVILIZED PLACE.

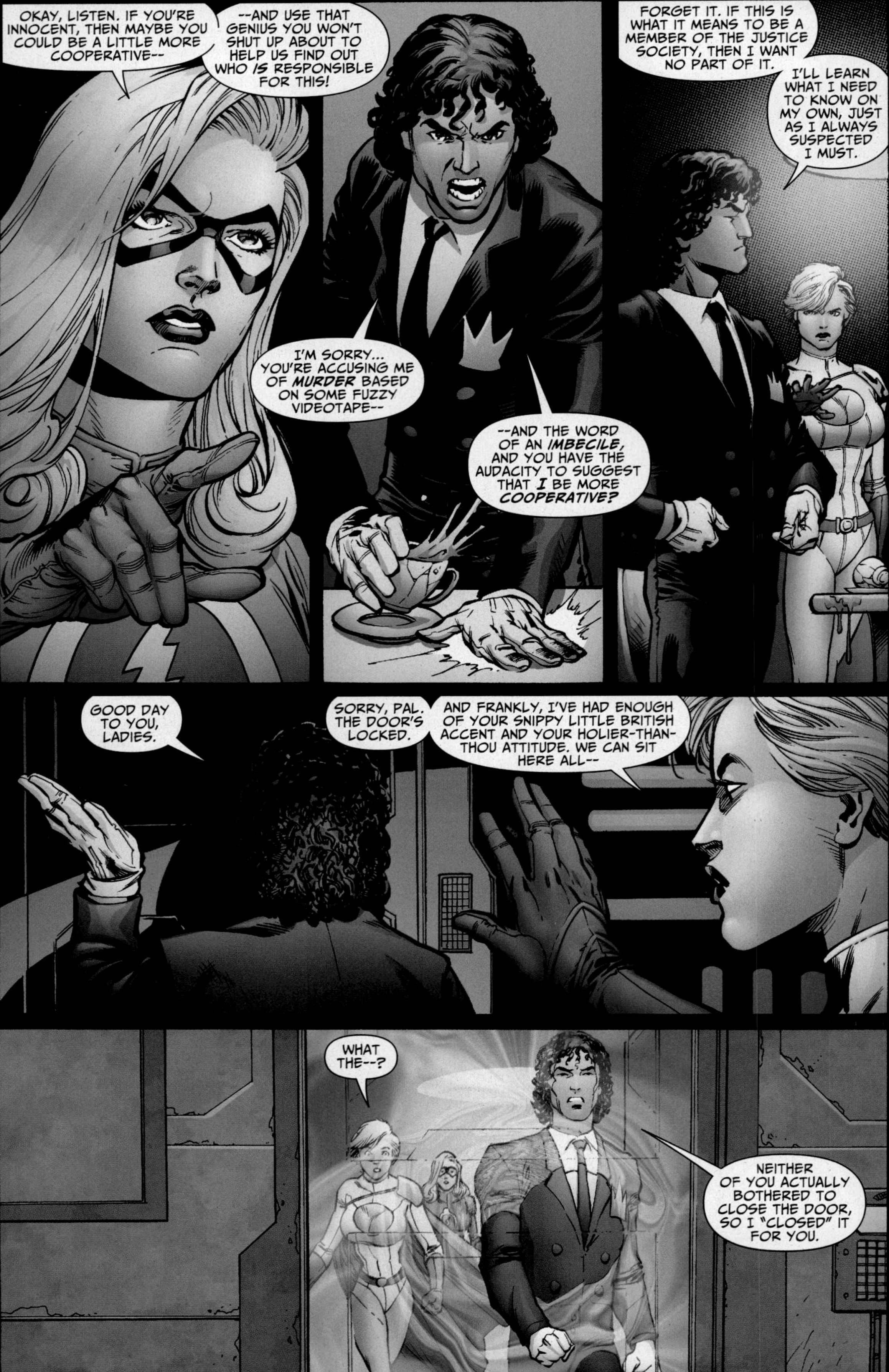
OKAY, LISTEN. IF YOU'RE INNOCENT, THEN MAYBE YOU COULD BE A LITTLE MORE COOPERATIVE--
--AND USE THAT GENIUS YOU WON'T SHUT UP ABOUT TO HELP US FIND OUT WHO IS RESPONSIBLE FOR THIS!
I'M SORRY... YOU'RE ACCUSING ME OF MURDER BASED ON SOME FUZZY VIDEOTAPE--
--AND THE WORD OF AN IMBECILE, AND YOU HAVE THE AUDACITY TO SUGGEST THAT I BE MORE COOPERATIVE?
FORGET IT. IF THIS IS WHAT IT MEANS TO BE A MEMBER OF THE JUSTICE SOCIETY, THEN I WANT NO PART OF IT.
I'LL LEARN WHAT I NEED TO KNOW ON MY OWN, JUST AS I ALWAYS SUSPECTED I MUST.
GOOD DAY TO YOU, LADIES.
SORRY, PAL. THE DOOR'S LOCKED.
AND FRANKLY, I'VE HAD ENOUGH OF YOUR SNIPPY LITTLE BRITISH ACCENT AND YOUR HOLIER-THAN-THOU ATTITUDE. WE CAN SIT HERE ALL--
WHAT THE--?
NEITHER OF YOU ACTUALLY BOTHERED TO CLOSE THE DOOR, SO I "CLOSED" IT FOR YOU.

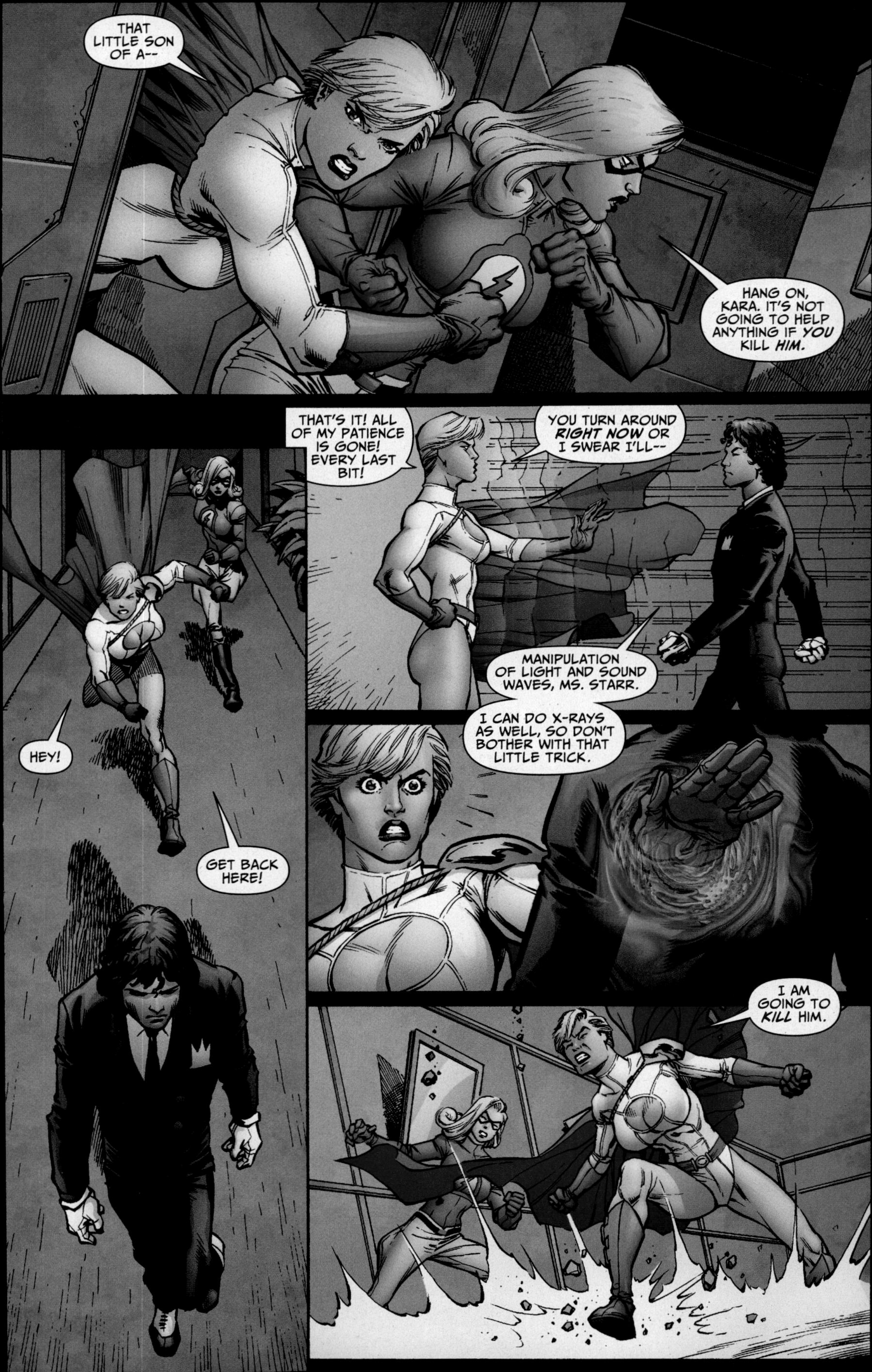
THAT LITTLE SON OF A--
HANG ON, KARA. IT'S NOT GOING TO HELP ANYTHING IF *YOU* KILL *HIM*.
HEY!
GET BACK HERE!
THAT'S IT! ALL OF MY PATIENCE IS GONE! EVERY LAST BIT!
YOU TURN AROUND *RIGHT NOW* OR I SWEAR I'LL--
MANIPULATION OF LIGHT AND SOUND WAVES, MS. STARR.
I CAN DO X-RAYS AS WELL, SO DON'T BOTHER WITH THAT LITTLE TRICK.
I AM GOING TO *KILL* HIM.

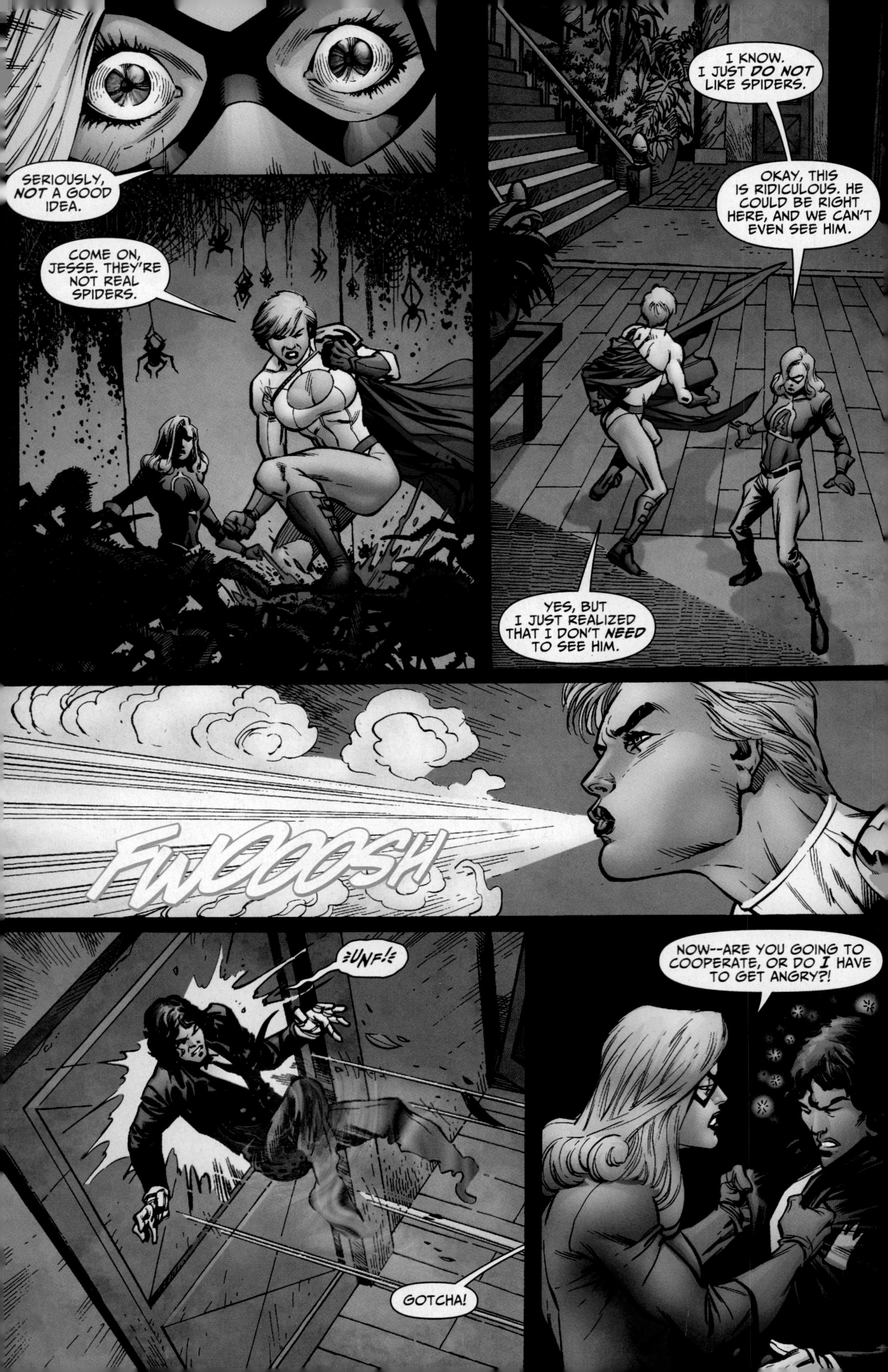
SERIOUSLY, NOT A GOOD IDEA.
COME ON, JESSE. THEY'RE NOT REAL SPIDERS.
I KNOW. I JUST DO NOT LIKE SPIDERS.
OKAY, THIS IS RIDICULOUS. HE COULD BE RIGHT HERE, AND WE CAN'T EVEN SEE HIM.
YES, BUT I JUST REALIZED THAT I DON'T NEED TO SEE HIM.
FWOOOSH!
UNF!
GOTCHA!
NOW--ARE YOU GOING TO COOPERATE, OR DO I HAVE TO GET ANGRY?!

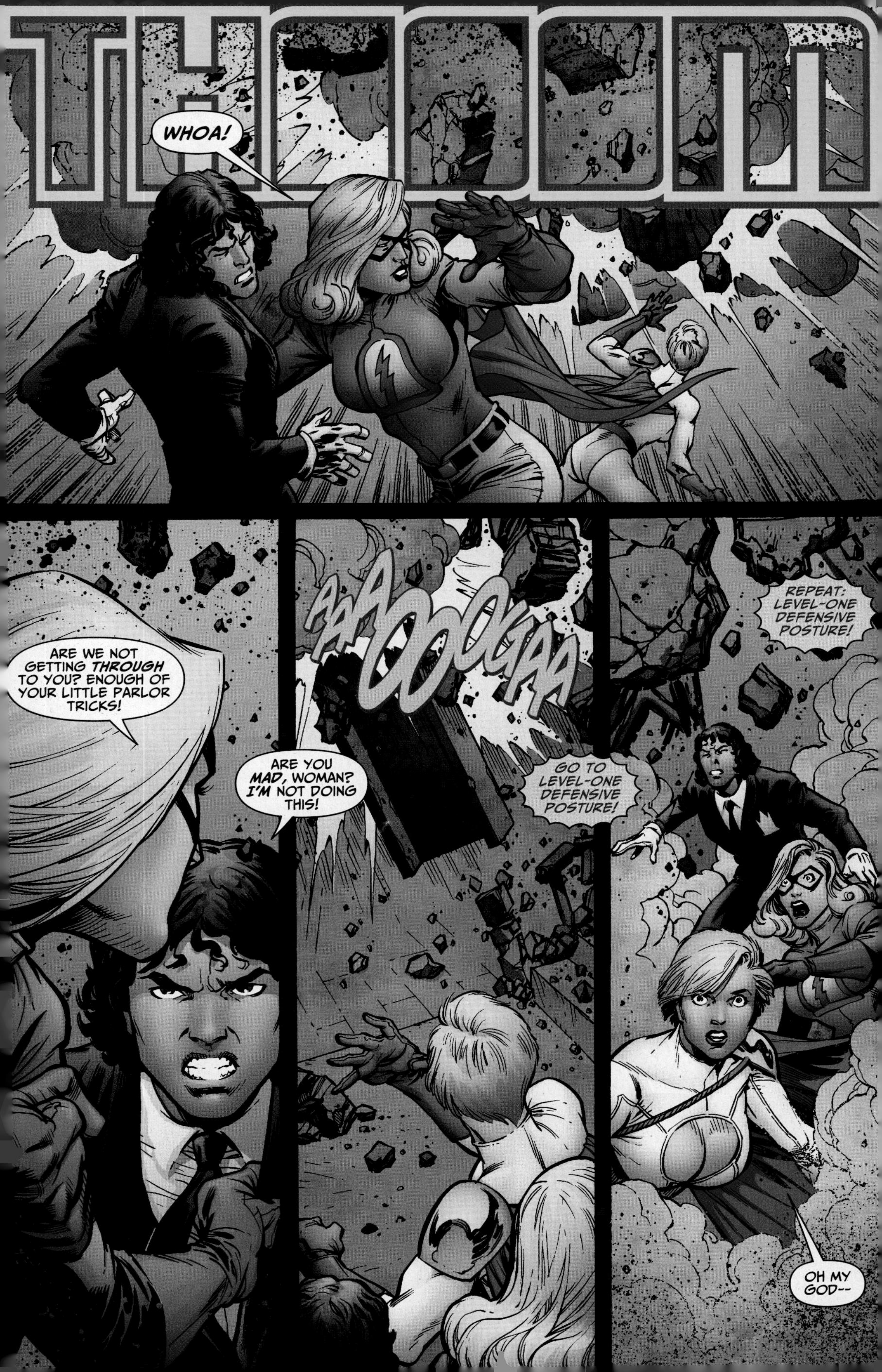
THOOOM
WHOA!
ARE WE NOT GETTING *THROUGH* TO YOU? ENOUGH OF YOUR LITTLE PARLOR TRICKS!
ARE YOU *MAD*, WOMAN? *I'M* NOT DOING THIS!
AAAOOOGAA
GO TO LEVEL-ONE DEFENSIVE POSTURE!
REPEAT: LEVEL-ONE DEFENSIVE POSTURE!
OH MY GOD--

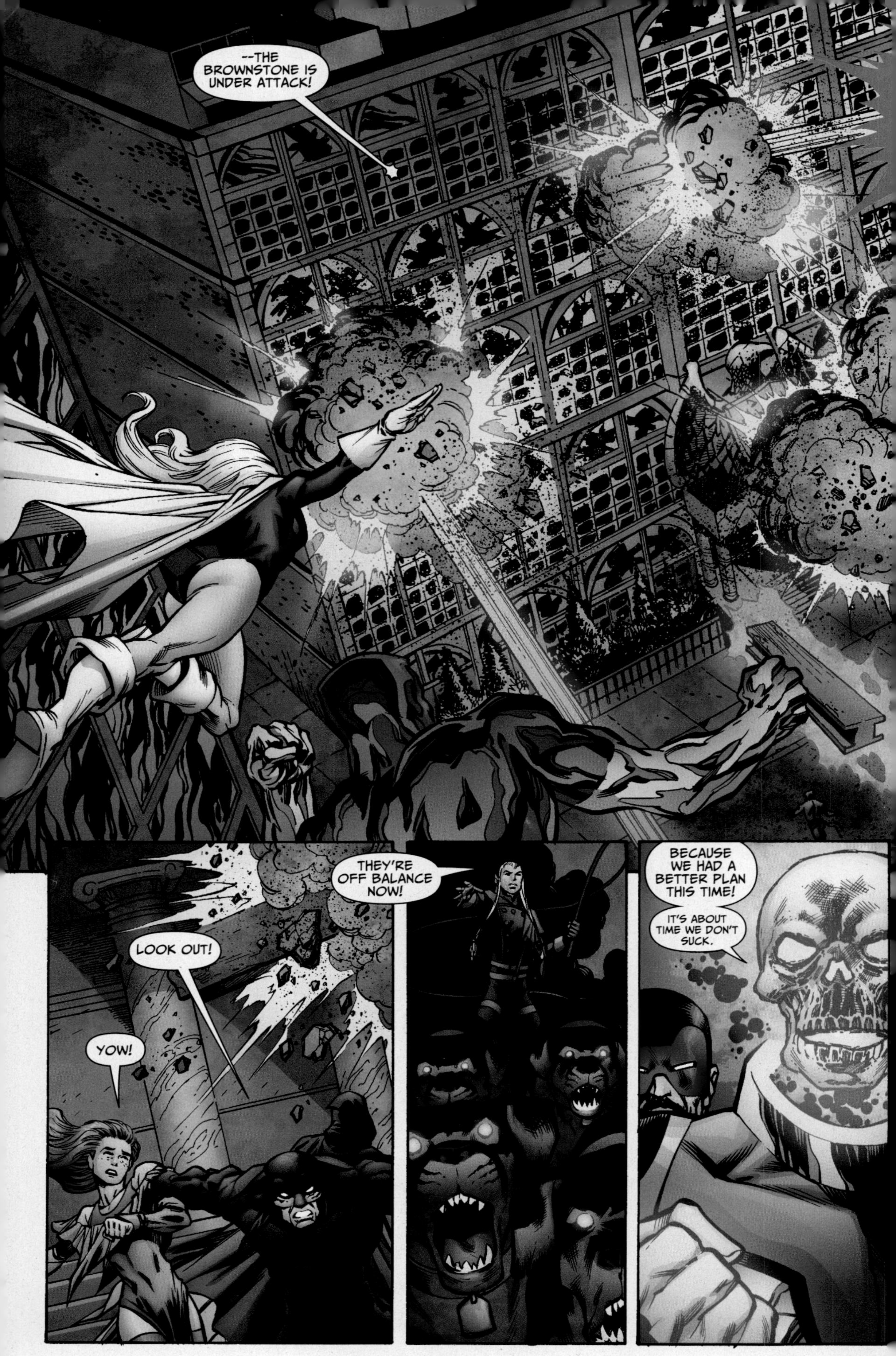
--THE BROWNSTONE IS UNDER ATTACK!
LOOK OUT!
YOW!
THEY'RE OFF BALANCE NOW!
BECAUSE WE HAD A BETTER PLAN THIS TIME!
IT'S ABOUT TIME WE DON'T SUCK.

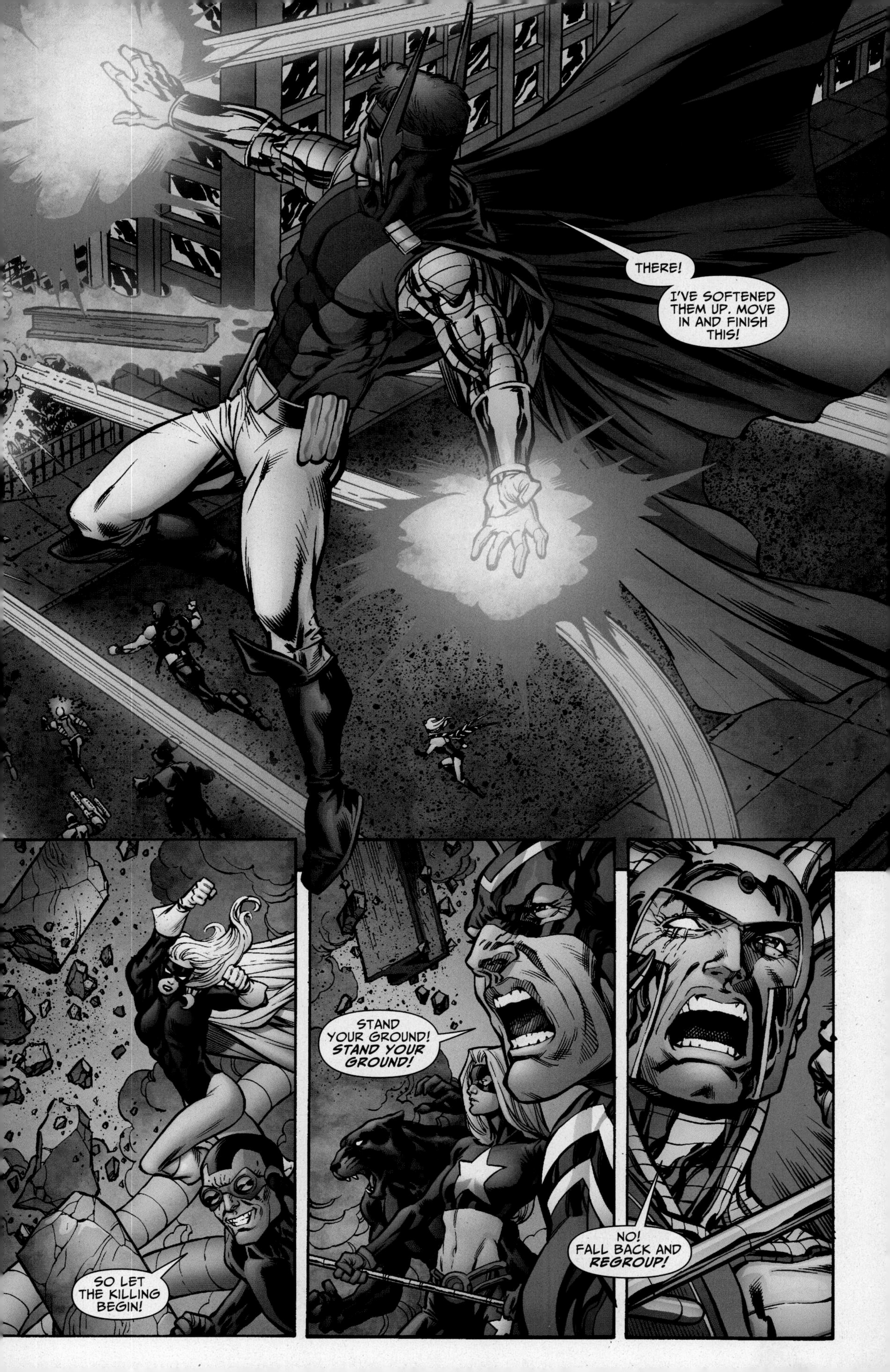
THERE!
I'VE SOFTENED THEM UP. MOVE IN AND FINISH THIS!
SO LET THE KILLING BEGIN!
STAND YOUR GROUND! *STAND YOUR GROUND!*
NO! FALL BACK AND *REGROUP!*

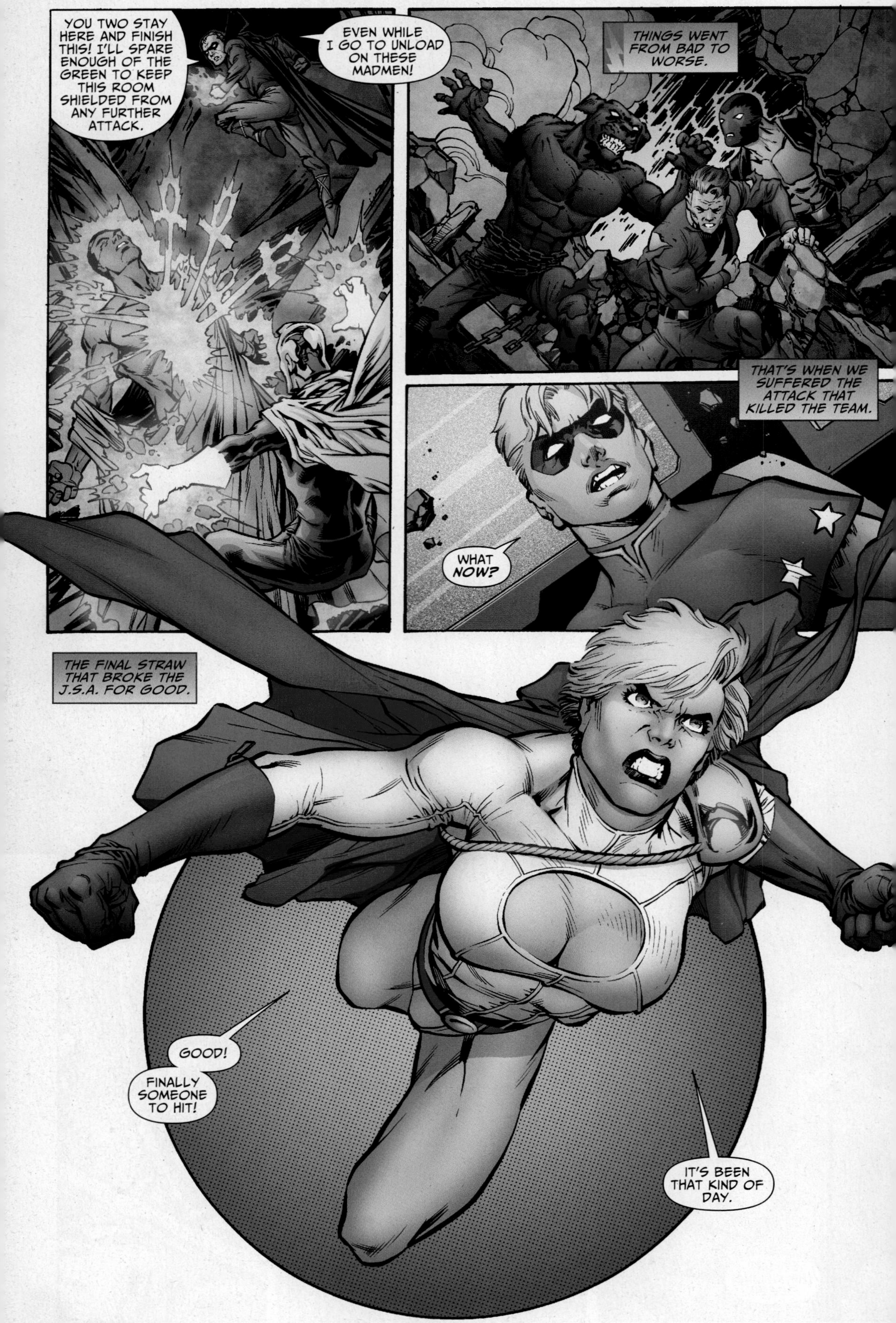
YOU TWO STAY HERE AND FINISH THIS! I'LL SPARE ENOUGH OF THE GREEN TO KEEP THIS ROOM SHIELDED FROM ANY FURTHER ATTACK.
EVEN WHILE I GO TO UNLOAD ON THESE MADMEN!
THINGS WENT FROM BAD TO WORSE.
THAT'S WHEN WE SUFFERED THE ATTACK THAT KILLED THE TEAM.
WHAT NOW?
THE FINAL STRAW THAT BROKE THE J.S.A. FOR GOOD.
GOOD!
FINALLY SOMEONE TO HIT!
IT'S BEEN THAT KIND OF DAY.

THE BAD SEED Part Five

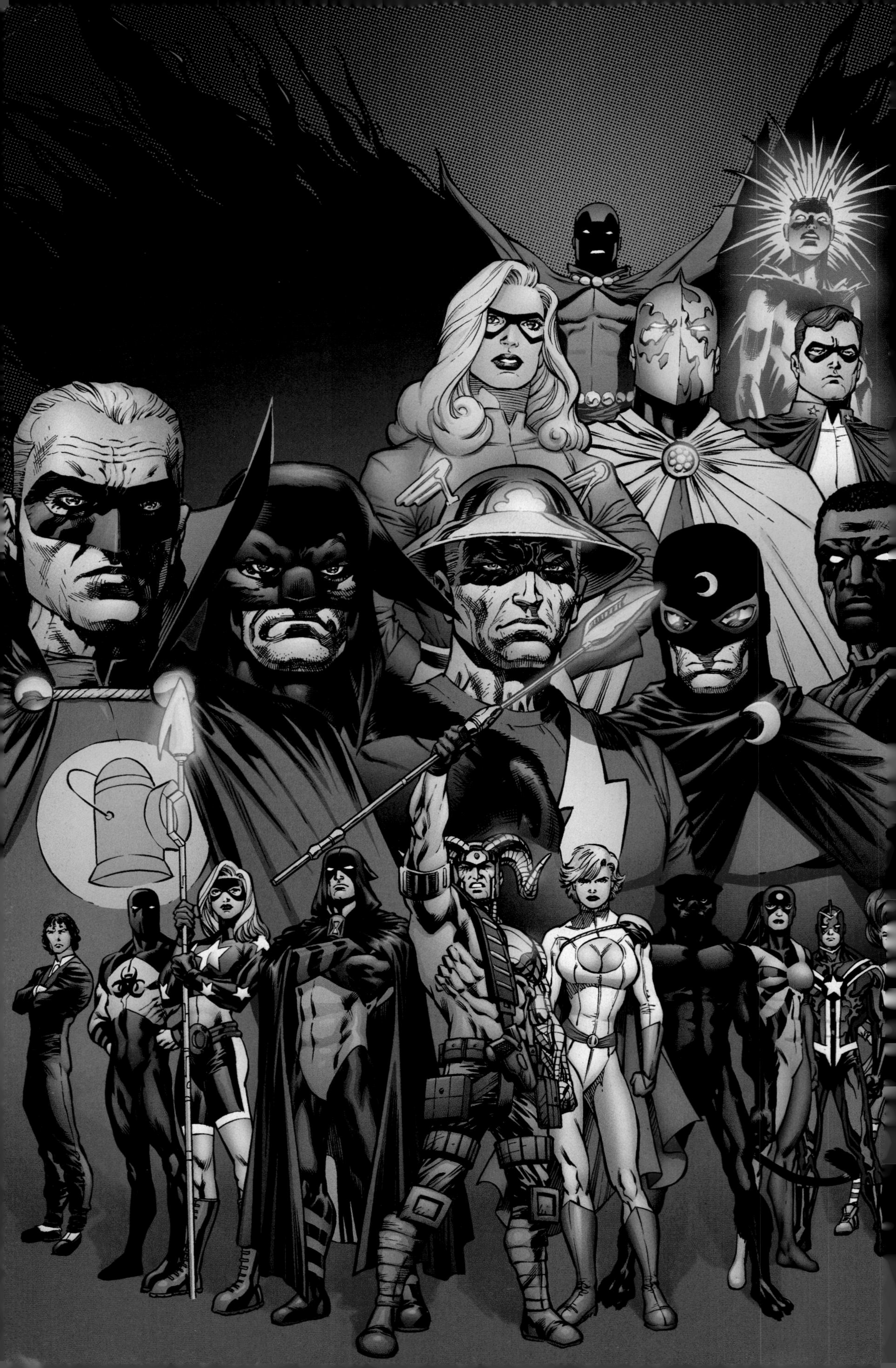

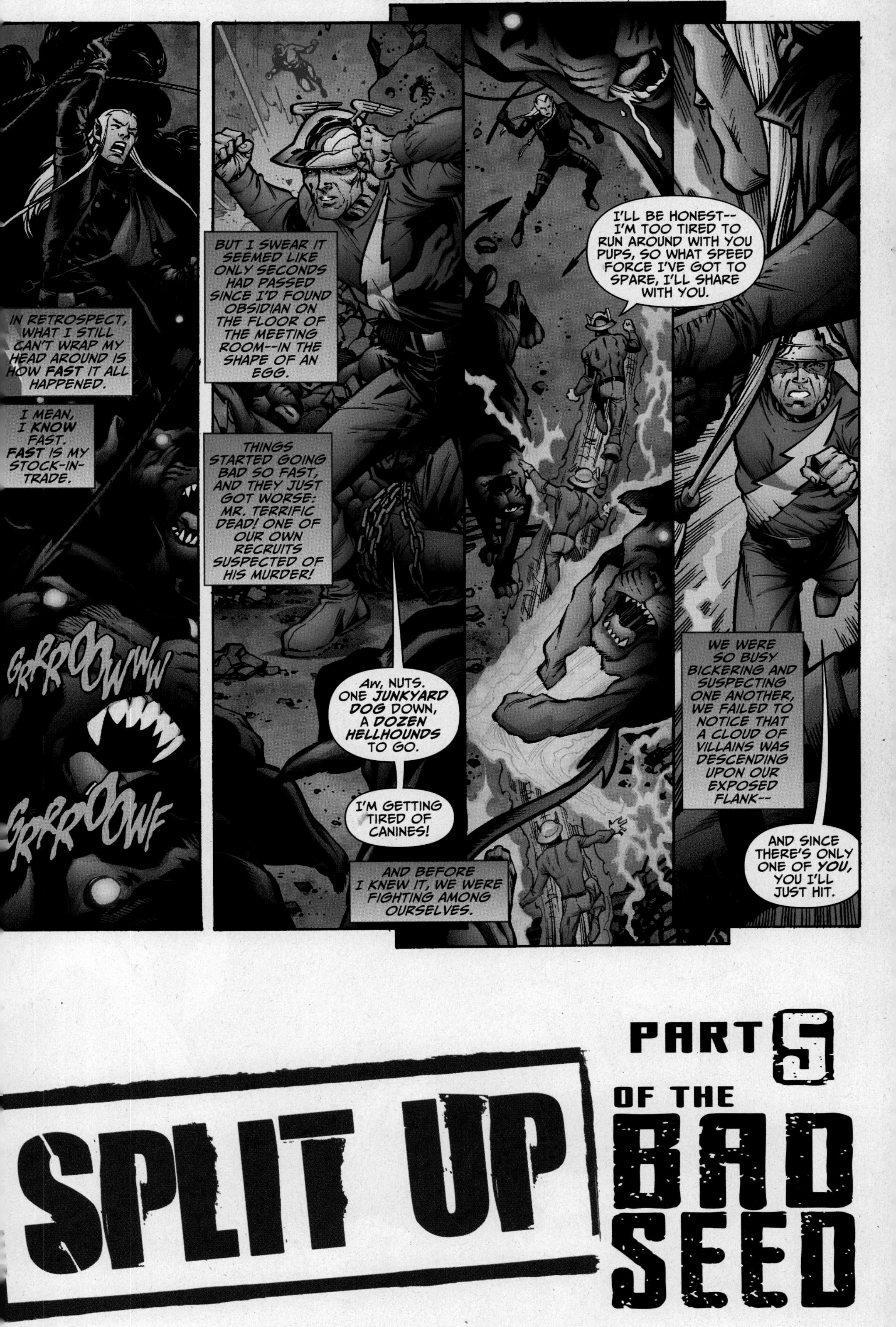
IN RETROSPECT, WHAT I STILL CAN'T WRAP MY HEAD AROUND IS HOW FAST IT ALL HAPPENED.
I MEAN, I KNOW FAST. FAST IS MY STOCK-IN-TRADE.
GRRROOWWW
GRRROOWF
BUT I SWEAR IT SEEMED LIKE ONLY SECONDS HAD PASSED SINCE I'D FOUND OBSIDIAN ON THE FLOOR OF THE MEETING ROOM--IN THE SHAPE OF AN EGG.
THINGS STARTED GOING BAD SO FAST, AND THEY JUST GOT WORSE: MR. TERRIFIC DEAD! ONE OF OUR OWN RECRUITS SUSPECTED OF HIS MURDER!
AW, NUTS. ONE JUNKYARD DOG DOWN, A DOZEN HELLHOUNDS TO GO.
I'M GETTING TIRED OF CANINES!
AND BEFORE I KNEW IT, WE WERE FIGHTING AMONG OURSELVES.
I'LL BE HONEST-- I'M TOO TIRED TO RUN AROUND WITH YOU PUPS, SO WHAT SPEED FORCE I'VE GOT TO SPARE, I'LL SHARE WITH YOU.
WE WERE SO BUSY BICKERING AND SUSPECTING ONE ANOTHER, WE FAILED TO NOTICE THAT A CLOUD OF VILLAINS WAS DESCENDING UPON OUR EXPOSED FLANK--
AND SINCE THERE'S ONLY ONE OF YOU, YOU I'LL JUST HIT.

SPLIT UP

PART 5 OF THE BAD SEED

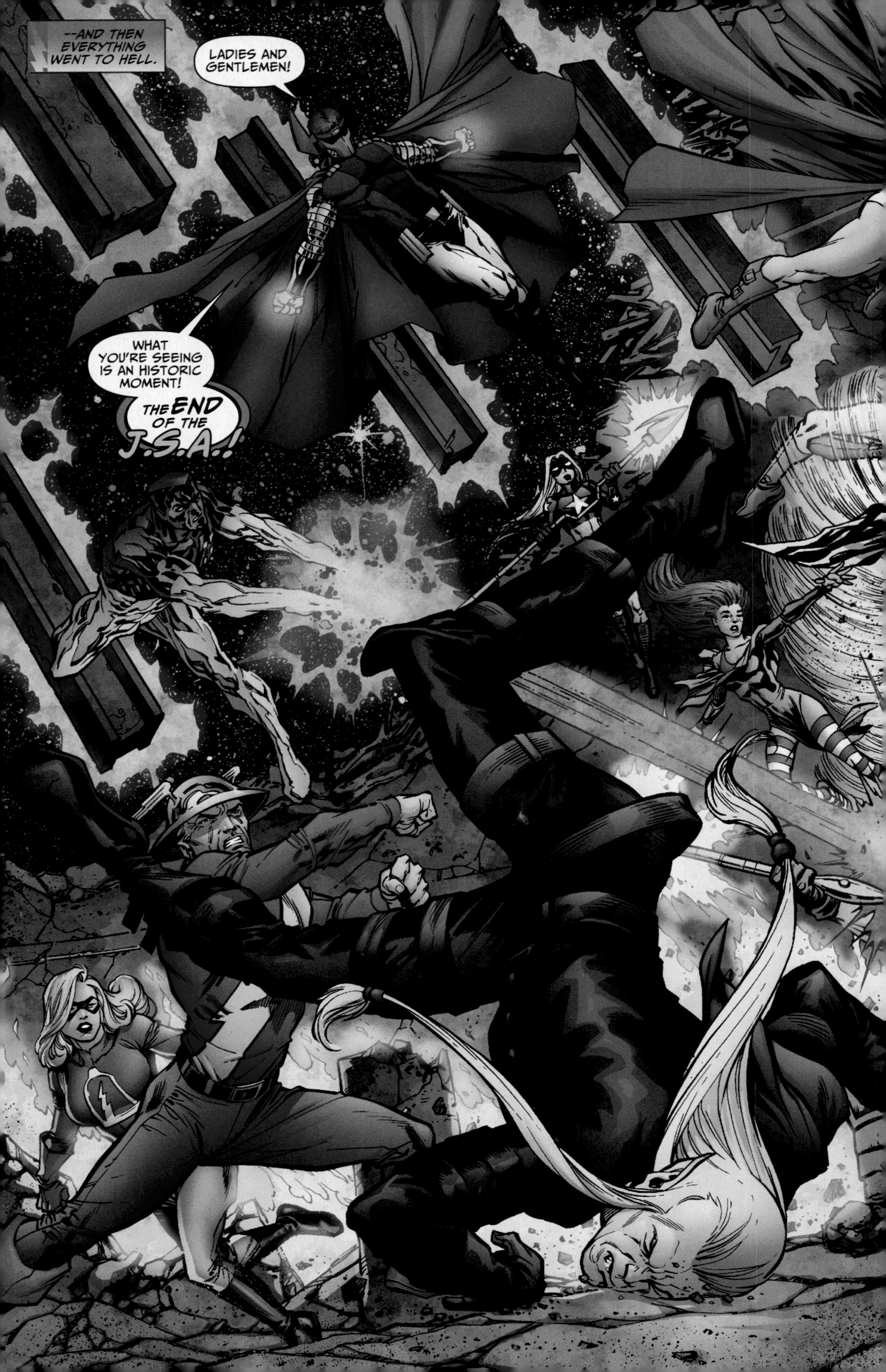
--AND THEN EVERYTHING WENT TO HELL.
LADIES AND GENTLEMEN!
WHAT YOU'RE SEEING IS AN HISTORIC MOMENT!
THE END OF THE J.S.A.!

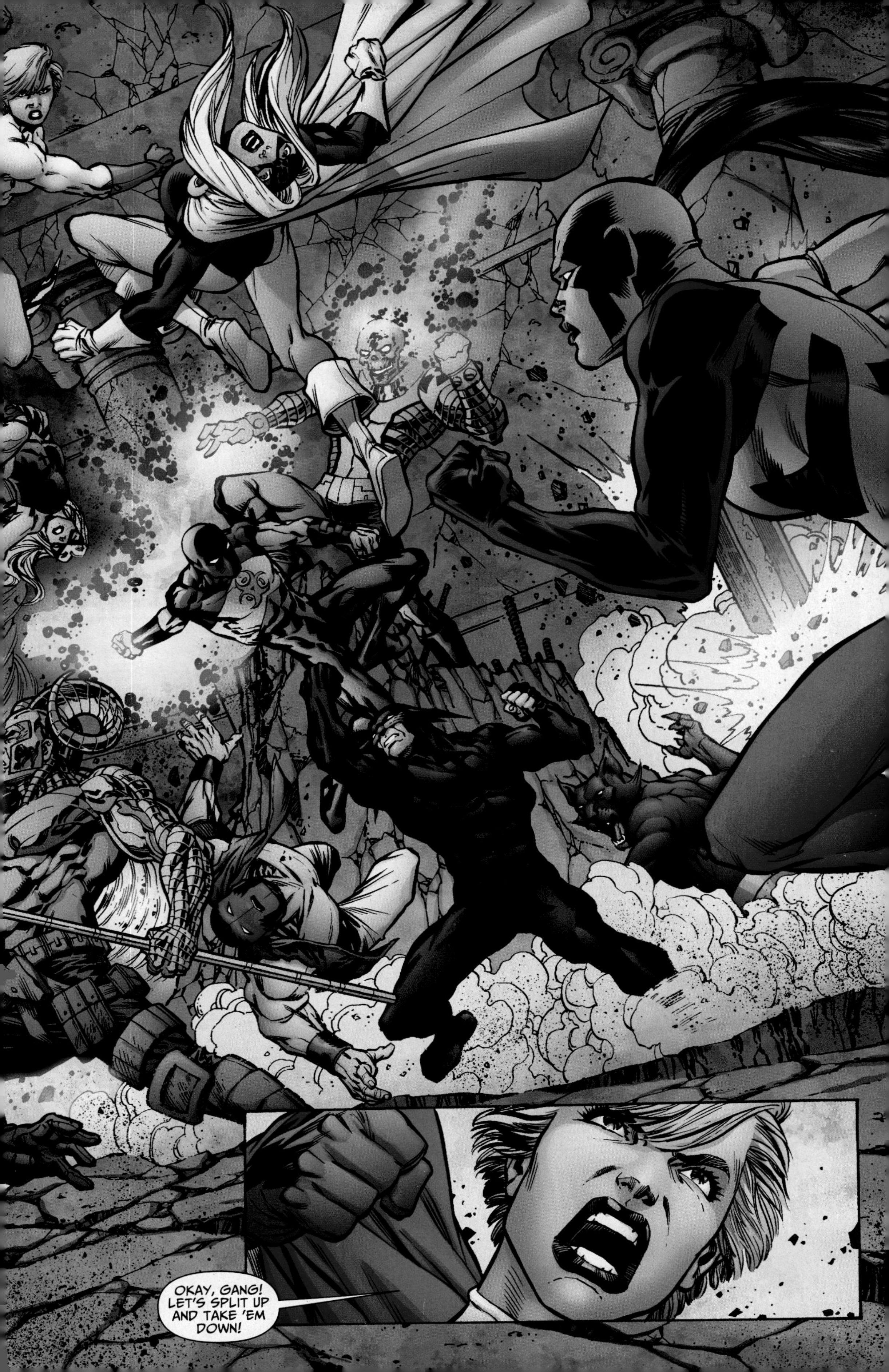
OKAY, GANG! LET'S SPLIT UP AND TAKE 'EM DOWN!

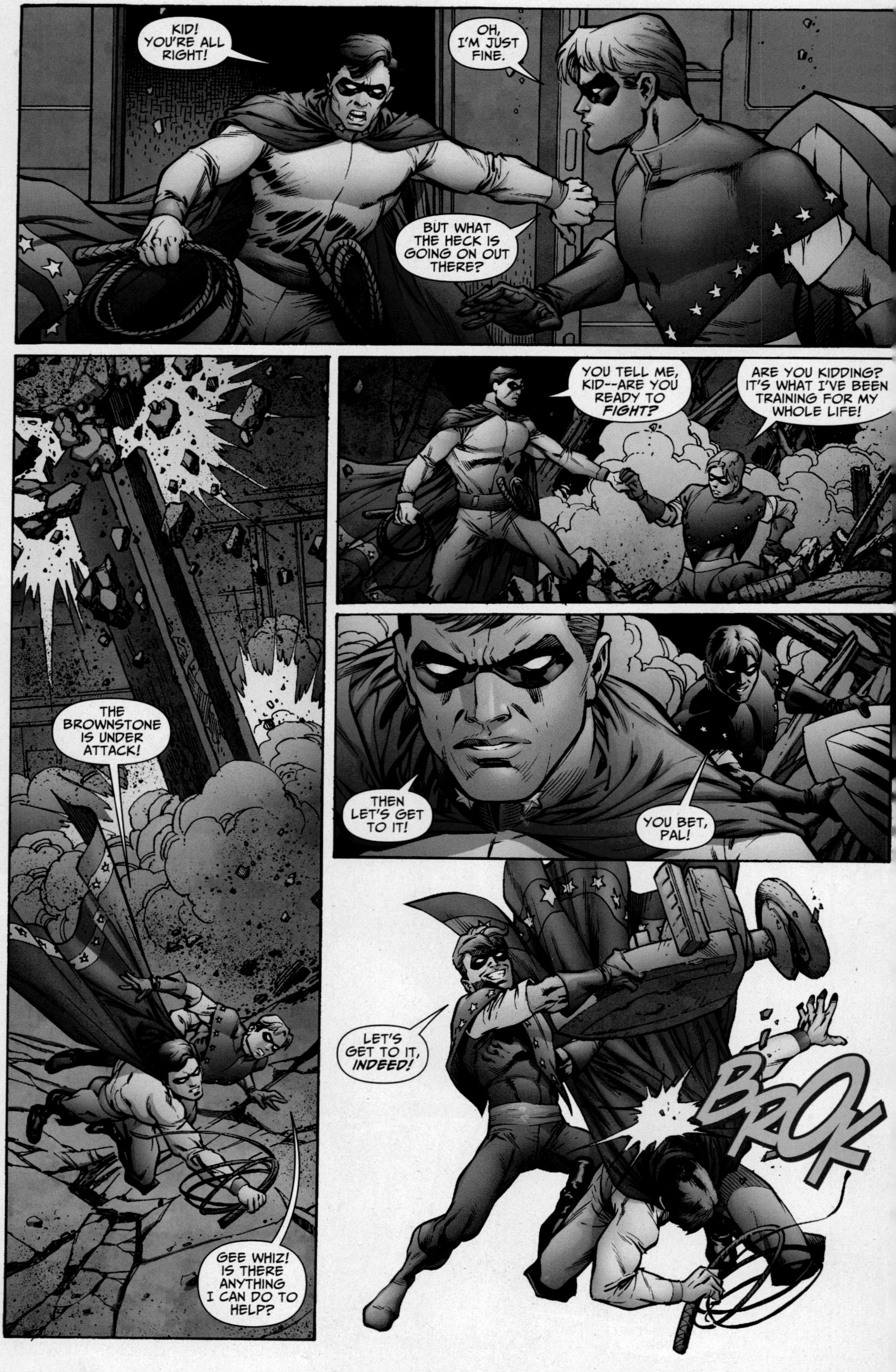
KID! YOU'RE ALL RIGHT!
OH, I'M JUST FINE.
BUT WHAT THE HECK IS GOING ON OUT THERE?
THE BROWNSTONE IS UNDER ATTACK!
GEE WHIZ! IS THERE ANYTHING I CAN DO TO HELP?
YOU TELL ME, KID--ARE YOU READY TO FIGHT?
ARE YOU KIDDING? IT'S WHAT I'VE BEEN TRAINING FOR MY WHOLE LIFE!
THEN LET'S GET TO IT!
YOU BET, PAL!
LET'S GET TO IT, INDEED!
BROK

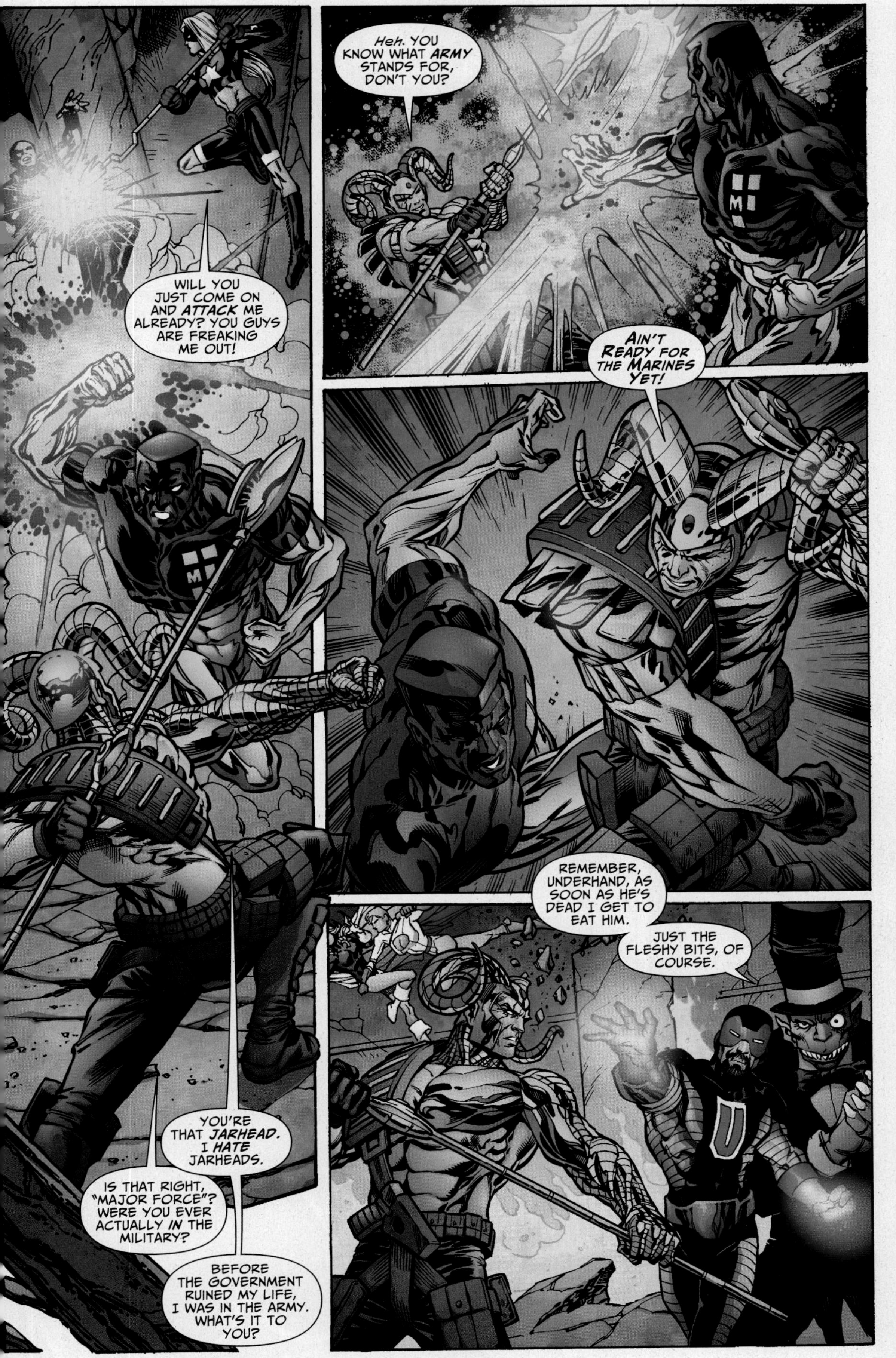
Heh. YOU KNOW WHAT ARMY STANDS FOR, DON'T YOU?
WILL YOU JUST COME ON AND ATTACK ME ALREADY? YOU GUYS ARE FREAKING ME OUT!
AIN'T READY FOR THE MARINES YET!
YOU'RE THAT JARHEAD. I HATE JARHEADS.
IS THAT RIGHT, "MAJOR FORCE"? WERE YOU EVER ACTUALLY IN THE MILITARY?
BEFORE THE GOVERNMENT RUINED MY LIFE, I WAS IN THE ARMY. WHAT'S IT TO YOU?
REMEMBER, UNDERHAND, AS SOON AS HE'S DEAD I GET TO EAT HIM.
JUST THE FLESHY BITS, OF COURSE.

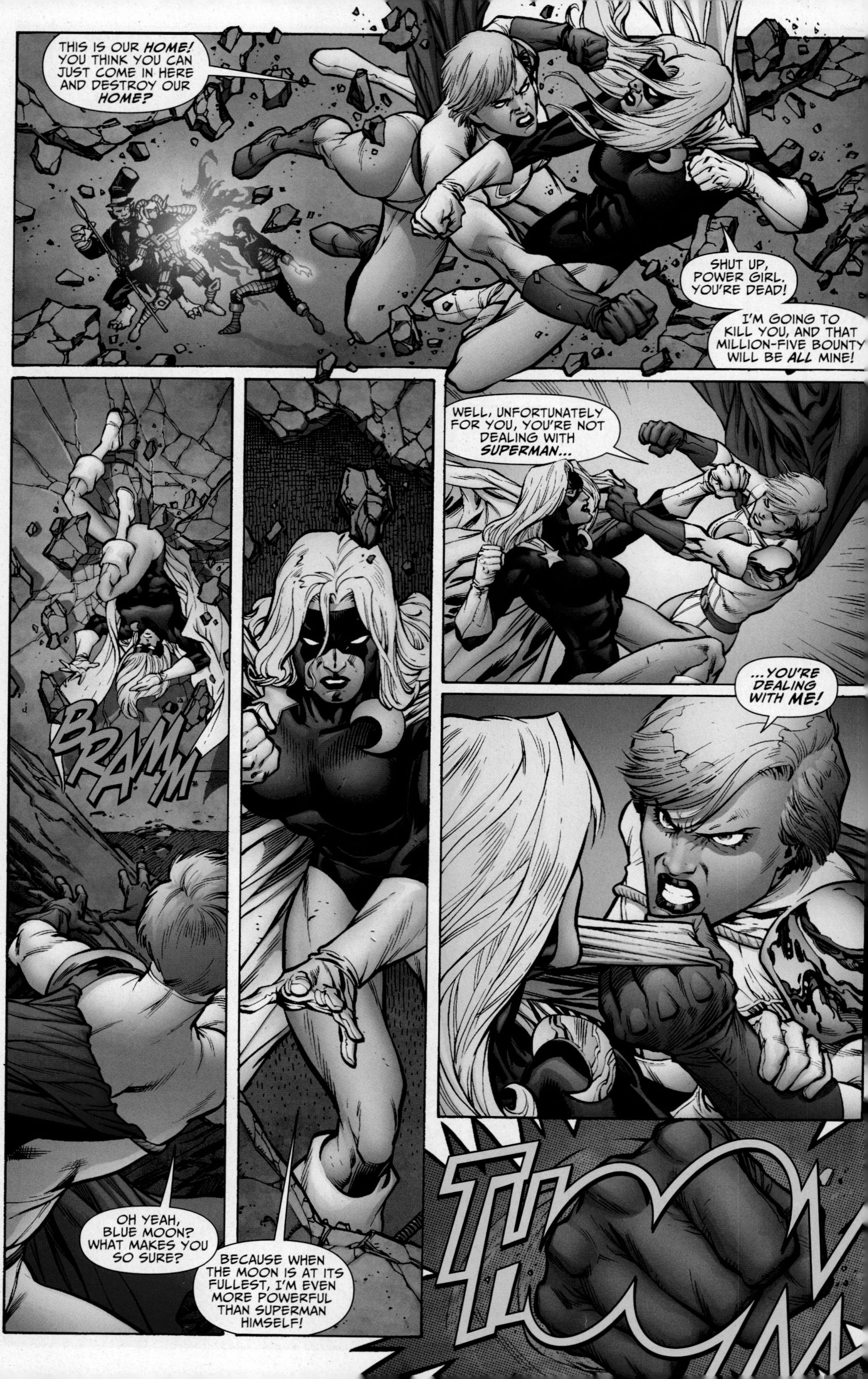
THIS IS OUR HOME! YOU THINK YOU CAN JUST COME IN HERE AND DESTROY OUR HOME?
SHUT UP, POWER GIRL. YOU'RE DEAD!
I'M GOING TO KILL YOU, AND THAT MILLION-FIVE BOUNTY WILL BE ALL MINE!
BRAMM
OH YEAH, BLUE MOON? WHAT MAKES YOU SO SURE?
BECAUSE WHEN THE MOON IS AT ITS FULLEST, I'M EVEN MORE POWERFUL THAN SUPERMAN HIMSELF!
WELL, UNFORTUNATELY FOR YOU, YOU'RE NOT DEALING WITH SUPERMAN...
...YOU'RE DEALING WITH ME!

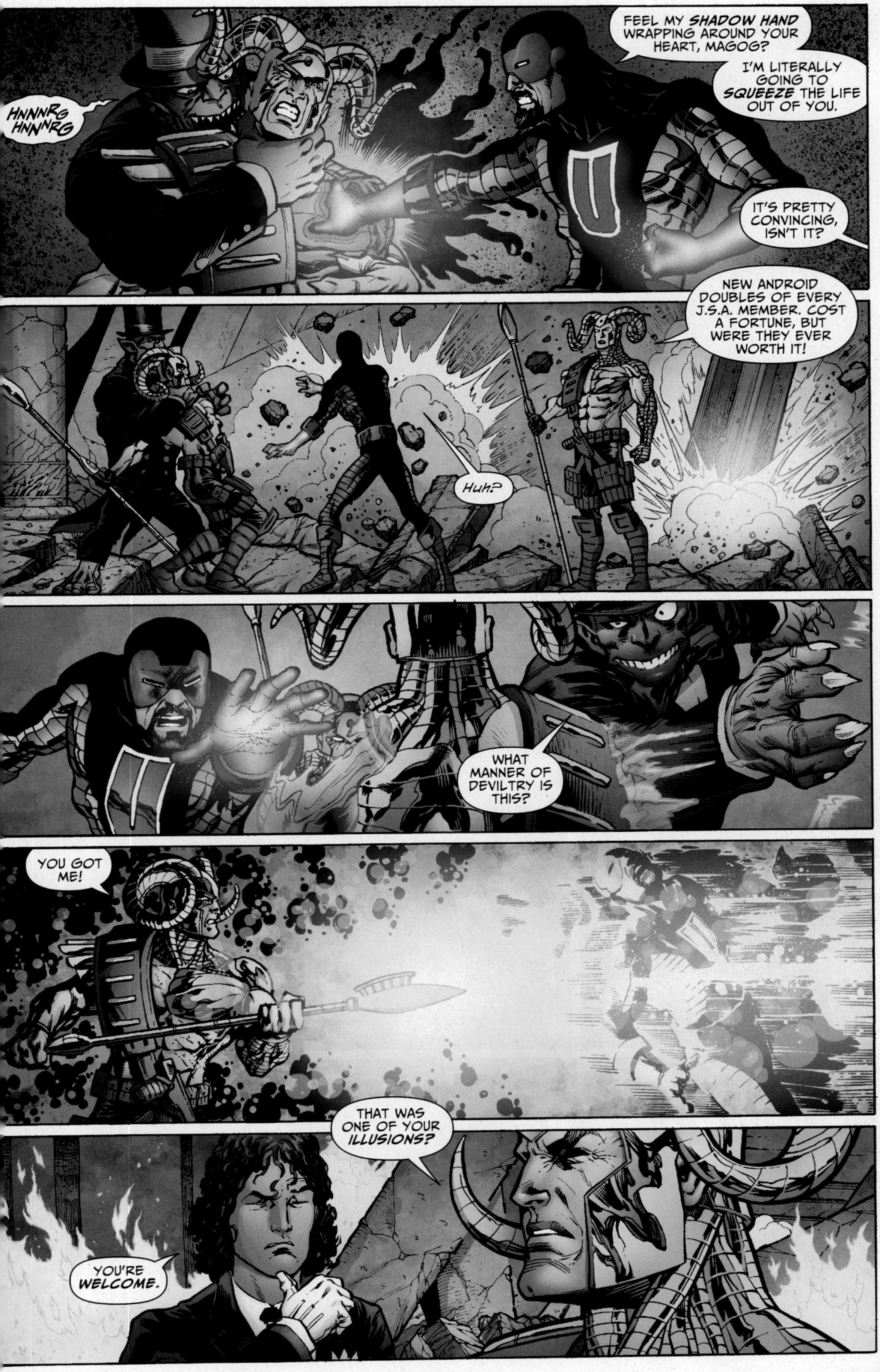

FEEL MY SHADOW HAND WRAPPING AROUND YOUR HEART, MAGOG?
I'M LITERALLY GOING TO SQUEEZE THE LIFE OUT OF YOU.
HNNNRG HNNNRG
IT'S PRETTY CONVINCING, ISN'T IT?
NEW ANDROID DOUBLES OF EVERY J.S.A. MEMBER. COST A FORTUNE, BUT WERE THEY EVER WORTH IT!
Huh?
WHAT MANNER OF DEVILTRY IS THIS?
YOU GOT ME!
THAT WAS ONE OF YOUR ILLUSIONS?
YOU'RE WELCOME.

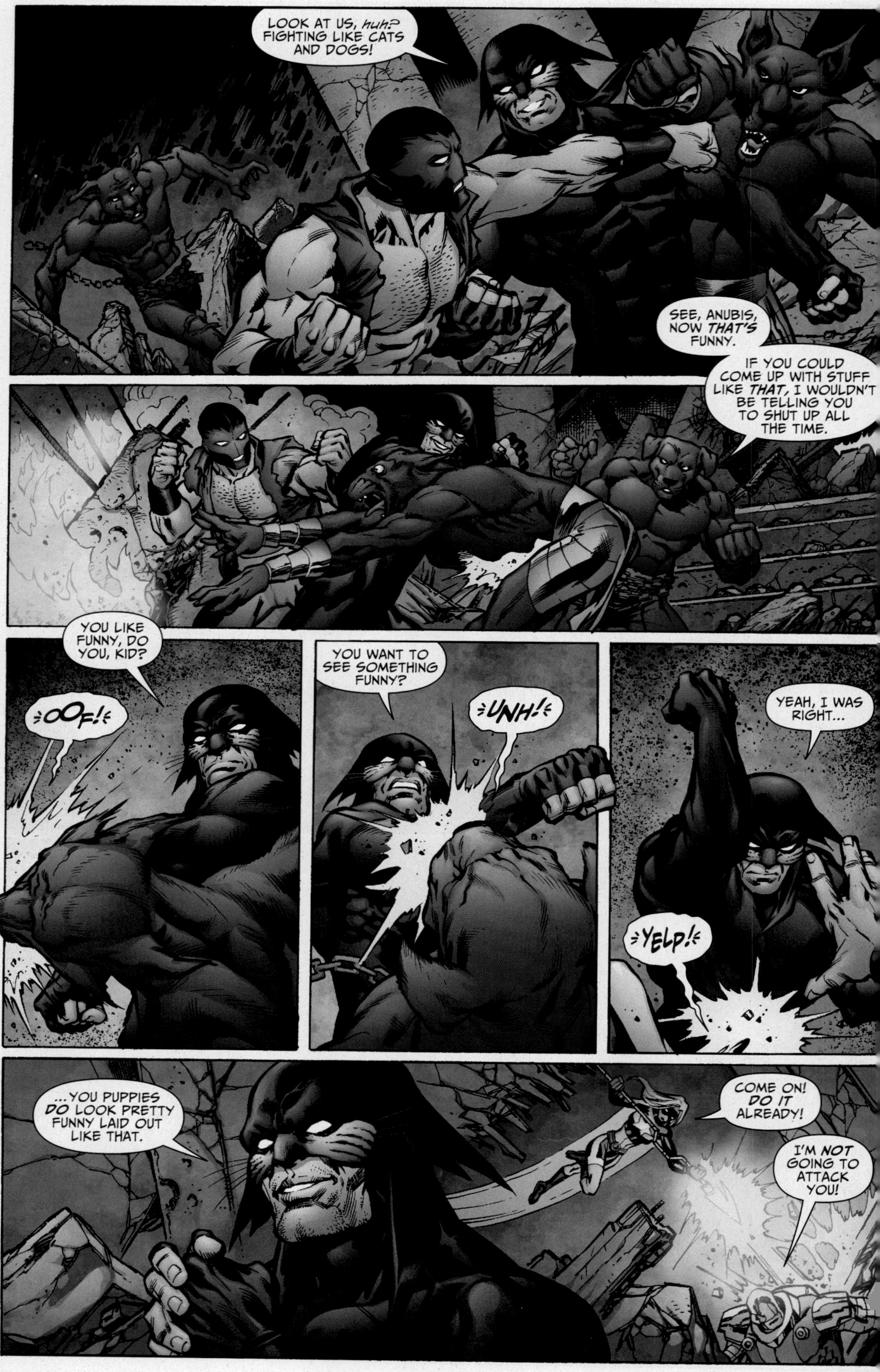
LOOK AT US, huh? FIGHTING LIKE CATS AND DOGS!
SEE, ANUBIS, NOW THAT'S FUNNY.
IF YOU COULD COME UP WITH STUFF LIKE THAT, I WOULDN'T BE TELLING YOU TO SHUT UP ALL THE TIME.
YOU LIKE FUNNY, DO YOU, KID?
OOF!
YOU WANT TO SEE SOMETHING FUNNY?
UNH!
YEAH, I WAS RIGHT...
YELP!
...YOU PUPPIES DO LOOK PRETTY FUNNY LAID OUT LIKE THAT.
COME ON! DO IT ALREADY!
I'M NOT GOING TO ATTACK YOU!

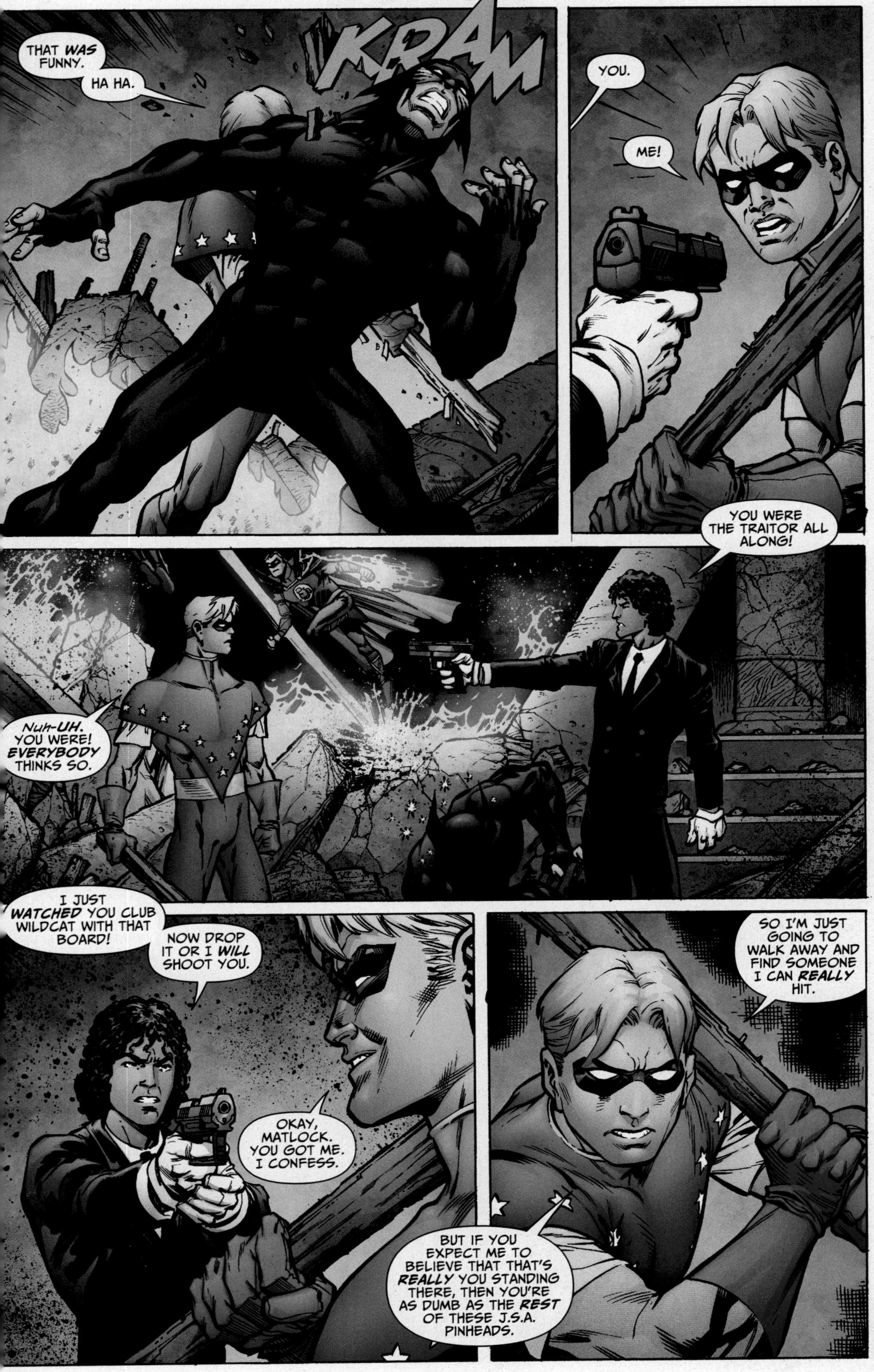
KRAM
THAT WAS FUNNY.
HA HA.
YOU.
ME!
YOU WERE THE TRAITOR ALL ALONG!
Nuh-UH. YOU WERE! EVERYBODY THINKS SO.
I JUST WATCHED YOU CLUB WILDCAT WITH THAT BOARD!
NOW DROP IT OR I WILL SHOOT YOU.
OKAY, MATLOCK. YOU GOT ME. I CONFESS.
SO I'M JUST GOING TO WALK AWAY AND FIND SOMEONE I CAN REALLY HIT.
BUT IF YOU EXPECT ME TO BELIEVE THAT THAT'S REALLY YOU STANDING THERE, THEN YOU'RE AS DUMB AS THE REST OF THESE J.S.A. PINHEADS.

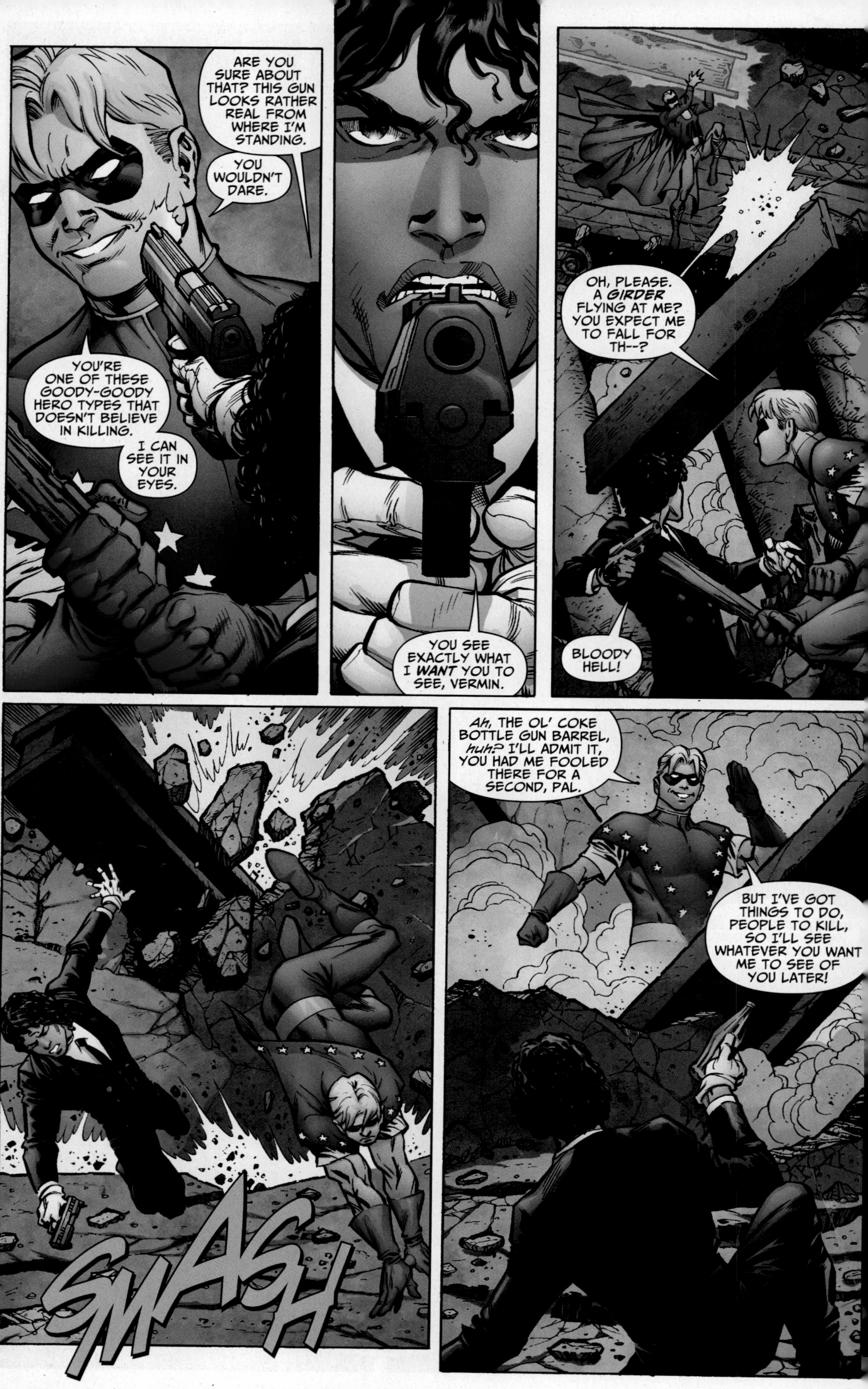
ARE YOU SURE ABOUT THAT? THIS GUN LOOKS RATHER REAL FROM WHERE I'M STANDING.
YOU WOULDN'T DARE.
YOU'RE ONE OF THESE GOODY-GOODY HERO TYPES THAT DOESN'T BELIEVE IN KILLING.
I CAN SEE IT IN YOUR EYES.
YOU SEE EXACTLY WHAT I *WANT* YOU TO SEE, VERMIN.
OH, PLEASE. A *GIRDER* FLYING AT ME? YOU EXPECT ME TO FALL FOR TH--?
BLOODY HELL!
SMASH
Ah, THE OL' COKE BOTTLE GUN BARREL, *huh?* I'LL ADMIT IT, YOU HAD ME FOOLED THERE FOR A SECOND, PAL.
BUT I'VE GOT THINGS TO DO, PEOPLE TO KILL, SO I'LL SEE WHATEVER YOU WANT ME TO SEE OF YOU LATER!

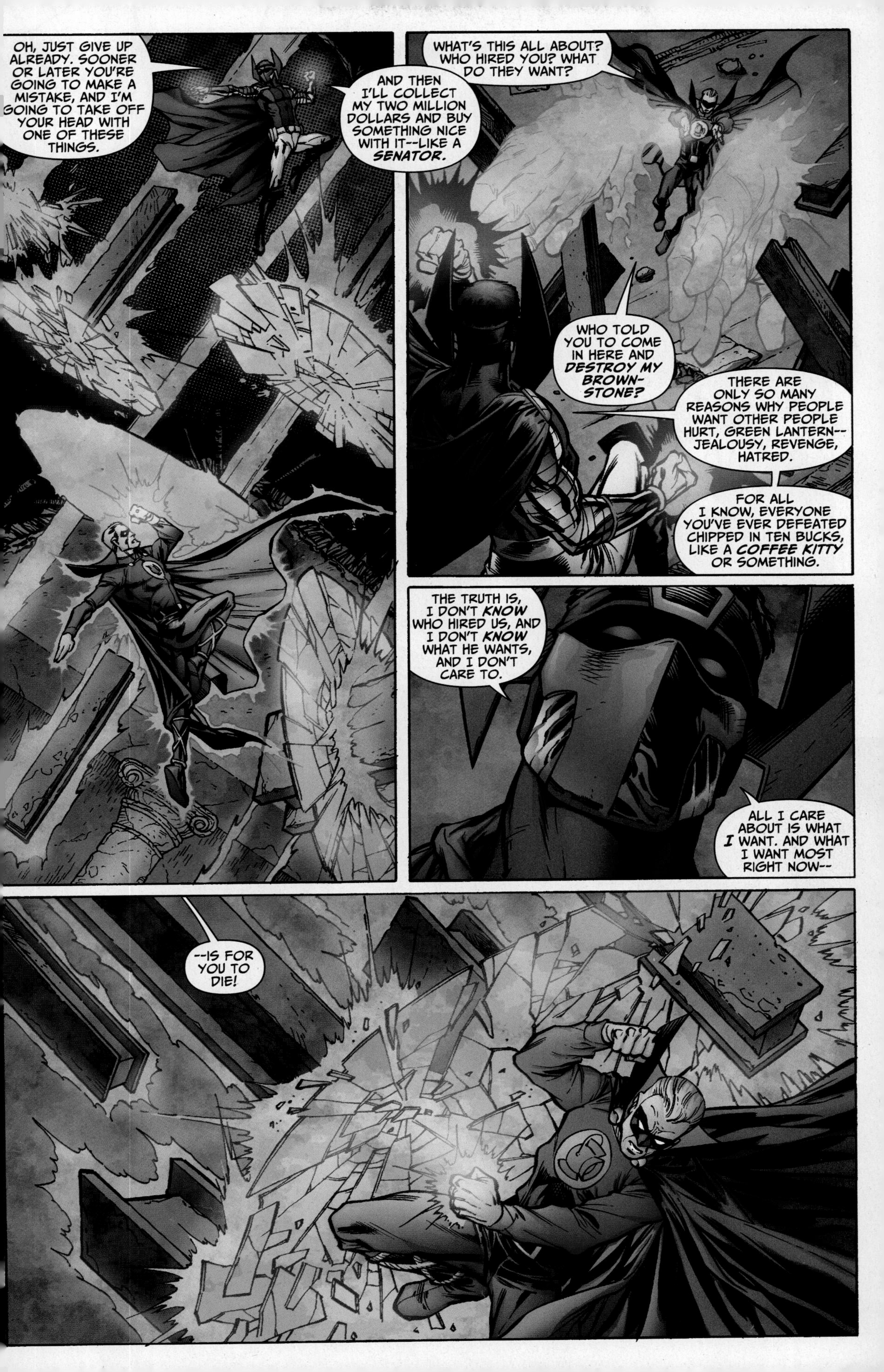

OH, JUST GIVE UP ALREADY. SOONER OR LATER YOU'RE GOING TO MAKE A MISTAKE, AND I'M GOING TO TAKE OFF YOUR HEAD WITH ONE OF THESE THINGS.
AND THEN I'LL COLLECT MY TWO MILLION DOLLARS AND BUY SOMETHING NICE WITH IT--LIKE A SENATOR.
WHAT'S THIS ALL ABOUT? WHO HIRED YOU? WHAT DO THEY WANT?
WHO TOLD YOU TO COME IN HERE AND DESTROY MY BROWN-STONE?
THERE ARE ONLY SO MANY REASONS WHY PEOPLE WANT OTHER PEOPLE HURT, GREEN LANTERN-- JEALOUSY, REVENGE, HATRED.
FOR ALL I KNOW, EVERYONE YOU'VE EVER DEFEATED CHIPPED IN TEN BUCKS, LIKE A COFFEE KITTY OR SOMETHING.
THE TRUTH IS, I DON'T KNOW WHO HIRED US, AND I DON'T KNOW WHAT HE WANTS, AND I DON'T CARE TO.
ALL I CARE ABOUT IS WHAT I WANT. AND WHAT I WANT MOST RIGHT NOW--
--IS FOR YOU TO DIE!

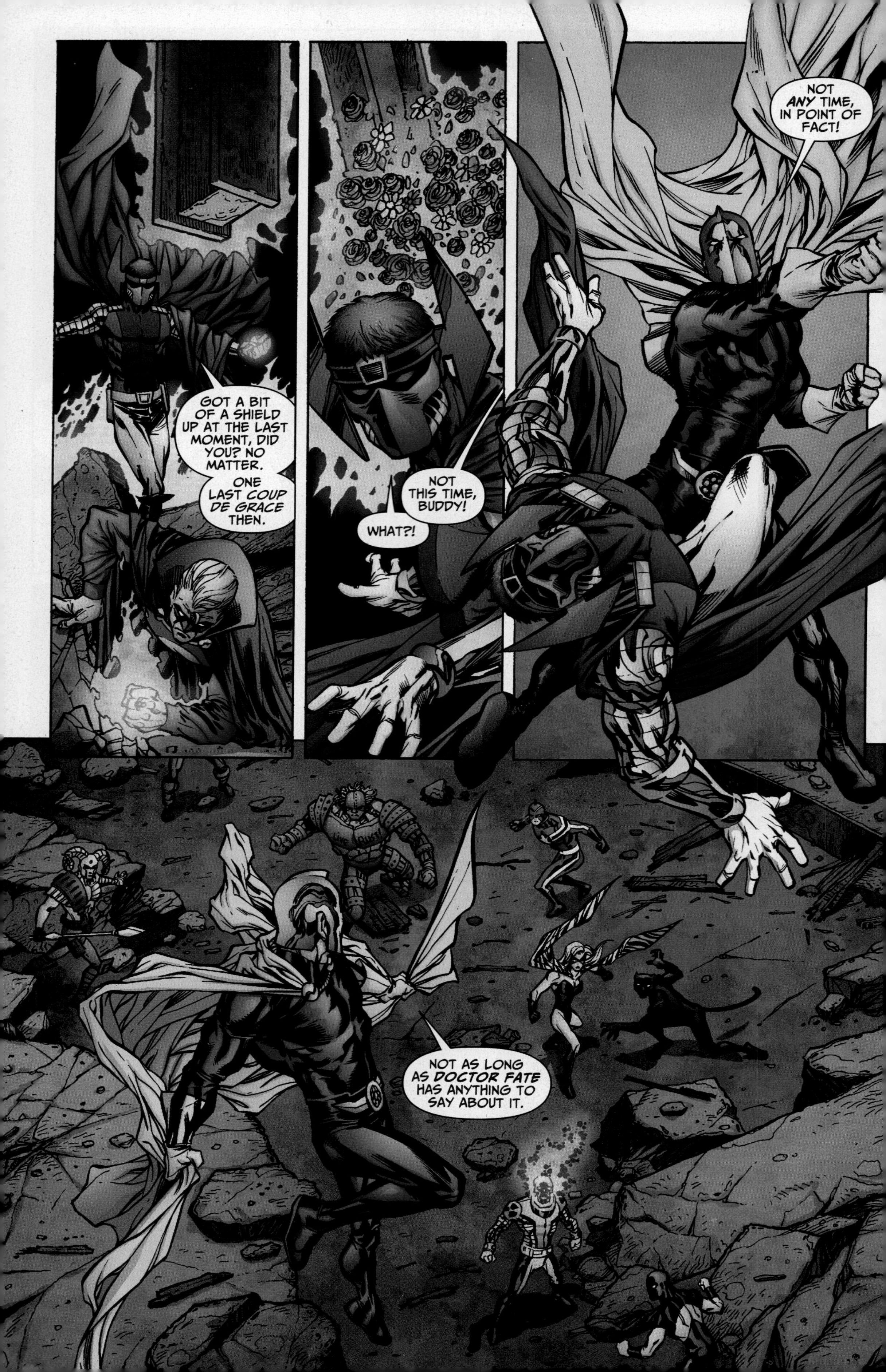
GOT A BIT OF A SHIELD UP AT THE LAST MOMENT, DID YOU? NO MATTER.
ONE LAST COUP DE GRACE THEN.
NOT THIS TIME, BUDDY!
WHAT?!
NOT ANY TIME, IN POINT OF FACT!
NOT AS LONG AS DOCTOR FATE HAS ANYTHING TO SAY ABOUT IT.

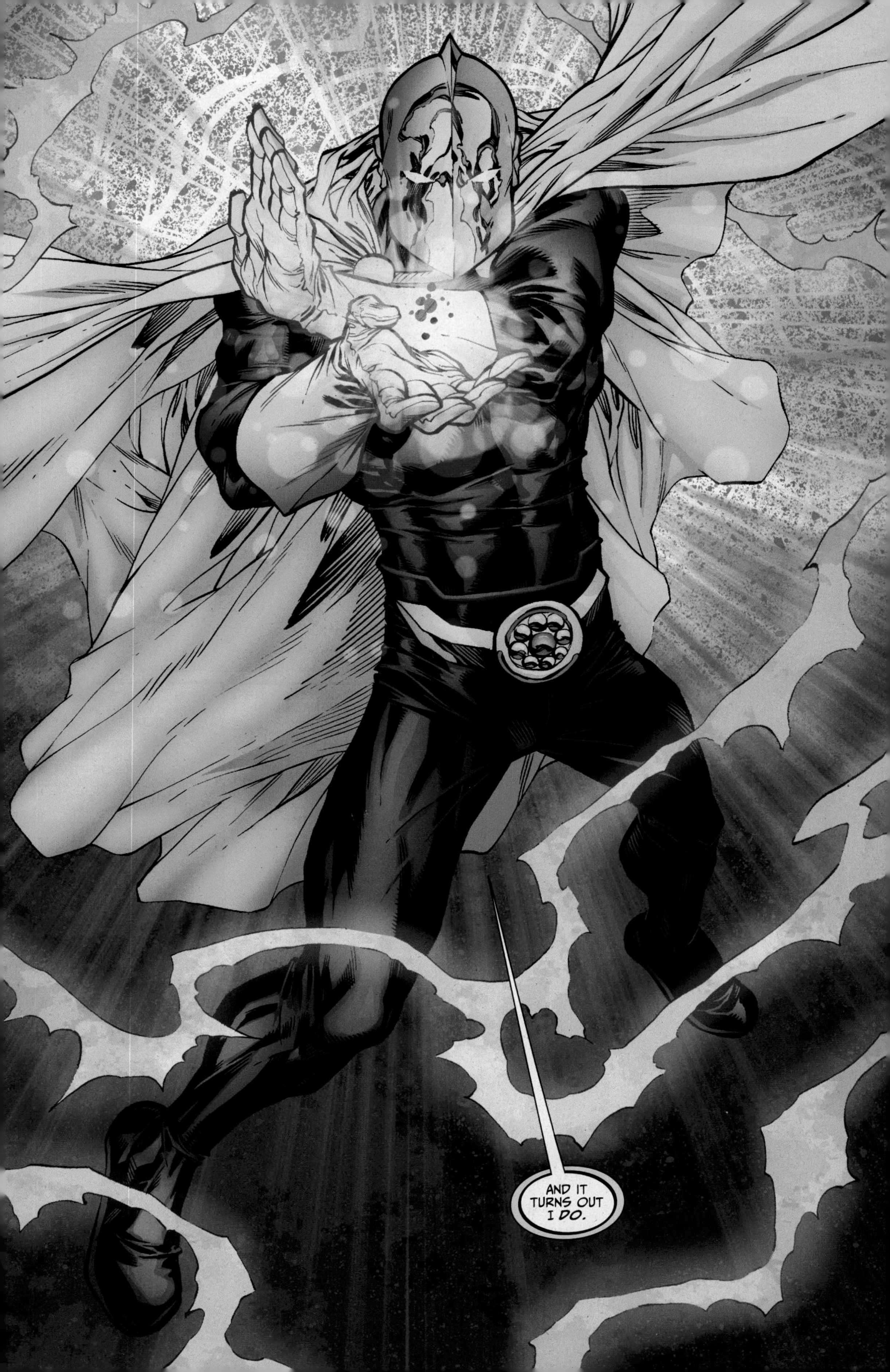
AND IT TURNS OUT I DO.

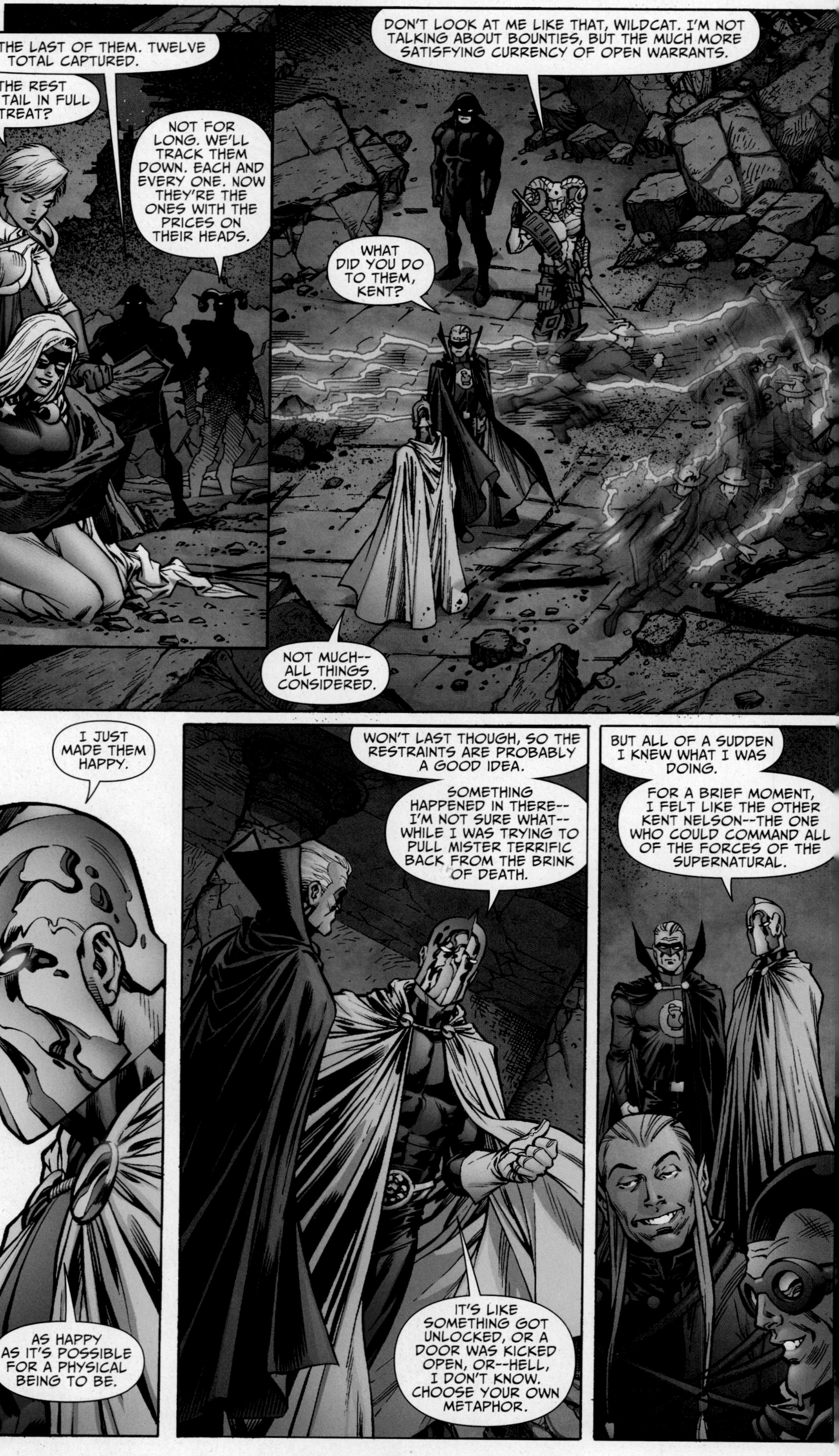
THIS IS THE LAST OF THEM. TWELVE TOTAL CAPTURED.
AND THE REST TUCKED TAIL IN FULL RETREAT?
NOT FOR LONG. WE'LL TRACK THEM DOWN. EACH AND EVERY ONE. NOW THEY'RE THE ONES WITH THE PRICES ON THEIR HEADS.
DON'T LOOK AT ME LIKE THAT, WILDCAT. I'M NOT TALKING ABOUT BOUNTIES, BUT THE MUCH MORE SATISFYING CURRENCY OF OPEN WARRANTS.
WHAT DID YOU DO TO THEM, KENT?
NOT MUCH-- ALL THINGS CONSIDERED.
I JUST MADE THEM HAPPY.
AS HAPPY AS IT'S POSSIBLE FOR A PHYSICAL BEING TO BE.
WON'T LAST THOUGH, SO THE RESTRAINTS ARE PROBABLY A GOOD IDEA.
SOMETHING HAPPENED IN THERE-- I'M NOT SURE WHAT-- WHILE I WAS TRYING TO PULL MISTER TERRIFIC BACK FROM THE BRINK OF DEATH.
IT'S LIKE SOMETHING GOT UNLOCKED, OR A DOOR WAS KICKED OPEN, OR--HELL, I DON'T KNOW. CHOOSE YOUR OWN METAPHOR.
BUT ALL OF A SUDDEN I KNEW WHAT I WAS DOING.
FOR A BRIEF MOMENT, I FELT LIKE THE OTHER KENT NELSON--THE ONE WHO COULD COMMAND ALL OF THE FORCES OF THE SUPERNATURAL.

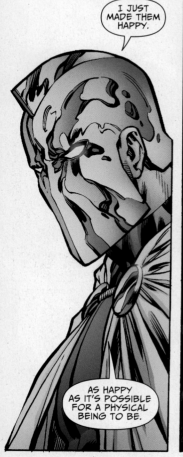

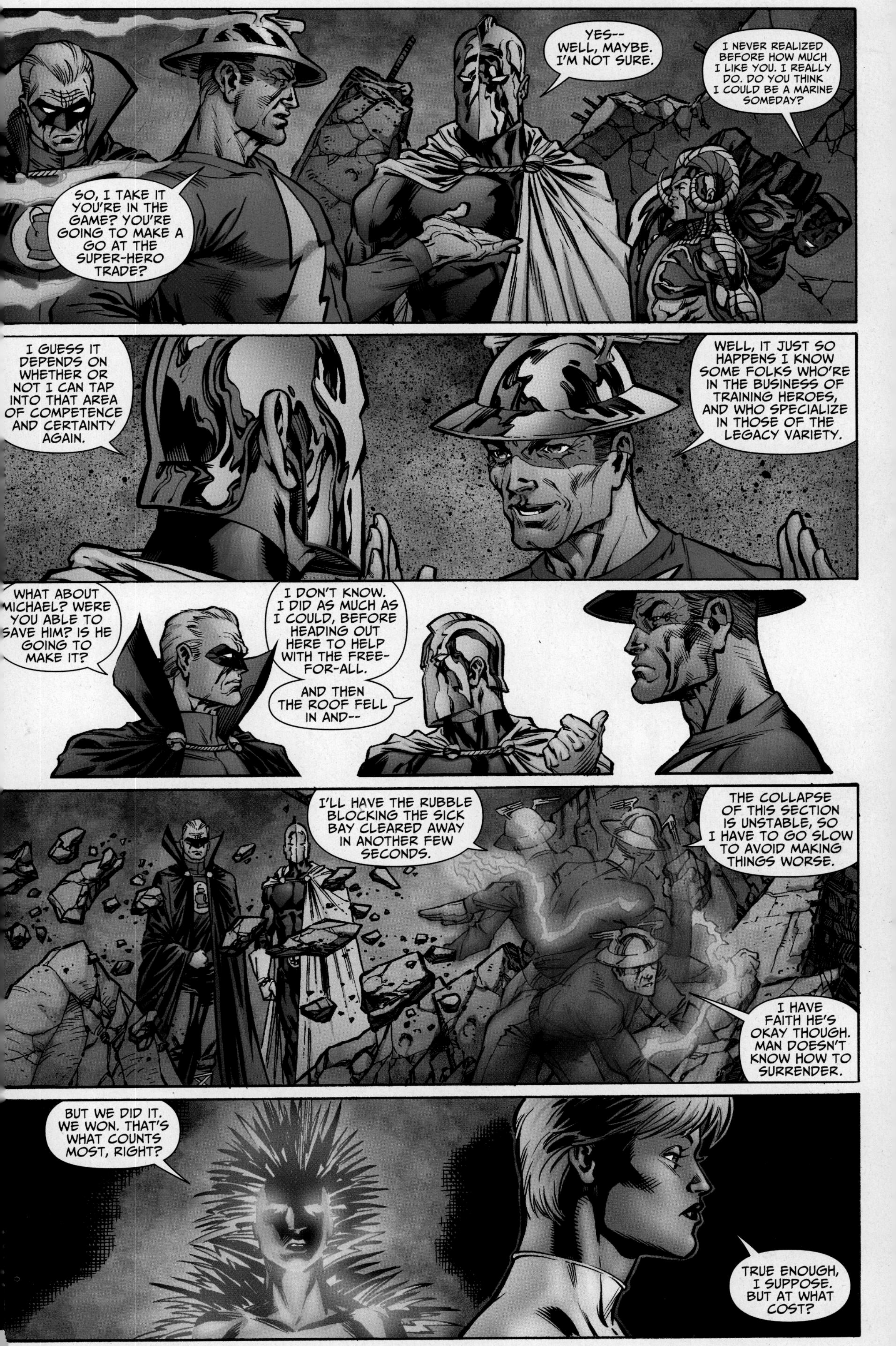

YES-- WELL, MAYBE. I'M NOT SURE.
I NEVER REALIZED BEFORE HOW MUCH I LIKE YOU. I REALLY DO. DO YOU THINK I COULD BE A MARINE SOMEDAY?
SO, I TAKE IT YOU'RE IN THE GAME? YOU'RE GOING TO MAKE A GO AT THE SUPER-HERO TRADE?
I GUESS IT DEPENDS ON WHETHER OR NOT I CAN TAP INTO THAT AREA OF COMPETENCE AND CERTAINTY AGAIN.
WELL, IT JUST SO HAPPENS I KNOW SOME FOLKS WHO'RE IN THE BUSINESS OF TRAINING HEROES, AND WHO SPECIALIZE IN THOSE OF THE LEGACY VARIETY.
WHAT ABOUT MICHAEL? WERE YOU ABLE TO SAVE HIM? IS HE GOING TO MAKE IT?
I DON'T KNOW. I DID AS MUCH AS I COULD, BEFORE HEADING OUT HERE TO HELP WITH THE FREE-FOR-ALL.
AND THEN THE ROOF FELL IN AND--
I'LL HAVE THE RUBBLE BLOCKING THE SICK BAY CLEARED AWAY IN ANOTHER FEW SECONDS.
THE COLLAPSE OF THIS SECTION IS UNSTABLE, SO I HAVE TO GO SLOW TO AVOID MAKING THINGS WORSE.
I HAVE FAITH HE'S OKAY THOUGH. MAN DOESN'T KNOW HOW TO SURRENDER.
BUT WE DID IT. WE WON. THAT'S WHAT COUNTS MOST, RIGHT?
TRUE ENOUGH, I SUPPOSE. BUT AT WHAT COST?

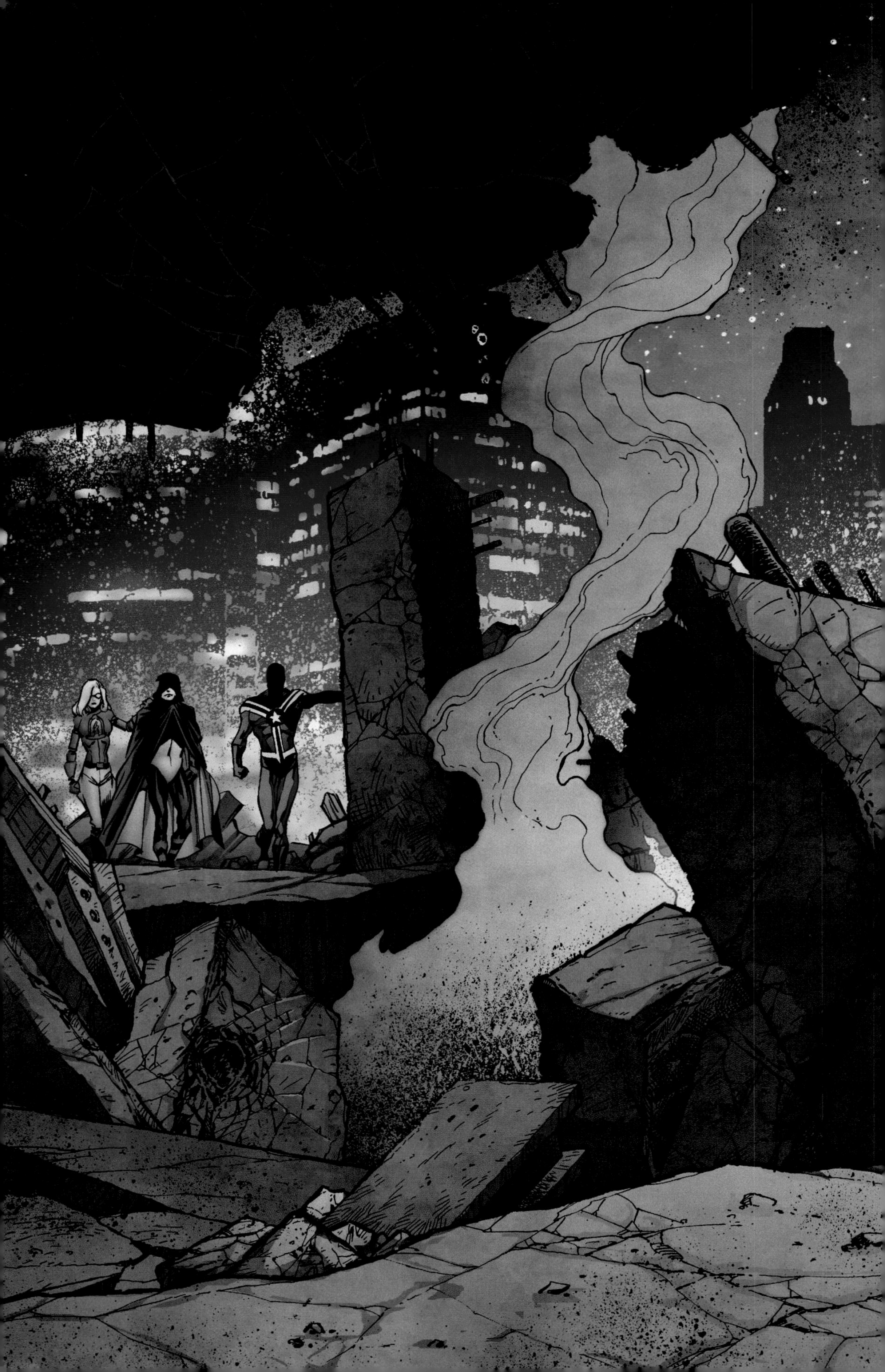

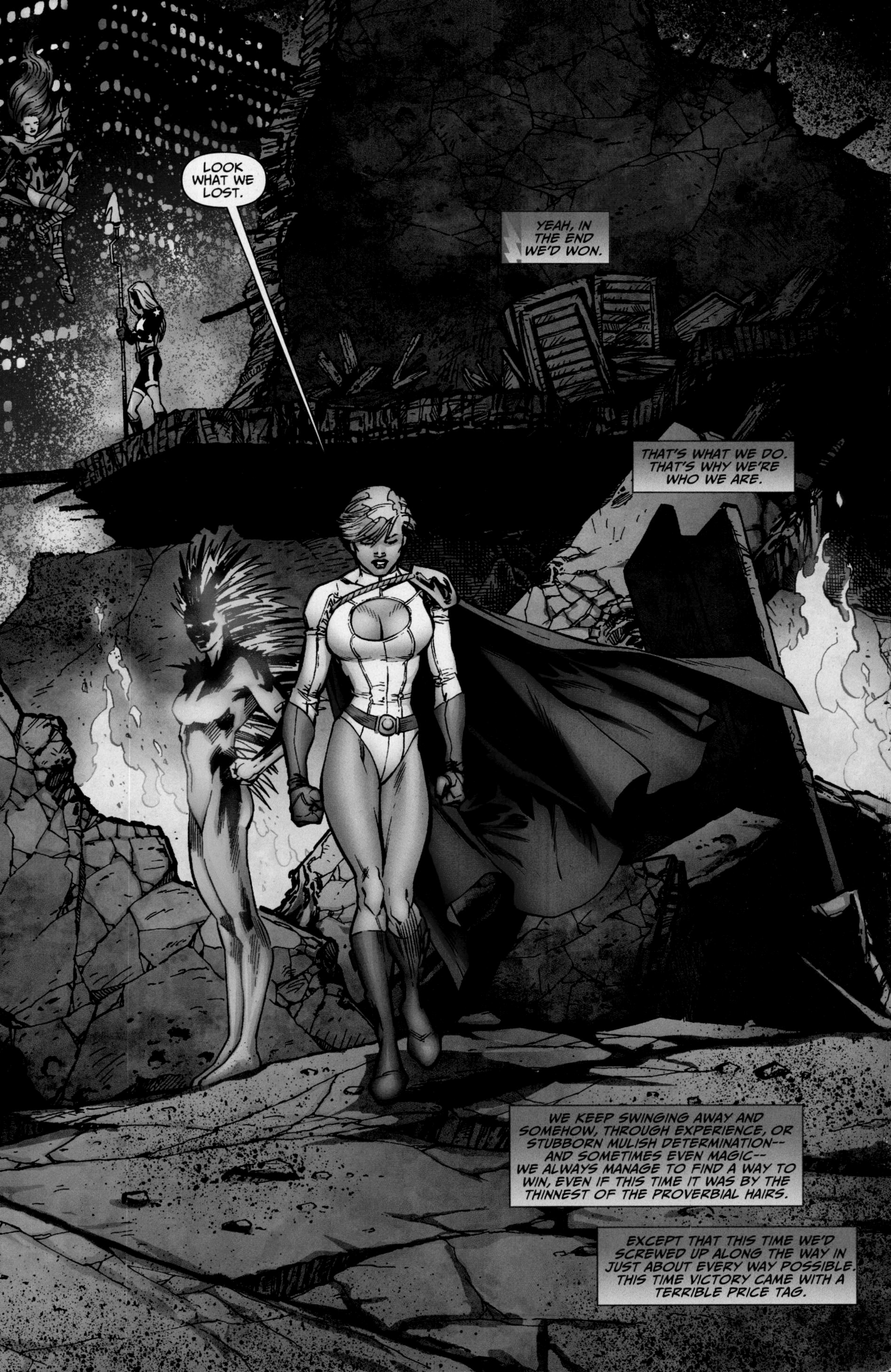
LOOK WHAT WE LOST.
YEAH, IN THE END WE'D WON.
THAT'S WHAT WE DO. THAT'S WHY WE'RE WHO WE ARE.
WE KEEP SWINGING AWAY AND SOMEHOW, THROUGH EXPERIENCE, OR STUBBORN MULISH DETERMINATION-- AND SOMETIMES EVEN MAGIC-- WE ALWAYS MANAGE TO FIND A WAY TO WIN, EVEN IF THIS TIME IT WAS BY THE THINNEST OF THE PROVERBIAL HAIRS.
EXCEPT THAT THIS TIME WE'D SCREWED UP ALONG THE WAY IN JUST ABOUT EVERY WAY POSSIBLE. THIS TIME VICTORY CAME WITH A TERRIBLE PRICE TAG.

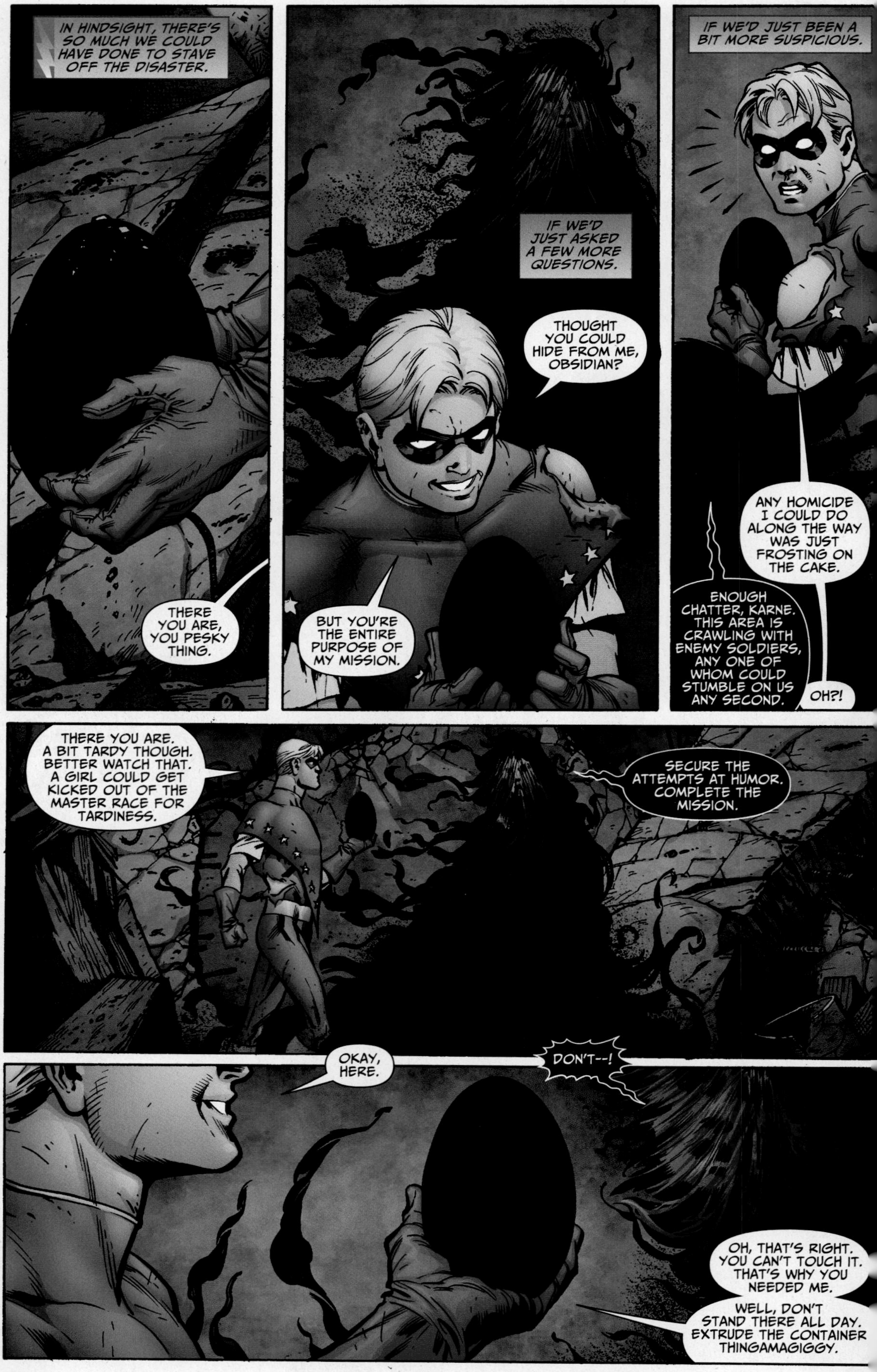
IN HINDSIGHT, THERE'S SO MUCH WE COULD HAVE DONE TO STAVE OFF THE DISASTER.
THERE YOU ARE, YOU PESKY THING.
IF WE'D JUST ASKED A FEW MORE QUESTIONS.
THOUGHT YOU COULD HIDE FROM ME, OBSIDIAN?
BUT YOU'RE THE ENTIRE PURPOSE OF MY MISSION.
IF WE'D JUST BEEN A BIT MORE SUSPICIOUS.
ANY HOMICIDE I COULD DO ALONG THE WAY WAS JUST FROSTING ON THE CAKE.
ENOUGH CHATTER, KARNE. THIS AREA IS CRAWLING WITH ENEMY SOLDIERS, ANY ONE OF WHOM COULD STUMBLE ON US ANY SECOND.
OH?!
THERE YOU ARE. A BIT TARDY THOUGH. BETTER WATCH THAT. A GIRL COULD GET KICKED OUT OF THE MASTER RACE FOR TARDINESS.
SECURE THE ATTEMPTS AT HUMOR. COMPLETE THE MISSION.
OKAY, HERE.
DON'T--!
OH, THAT'S RIGHT. YOU CAN'T TOUCH IT. THAT'S WHY YOU NEEDED ME.
WELL, DON'T STAND THERE ALL DAY. EXTRUDE THE CONTAINER THINGAMAGIGGY.

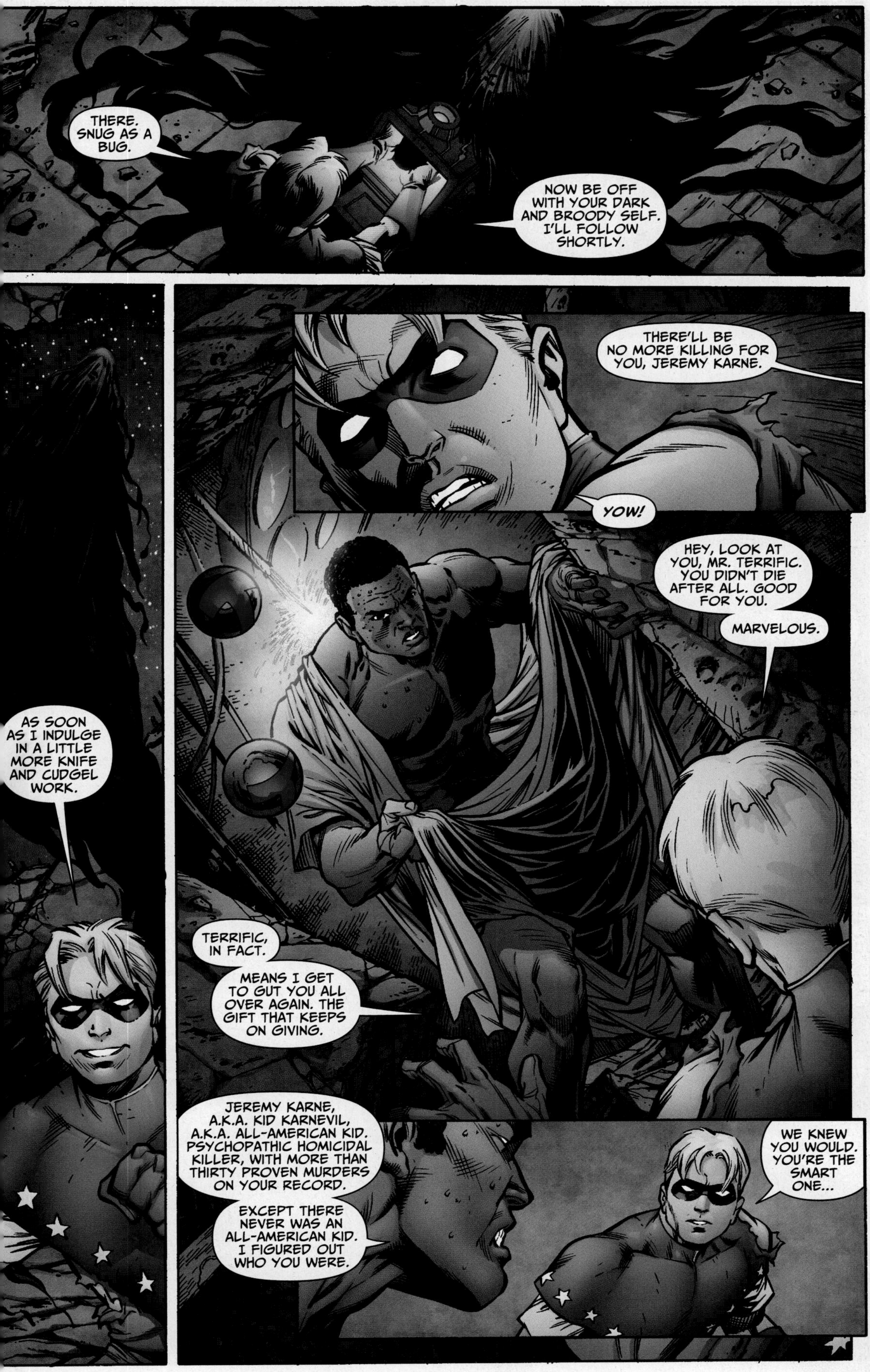
THERE. SNUG AS A BUG.
NOW BE OFF WITH YOUR DARK AND BROODY SELF. I'LL FOLLOW SHORTLY.
AS SOON AS I INDULGE IN A LITTLE MORE KNIFE AND CUDGEL WORK.
THERE'LL BE NO MORE KILLING FOR YOU, JEREMY KARNE.
YOW!
HEY, LOOK AT YOU, MR. TERRIFIC. YOU DIDN'T DIE AFTER ALL. GOOD FOR YOU.
MARVELOUS.
TERRIFIC, IN FACT.
MEANS I GET TO GUT YOU ALL OVER AGAIN. THE GIFT THAT KEEPS ON GIVING.
JEREMY KARNE, A.K.A. KID KARNEVIL, A.K.A. ALL-AMERICAN KID. PSYCHOPATHIC HOMICIDAL KILLER, WITH MORE THAN THIRTY PROVEN MURDERS ON YOUR RECORD.
EXCEPT THERE NEVER WAS AN ALL-AMERICAN KID. I FIGURED OUT WHO YOU WERE.
WE KNEW YOU WOULD. YOU'RE THE SMART ONE...

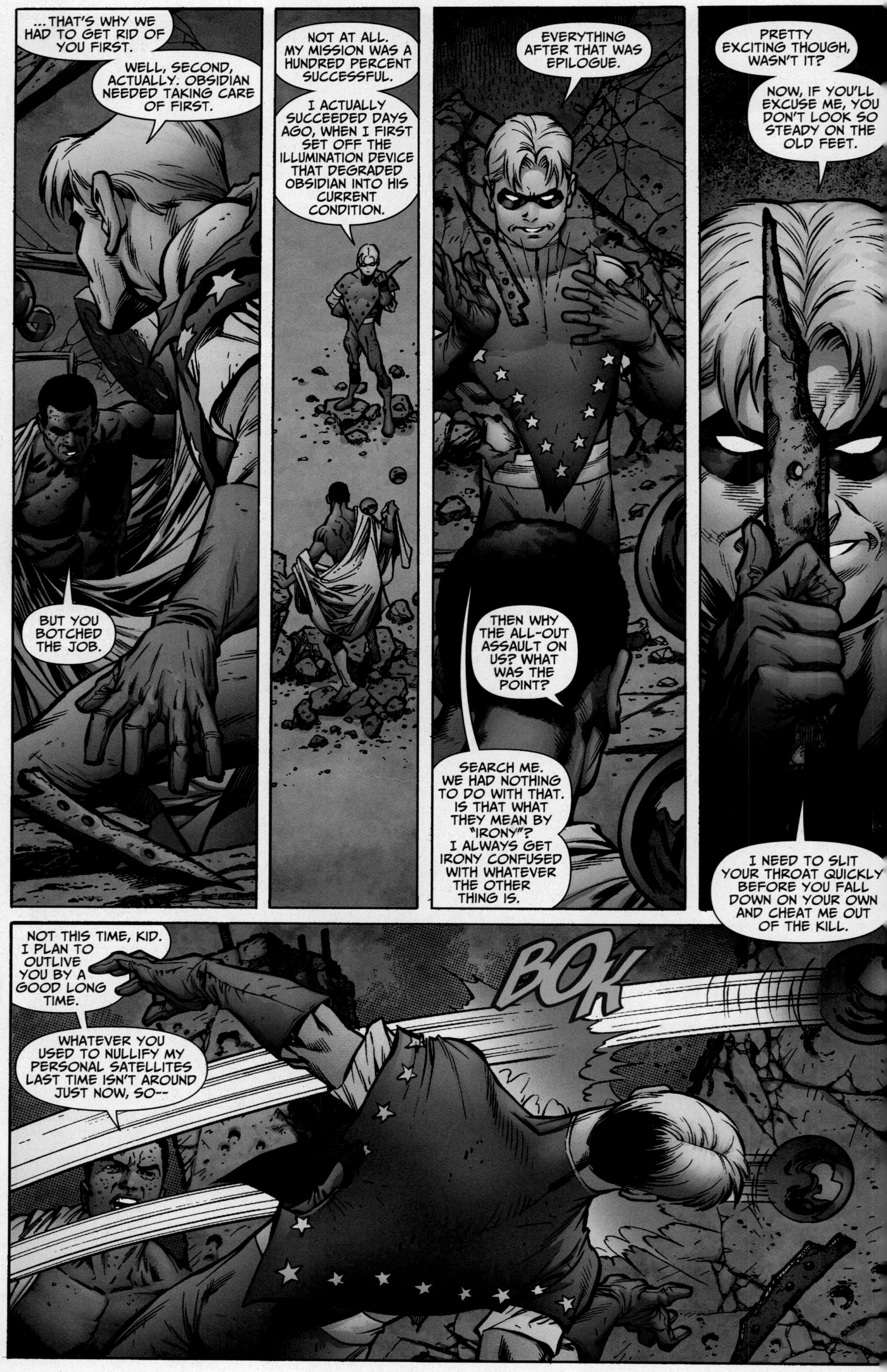
...THAT'S WHY WE HAD TO GET RID OF YOU FIRST.
WELL, SECOND, ACTUALLY. OBSIDIAN NEEDED TAKING CARE OF FIRST.
BUT YOU BOTCHED THE JOB.
NOT AT ALL. MY MISSION WAS A HUNDRED PERCENT SUCCESSFUL.
I ACTUALLY SUCCEEDED DAYS AGO, WHEN I FIRST SET OFF THE ILLUMINATION DEVICE THAT DEGRADED OBSIDIAN INTO HIS CURRENT CONDITION.
EVERYTHING AFTER THAT WAS EPILOGUE.
THEN WHY THE ALL-OUT ASSAULT ON US? WHAT WAS THE POINT?
SEARCH ME. WE HAD NOTHING TO DO WITH THAT. IS THAT WHAT THEY MEAN BY "IRONY"? I ALWAYS GET IRONY CONFUSED WITH WHATEVER THE OTHER THING IS.
PRETTY EXCITING THOUGH, WASN'T IT?
NOW, IF YOU'LL EXCUSE ME, YOU DON'T LOOK SO STEADY ON THE OLD FEET.
I NEED TO SLIT YOUR THROAT QUICKLY BEFORE YOU FALL DOWN ON YOUR OWN AND CHEAT ME OUT OF THE KILL.
NOT THIS TIME, KID. I PLAN TO OUTLIVE YOU BY A GOOD LONG TIME.
WHATEVER YOU USED TO NULLIFY MY PERSONAL SATELLITES LAST TIME ISN'T AROUND JUST NOW, SO--
BOK

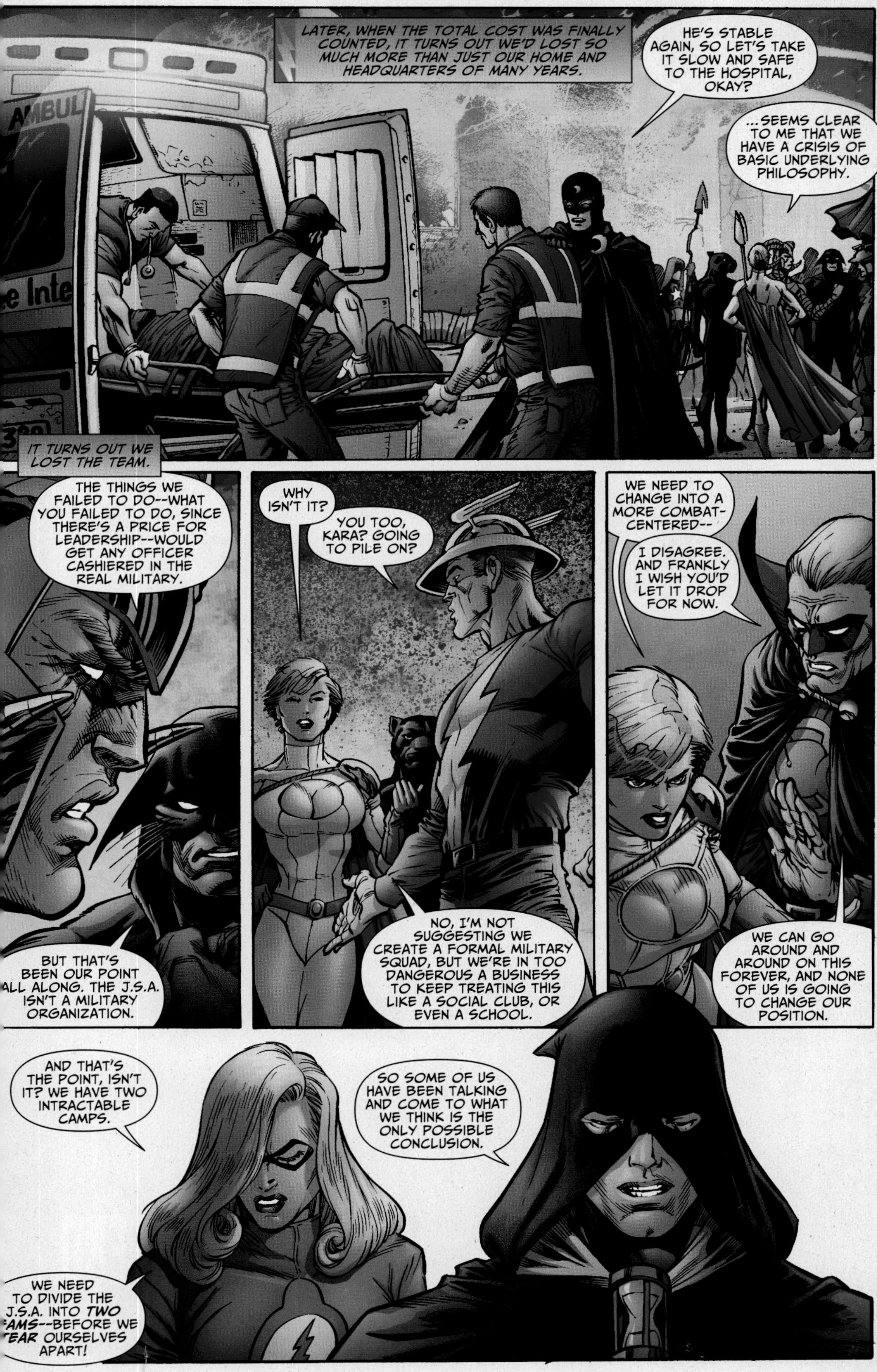
LATER, WHEN THE TOTAL COST WAS FINALLY COUNTED, IT TURNS OUT WE'D LOST SO MUCH MORE THAN JUST OUR HOME AND HEADQUARTERS OF MANY YEARS.
HE'S STABLE AGAIN, SO LET'S TAKE IT SLOW AND SAFE TO THE HOSPITAL, OKAY?
...SEEMS CLEAR TO ME THAT WE HAVE A CRISIS OF BASIC UNDERLYING PHILOSOPHY.
IT TURNS OUT WE LOST THE TEAM.
THE THINGS WE FAILED TO DO--WHAT YOU FAILED TO DO, SINCE THERE'S A PRICE FOR LEADERSHIP--WOULD GET ANY OFFICER CASHIERED IN THE REAL MILITARY.
BUT THAT'S BEEN OUR POINT ALL ALONG. THE J.S.A. ISN'T A MILITARY ORGANIZATION.
WHY ISN'T IT?
YOU TOO, KARA? GOING TO PILE ON?
NO, I'M NOT SUGGESTING WE CREATE A FORMAL MILITARY SQUAD, BUT WE'RE IN TOO DANGEROUS A BUSINESS TO KEEP TREATING THIS LIKE A SOCIAL CLUB, OR EVEN A SCHOOL.
WE NEED TO CHANGE INTO A MORE COMBAT-CENTERED--
I DISAGREE. AND FRANKLY I WISH YOU'D LET IT DROP FOR NOW.
WE CAN GO AROUND AND AROUND ON THIS FOREVER, AND NONE OF US IS GOING TO CHANGE OUR POSITION.
AND THAT'S THE POINT, ISN'T IT? WE HAVE TWO INTRACTABLE CAMPS.
SO SOME OF US HAVE BEEN TALKING AND COME TO WHAT WE THINK IS THE ONLY POSSIBLE CONCLUSION.
WE NEED TO DIVIDE THE J.S.A. INTO *TWO* ...AMS--BEFORE WE ...TEAR OURSELVES APART!

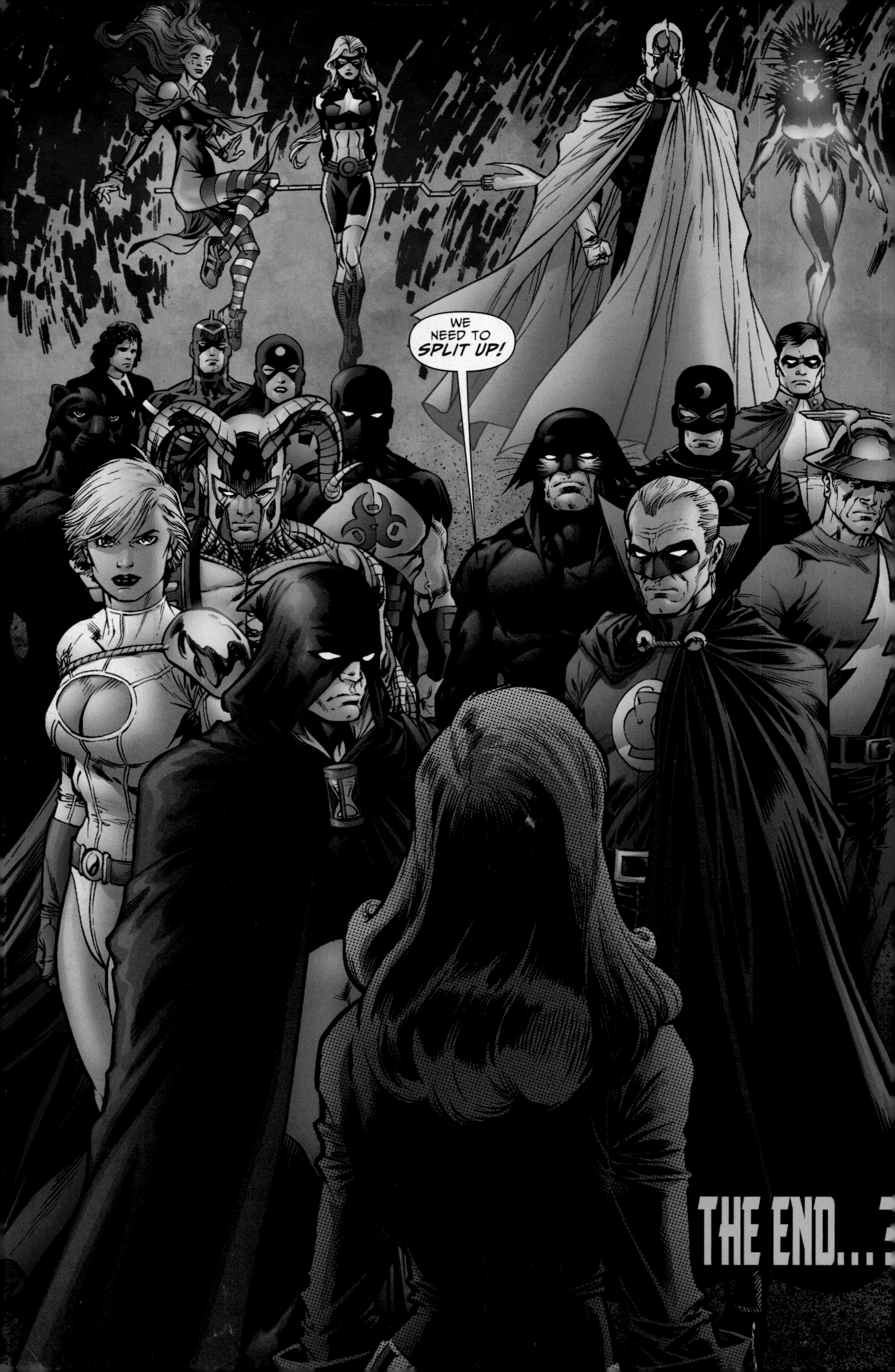
WE NEED TO SPLIT UP!
THE END...?

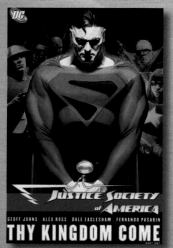

FROM THE WRITER OF
GREEN LANTERN *AND* THE FLASH

GEOFF JOHNS

During World War II, a group of costumed mystery men formed the first superhero team, the Justice Society of America. Today, the JSA lives again, as the surviving original members fight alongside a new generation of heroes.

DARKNESS FALLS
THE RETURN OF HAWKMAN
FAIR PLAY
STEALING THUNDER
SAVAGE TIMES
PRINCES OF DARKNESS
BLACK REIGN
LOST
BLACK VENGEANCE
MIXED SIGNALS

DC
JSA
GEOFF JOHNS
BLACK VENGEANCE
DON KRAMER · KEITH CHAMPAGNE

JSA:
THE RETURN OF HAWKMAN

DC
JSA
THE RETURN OF HAWKMAN

JSA:
BLACK REIGN

DC
JSA
BLACK REIGN
GEOFF JOHNS · RAGS MORALES
DON KRAMER · MICHAEL BAIR
KEITH CHAMPAGNE

JSA:
MIXED SIGNALS

DC
JSA
GEOFF JOHNS
MIXED SIGNALS
KEITH CHAMPAGNE · DON KRAMER

SEARCH THE GRAPHIC NOVELS SECTION OF
DCCOMICS.COM
FOR ART AND INFORMATION ON ALL OF OUR BOOKS!

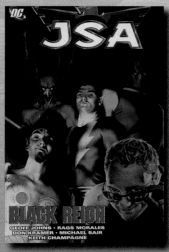